IMAGES
of America

OYSTERPONDS
EAST MARION AND ORIENT

ON THE COVER: THE POQUATUCK HOOK AND LADDER COMPANY, 1920S. In the early 1920s, the members of the fire department posed for a photograph by the Orient wharf in front of C.B. King's store. In 1930, the Poquatuck Hook and Ladder Company disbanded, and the fire department reformed as the Orient Fire Department. (Courtesy of the Oysterponds Historical Society.)

IMAGES
of America

OYSTERPONDS

EAST MARION AND ORIENT

Amy Kasuga-Folk

ARCADIA
PUBLISHING

ISBN 978-1-4671-2292-4

Published by Arcadia Publishing
Charleston, South Carolina

Printed in the United States of America

Library of Congress Control Number: 2014946362

For all general information, please contact Arcadia Publishing:
Telephone 843-853-2070
Fax 843-853-0044
E-mail sales@arcadiapublishing.com
For customer service and orders:
Toll-Free 1-888-313-2665

Visit us on the Internet at www.arcadiapublishing.com

To Donald Boerum, Elinor Williams, and the late Gordon Rackett, three people whose love of history and generosity of spirit in passing on their knowledge of the area so it can be preserved for future generations has, for more than a decade, humbled and inspired me

Contents

ACKNOWLEDGMENTS

This book would not be possible without the extensive collection of the Oysterponds Historical Society. The author would like to thank the director and board of Oysterponds for giving the go-ahead to create this book. The author would also like to thank the following for helping in the creation of this book: Donald Boerum for sharing his remarkable depth of knowledge of the area and its inhabitants with me, as well as fact-checking all the details of each photograph; Ruthann Bramson for sharing her family history in East Marion; the East Marion Community Association for sharing information on the location of privately held images; Kristine McGroary, who assisted in checking the facts of every caption in the book; Carol Kalin, who willingly searched an extensive collection for specific images of East Marion; Jean Letty for allowing me to use one of the wonderful photographs taken by her father, L. Vinton Richard; Ellen Mitchell, who has collected and transcribed the oral histories of the Hill in Orient; Barb Pfanz and Robin Imandt, for accepting and calmly responding to all of my bizarre questions on East Marion history; the late Gordon Rackett, who for many years told me stories and the history of East Marion as we worked around the grounds of the historical society; Robert Reeves Jr. for patiently answering multiple emails on the events and locations of people and places in Orient; Joan Turturro for providing images of the Orient Inn; Diana Whitsit for not only her help over the years in the archives but also sharing her family history; Elinor Williams, who over the years not only shared her knowledge of Orient Point, but also provided details of family history in the area and answered all of my questions whenever they happen to occur to me; and Ellen Zimmerman for providing access to the East Marion Community Association's index images in local collections in the process of selecting images to create this book.

Unless otherwise noted, all images appear courtesy of the Oysterponds Historical Society.

INTRODUCTION

The history of Oysterponds, on the easternmost tip of the North Fork, begins with the settling of Southold in 1640. Rev. John Youngs and his followers arrived from Connecticut to found a plantation for the colony of New Haven on the shores of Peconic Bay. The new community spanned from what is now Wading River out to Orient Point. In 1649, the plantation gained its independence from New Haven. The area thrived, and with the arrival of an increasing number of new settlers, the physical size of the settlement became a burden on the church-led community. By 1661, Southold partitioned the lands on the western and eastern ends, forming three new sub-communities known as Occubogue (Aquebogue), Cutchogue, and Oysterponds.

The easternmost division, Oysterponds encompassed the area now known as East Marion and Orient. The name probably came from the lush oyster-filled ponds that divide the two communities. According to the records, when the town opened the area for private ownership, Oysterponds was divided into 40 lots, each about 50 acres. Prospective owners entered into a lottery to decide the order each would be allowed to choose what property to claim. The plots were taken by 16 owners, all of whom had drawn early numbers in the lottery. Rev. John Youngs, Capt. John Youngs, the widow of Joseph Youngs, Thomas Moore Sr., Thomas Moore Jr., Lieutenant Glover, Richard Brown, John Herbert, John Corey, Thomas Osman, John Conklin Sr., John Conklin Jr., John Payne, Geoffrey Jones, Abram Whitter, and Thomas Rider took up all of the land in the area. Most of these of new owners never moved to Oysterponds, instead selling or trading the lots for other properties. Augustus Griffin, a local 19th-century historian, tells the founding of Oysterponds somewhat differently. In his book *Griffins Journal*, he claims that Peter Hallock owned the whole area but soon left to get his family from England. During his absence, the land was taken by several others, including the Tuthill and Youngs families.

During the American Revolution, the North Fork was virtually deserted by all of the major landholders, who heeded George Washington's orders to flee to Connecticut to avoid the British forces. While some stayed on to harass the British troops stationed in the area, other locals determined to maintain ownership of their farms generally had a least one family member stay and swear loyalty to the crown while the rest of the family joined the resistance.

When the War of 1812 broke out, the inhabitants of Oysterponds, remembering the chaos and financial devastation of the American Revolution, were determined not to repeat the past. Instead of resisting the British, the village established a cooperative relationship with the warships controlling the area and profited from the association.

Locally, the area differentiated itself into two sections: the western end, known as Upper Neck, and the eastern area, known as Lower Neck. In 1826, the Upper Neck and Lower Neck formally split into two separate communities; the Lower Neck retained the name Oysterponds, and the Upper Neck chose the name Rocky Point.

When Oysterponds applied to the US Postal Service for a local office, it was told that the name Oysterponds was too similar to another Long Island community, Oyster Bay. The government then suggested the name Orient, as the community was on the far eastern end of Long Island. The name was formally adopted in 1836.

Rocky Point also faced a similar problem. In the early 1850s, the community applied to get its own post office, but the US Postal Service rejected the name Rocky Point, since the name was already in use by a community in western Suffolk County. During a meeting to discuss the situation, Warren Griffing suggested the name Marion in honor of his favorite general of the American Revolution, Gen. Francis Marion. Unfortunately, the post office already had a community named Marion in upstate New York and countered with East Marion, which stuck.

Both communities had been farming and fishing economies since their founding. Families frequently had business interests in both trades. While residents during the colonial period practiced subsistence farming and fishing, when the industrial revolution changed the economy in the North, it made little impact on the Oysterponds area. It was only with the discovery of a method to efficiently process the oily fish menhaden that the industrial revolution touched the communities. The fish, locally known as bunker, was processed in small factories into a cheap fertilizer as well as an inexpensive lamp oil. Many residents joined local bunker fishing companies as tons of bunker were pulled from the bays during the warmer seasons. After processing, the fertilizer and oil were then sold to customers across the country.

In 1861, when men were needed to fight in the Civil War, young men from the area volunteered, signing up with one of two groups recruited locally, the 127th Company H Infantry or 165th Duryée Zouaves. Several men who did not wish to fight on foot joined the 6th Calvary, which recruited volunteers in New York City. Each of the groups saw action in either South Carolina, Louisiana, or Virginia.

In the 1870s, the East End was discovered by city dwellers desperate to escape the summer heat. Tourism became a big business opportunity for the area. Many residents converted their homes into boardinghouses and took in visitors. Some started tea rooms, ice cream shops, candy and cigar stores, or other businesses that catered to the influx of tourists.

Just after World War I, the mass production of affordable automobiles changed the nature of the tourist trade on the North Fork from long-term summer rentals to short one-day trips. East Marion and Orient, for the most part, were left out of the new tourist boom. Many of the boardinghouses and small tourist businesses that flourished in local homes closed down, and the communities returned to being mostly residential, interspersed with a few farms, which remain today.

One

People

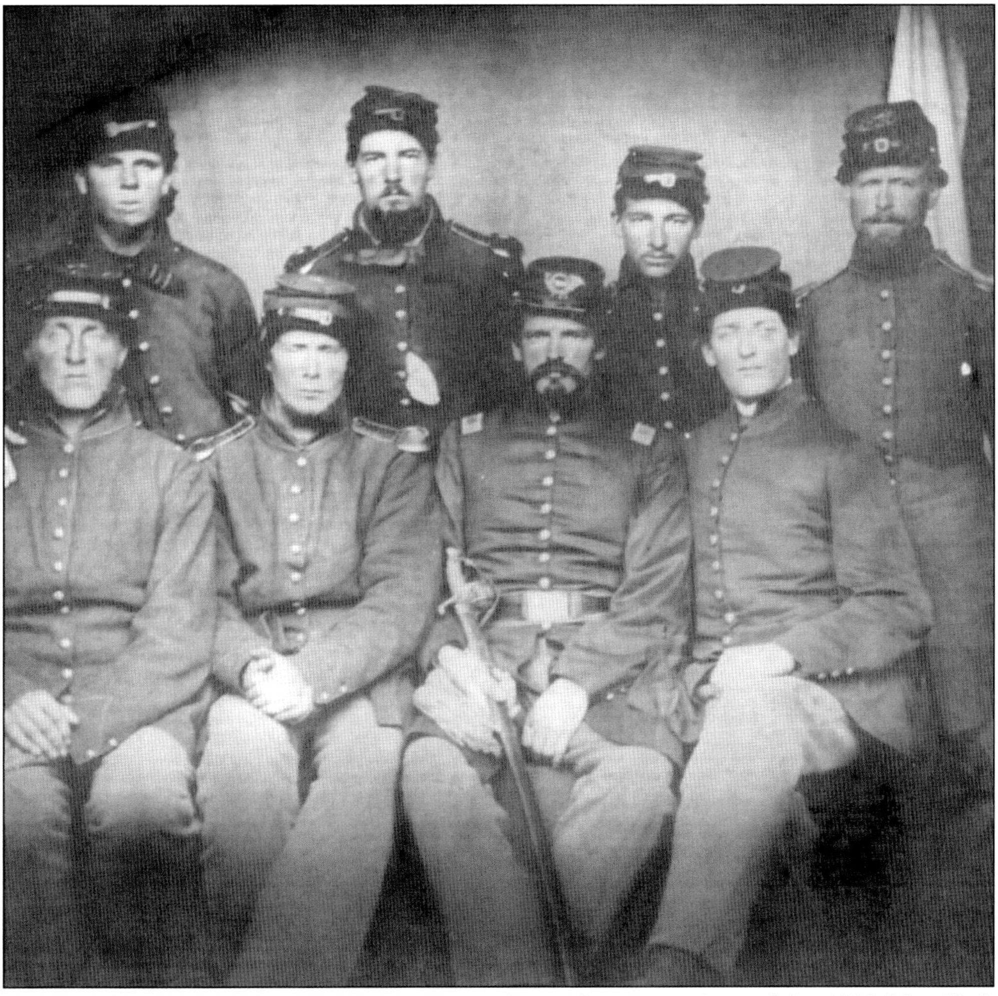

127TH NEW YORK STATE VOLUNTEERS, 1863. Some Orient members of the 127th New York Volunteers, Company H, were photograph on February 28, 1863, in Alexandria, Virginia. Pictured here are, from left to right, (first row) Sidney Petty, Robert Ebbits, James H. Young, and Napoleon B. Young; (second row) George E. Latham, John Henry Young, John S. Young, and Charles B. Moore. Of these men, John S. Young, Sidney Petty, and George E. Latham were killed in battle.

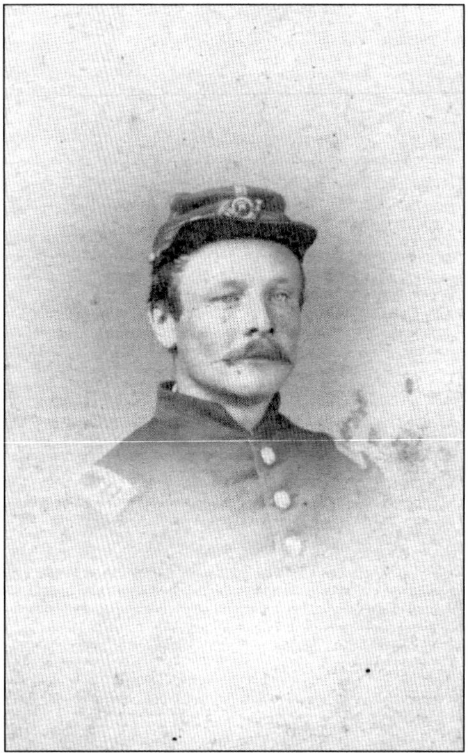

William Wilson Stephenson, c. 1863. Stephenson (1831–1889) was a resident of both Brooklyn and Orient. During the Civil War, Stephenson started as a private in the 7th Regiment, then transferred to the 165th Duryée Zouaves. He rose in the ranks to become a brevetted lieutenant colonel. Stephenson was among the recruiters looking for men during the Civil War on the North Fork. After the war, Stephenson became a lawyer and built a house in Orient.

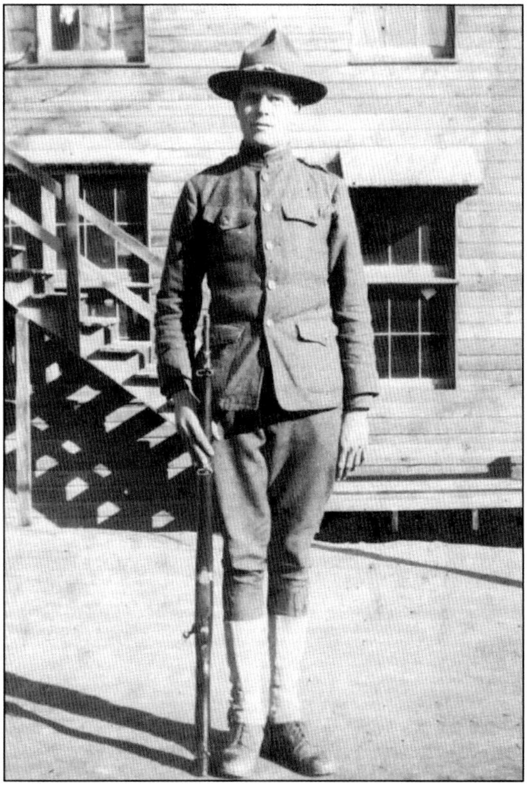

Stacy T. Brooks, 1918. Posted at Camp Upton, Brooks (1895–1918) had his photograph taken before being shipped out to Europe. Brooks was a private in the 326th machine gun company. On November 15, 1918, he died in France of wounds sustained from battle.

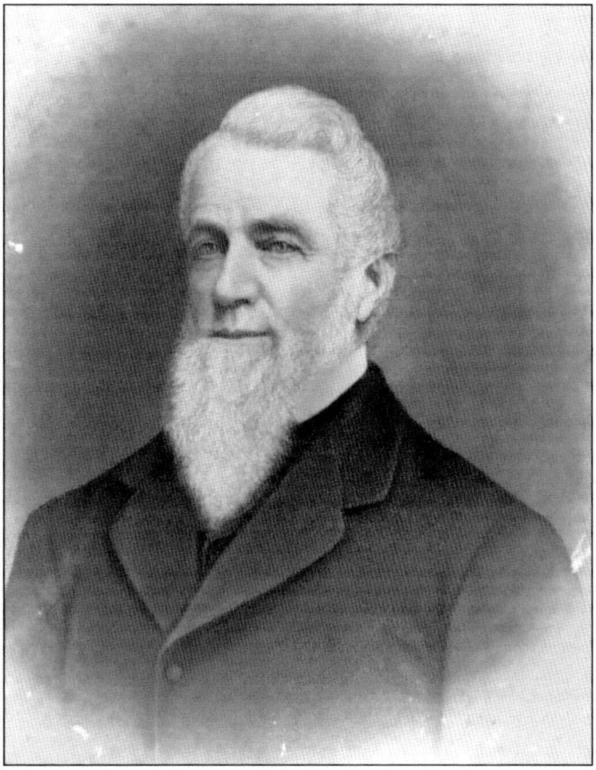

Lewis Edwards, c. 1870. Edwards (1811–1879) was the New York state senator representing the first district from 1868 to 1869. Edwards was born on Gardiner's Island, the oldest of nine children, and his father was the farm superintendent on the island. In addition to his political duties, Edwards was a farmer, an investor, and a part owner in the Atlantic and Virginia Fertilizer Company, which turned menhaden and bird guano into fertilizer.

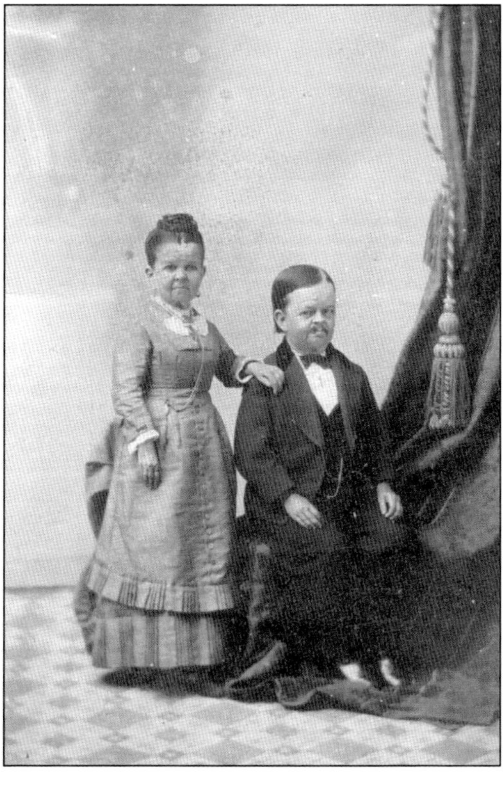

The Tiny Tuthills, c. 1865. Emma (1830–1884) and her brother Addison (1842–1894) as adults both measured less than 36 inches. P.T. Barnum heard about the Tuthills and traveled to Orient to ask Addison to join his troupe. Addison declined, stating that in Orient everyone treated him the same as everyone else, and he had no wish to be gawked at by the public. Emma worked as a seamstress in Orient Village, while Addison was a gentleman farmer.

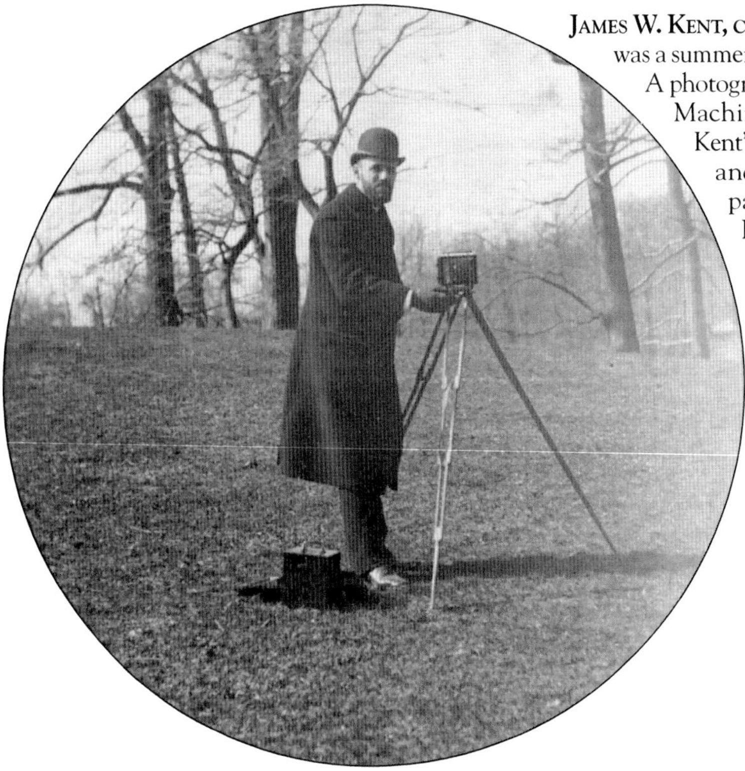

JAMES W. KENT, C. 1940. Kent (1863–1955) was a summer resident of East Marion. A photographer and owner of Kent Machine Works of Brooklyn, Kent's company made grinding and mixing machines for paint and printing inks. Kent was constantly experimenting, using different chemicals in developing his photographs. He often used a bromide print to add a misty, otherworldly effect to his images.

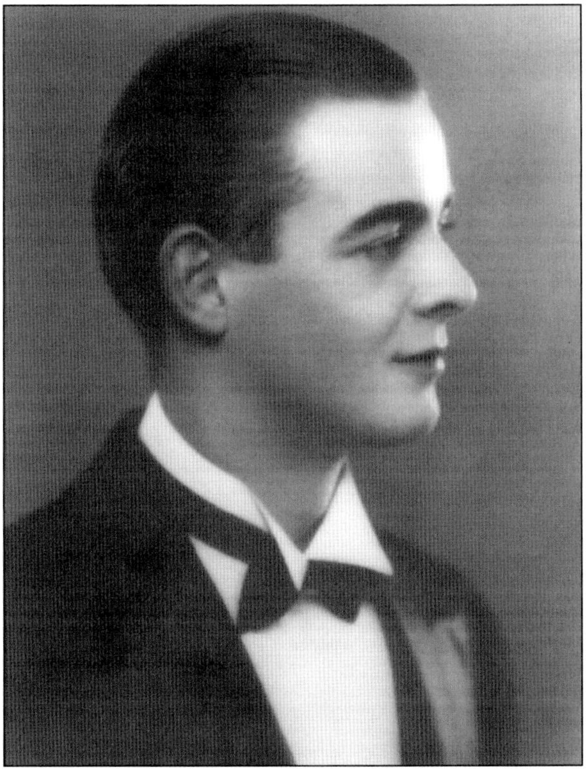

GEORGE W. HALLOCK, C. 1930. Hallock (1916–1984) was the heir of his farming family when he decided that he did not want to take over the reins of the family business. A talented artist, Hallock married a local girl, Lillian Vail, and worked as a printer. He eventually owned a gift shop in Greenport where he sold his paintings.

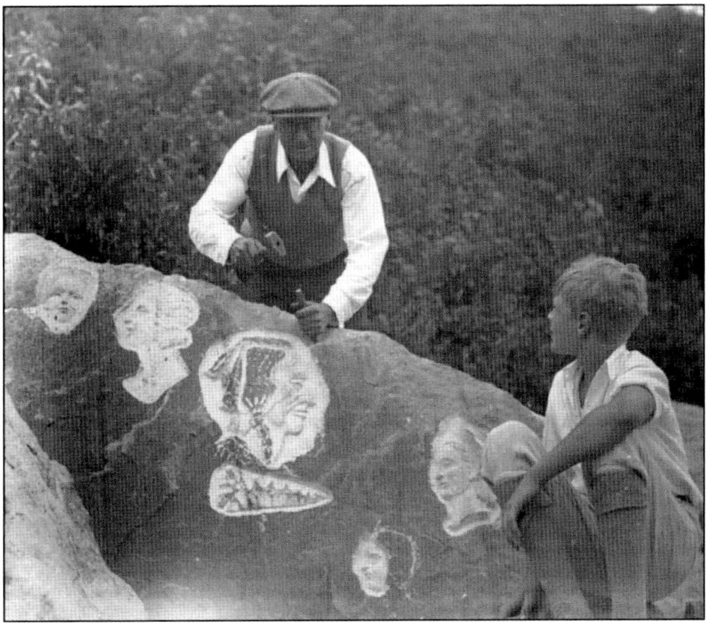

ELLIOT A. BROOKS, C. 1930. Fisherman and artist Elliot Brooks (1888–1949) is perhaps best known for his relief carvings on the rocks along Long Island Sound in Orient. Brooks, who had trained as an artist locally, painted mostly local scenes. He and his brother Frank, who was also an artist, were commercial fishermen by trade. The brothers would sell their catch daily at a stand along the causeway by Peconic Bay.

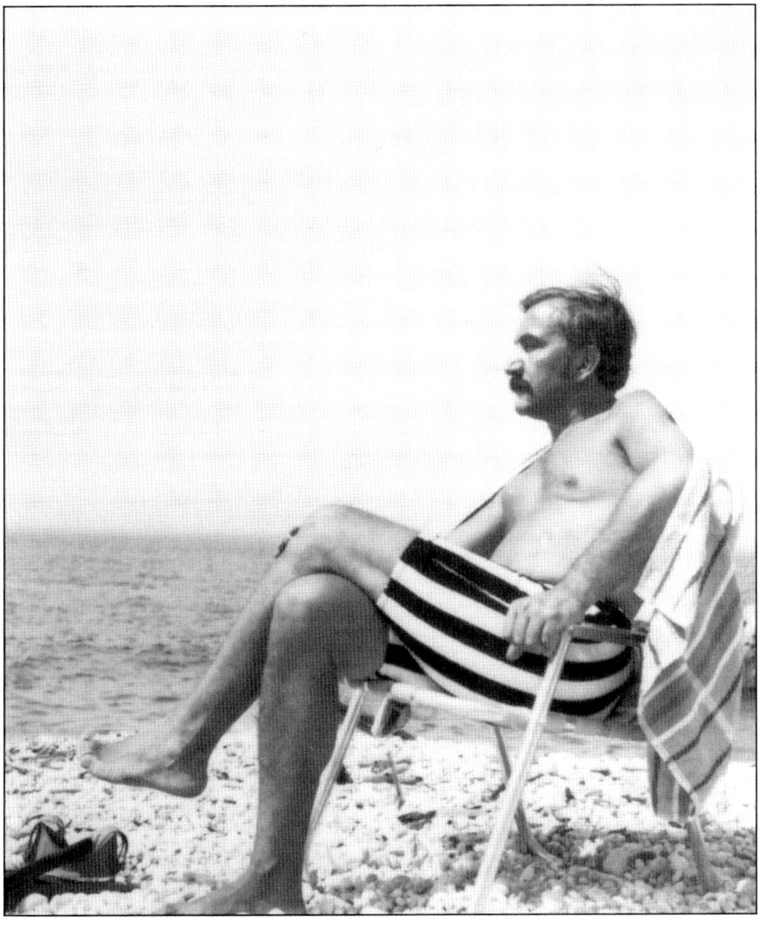

THEODOROS STAMOS, C. 1960. Stamos (1922–1997) was a New York City abstract expressionist artist and summer resident of East Marion. Stamos is remembered not only for his art, but also for his association with Mark Rothko and his family. Stamos and Rothko lived along Aquaview Avenue by Long Island Sound.

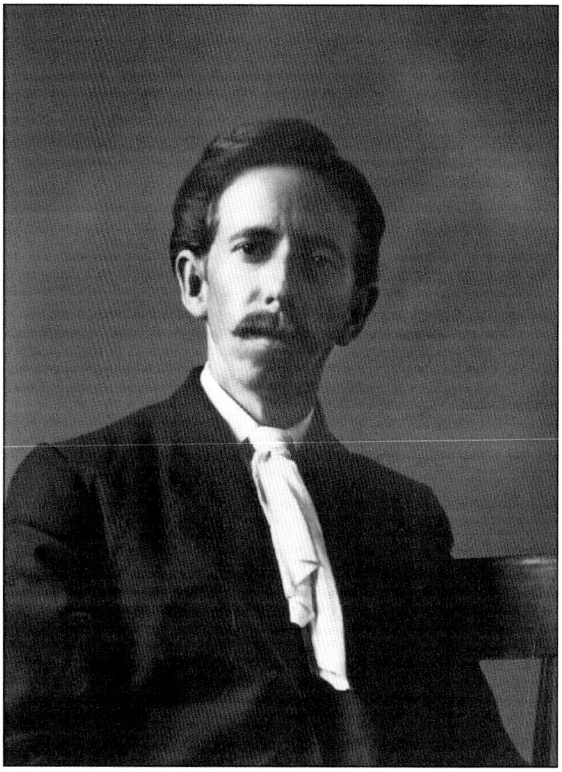

William Steeple Davis, c. 1910. Davis (1884–1961) was an artist and photographer who was born and raised in Orient. He is perhaps better known for his paintings of local scenes but was also an extraordinary photographer. The people of Orient recognized his talent and took up a collection and sent him to study art. However, it was not until after his parents died that Davis was able to take an extended trip to Europe.

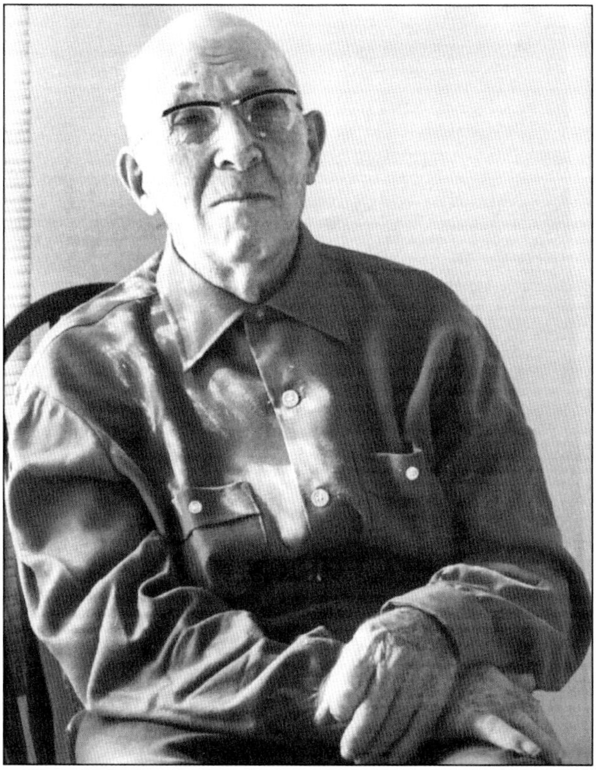

Angelo LeRoy Latham, c. 1970. Latham (1881–1979), better known as Roy Latham, was a naturalist, farmer, and amateur archeologist. Latham had a sixth-grade education and a passionate interest in the world around him. After studying the flora and fauna in the area, he turned to insects, remarking that there were so many kinds that he would never run out. Latham discovered the paleo-arrowhead known as the Orient fishtail. This photograph of Latham was taken by Sid B. Jones.

Two

Churches and Cemeteries

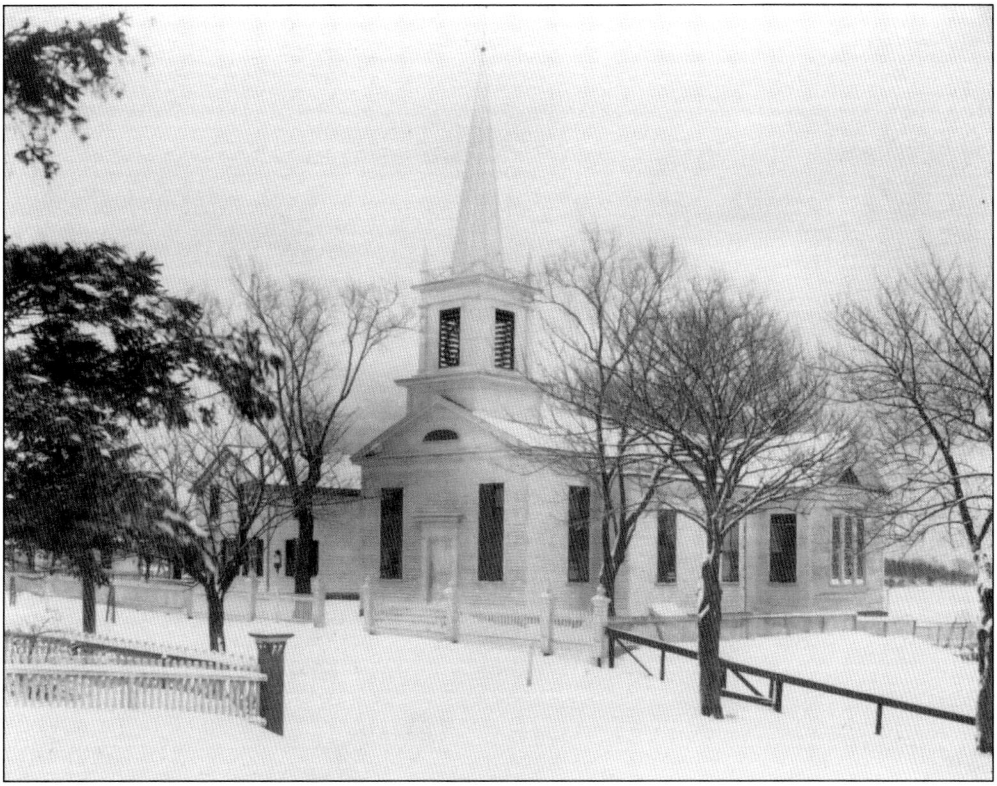

East Marion Baptist Church, c. 1870. The church was constructed in 1846 as a jointly owned building between the Baptists and the Methodists of the area. The first service was held in the new building in 1847. The new congregation was formally recognized not by the Greenport Baptist Church, but by the First Baptist Church of Groton, Connecticut. Several years later, after sharing the building, the Baptist congregation raised enough money and bought out their Methodist partners.

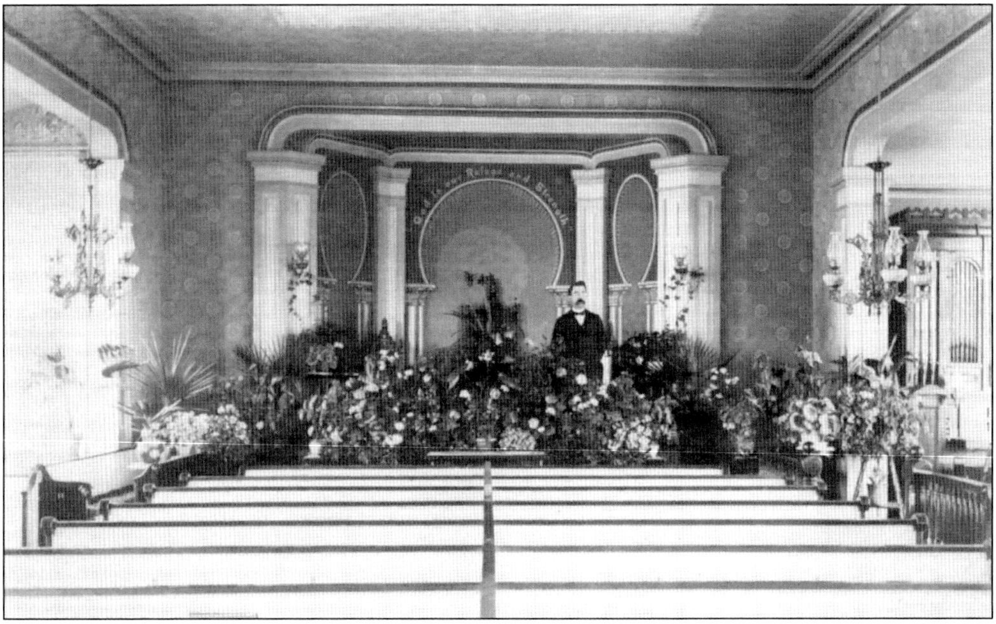

INTERIOR OF EAST MARION BAPTIST CHURCH WITH REV. LOREN ROWLEY, C. 1900. Rowley was minister from 1896 to 1904. A fiery speaker, he was praised for whipping up the members of the church to new heights of evangelism. Under his leadership, even the local stores began closing on Sundays, so the owners could listen to Rowley preach. Reverend Rowley, who was from upstate New York, was also a professional photographer and often sold copies of his photographs.

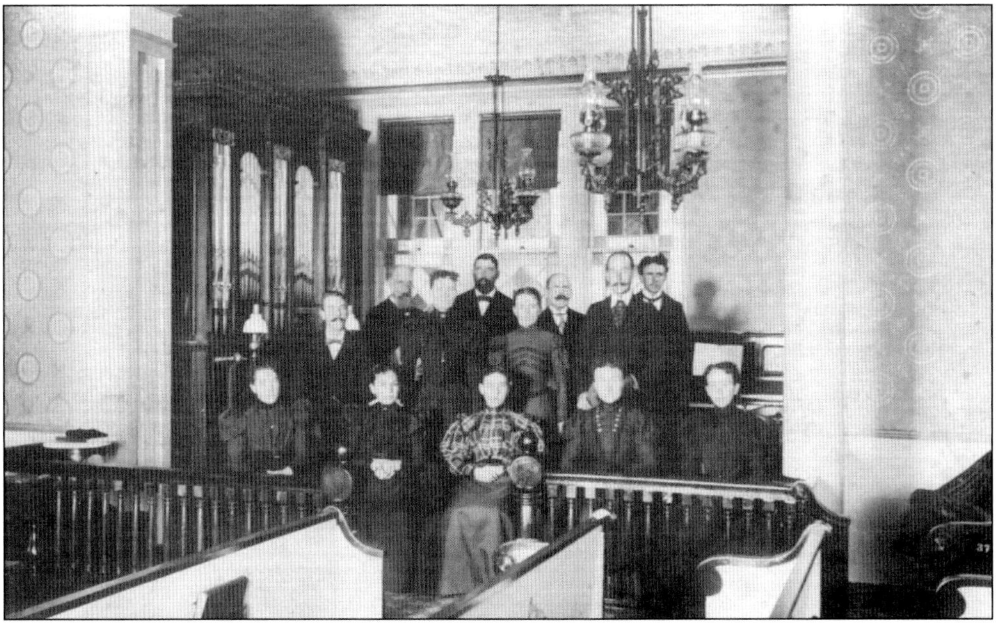

CHOIR OF THE EAST MARION BAPTIST CHURCH, C. 1880. The choir sits in the small alcove at the side of the church with the small pipe organ that originally served the congregation. Mary L. Furst was the first organist of the church.

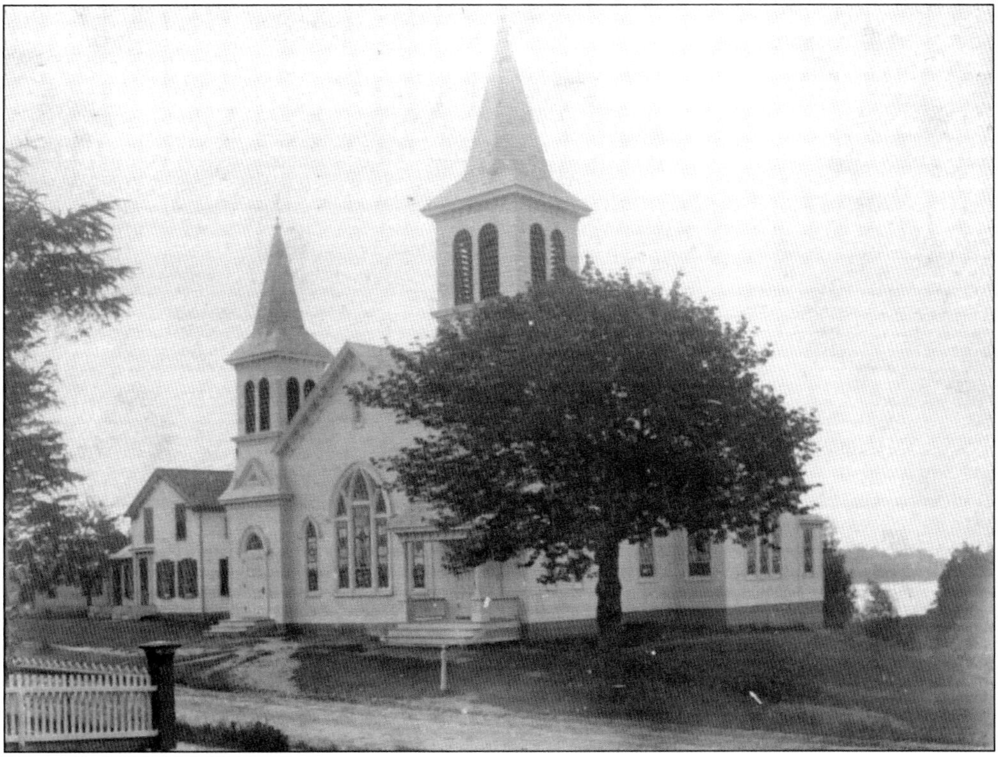

East Marion Baptist Church, c. 1890. By 1860, the East Marion Baptist Church was too small to accommodate the parishioners. The church expanded not only on both sides, but also in the back. A second spire and a bell were added to the building at the same time.

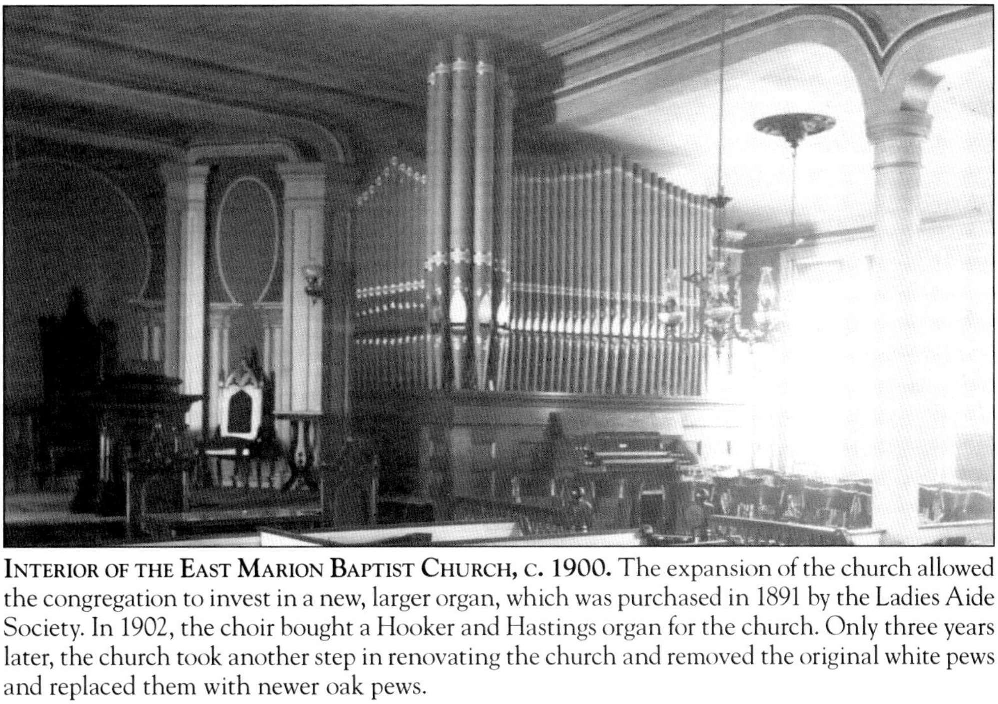

Interior of the East Marion Baptist Church, c. 1900. The expansion of the church allowed the congregation to invest in a new, larger organ, which was purchased in 1891 by the Ladies Aide Society. In 1902, the choir bought a Hooker and Hastings organ for the church. Only three years later, the church took another step in renovating the church and removed the original white pews and replaced them with newer oak pews.

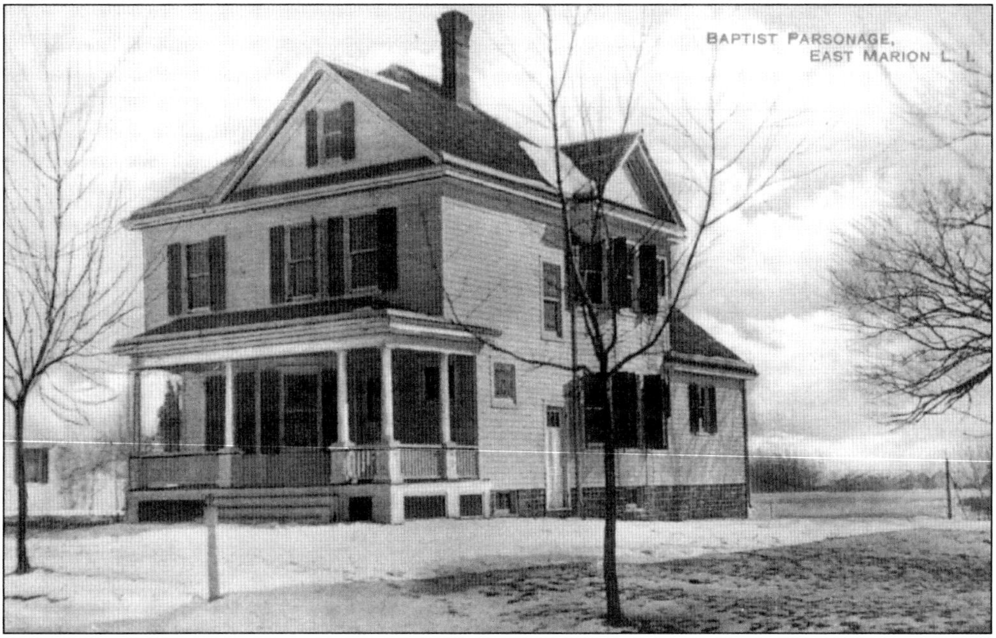

EAST MARION BAPTIST CHURCH PARSONAGE, C. 1910. Just to the east of the church sits the Baptist church parsonage. The congregation purchased the Orange Beebe house in 1861. In 1905, the old pastorate was torn down and a new house, seen here, was constructed.

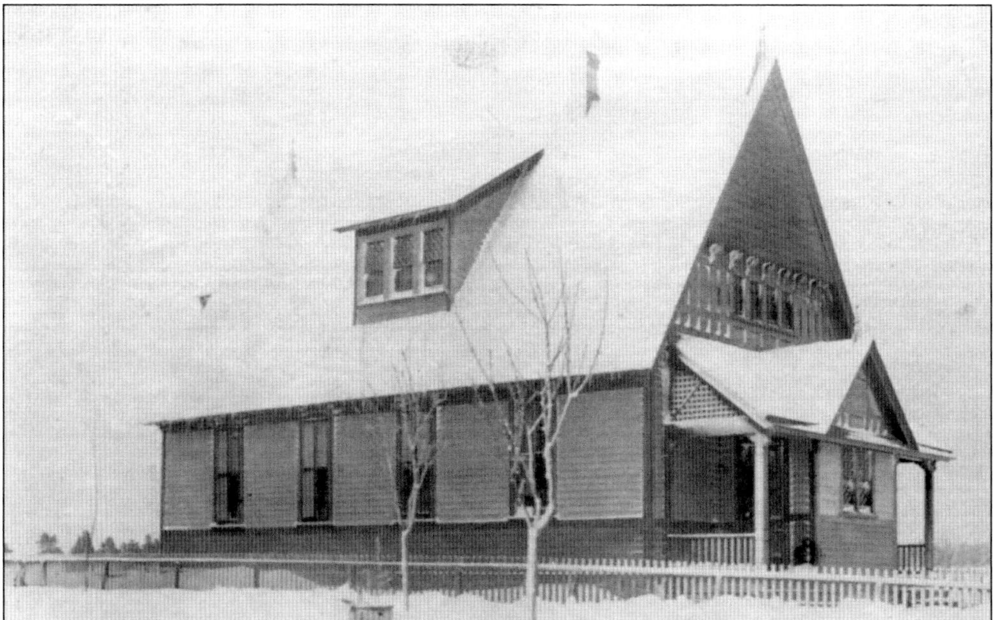

EAST MARION CHAPEL, C. 1890. In 1886, the church was given the property on the eastern corner of Main Road and Cemetery Road. The building that was on the site (known as Temperance Hall) was moved, and a new larger structure, East Marion Baptist Chapel, was constructed. The chapel was used for midweek services and meetings. In 1891, the Ladies Aide Society raised the money to retire the debt on the chapel.

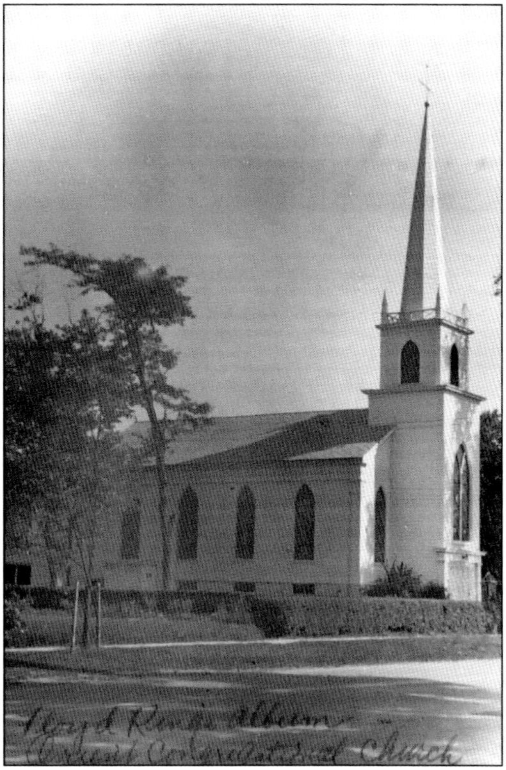

Orient Congregational Church, c. 1935. The Congregational church was built between 1717 and 1718 on land purchased from David Youngs. The congregation was organized in 1735. In 1817, additional land was acquired, and the simple wooden structure was replaced with a second building. Reorganized in 1828, the second church was demolished in 1843, and the current building was constructed.

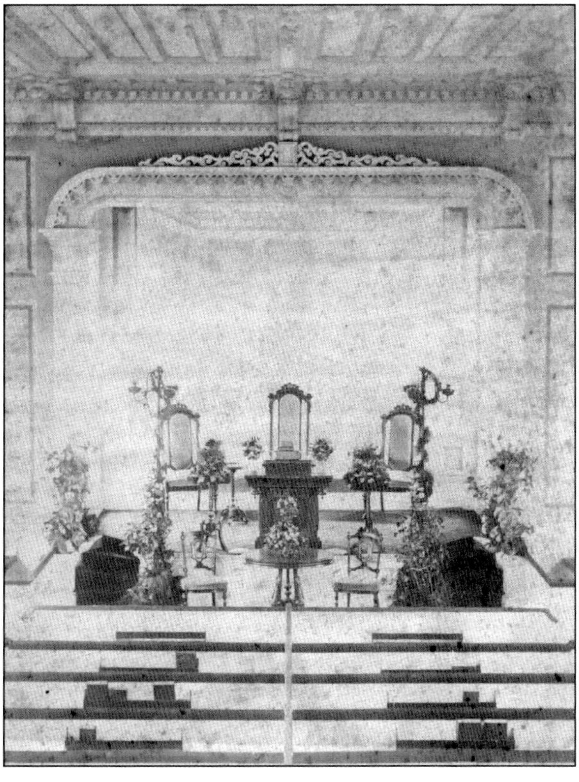

Congregational Church before Renovation, c. 1865. The ceiling of the 1843 structure was built to resemble the timbers of a ship, and the entryway of the church was built in the shape of a pilot house. This image was taken of the chancel area prior to 1868. It was this church that the famous revivalist preacher George Whitfield visited in 1740 and preached to the faithful in the area.

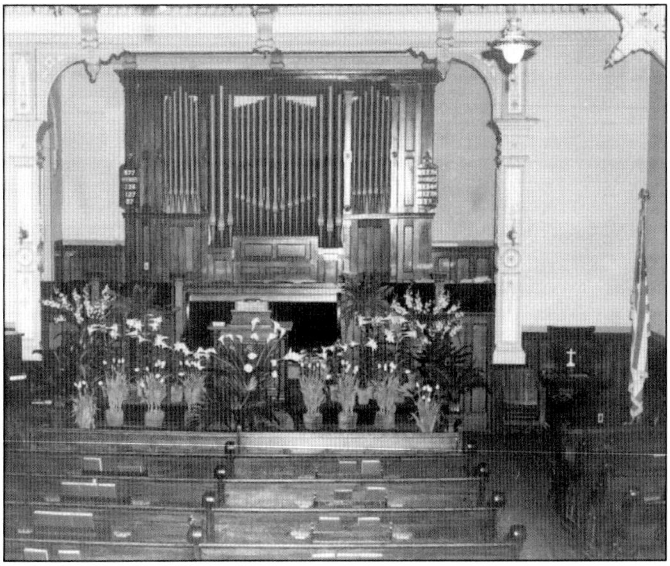

Congregational Church after Renovation, c. 1940. After the 1868 renovation, the church organ was moved to the front of the building and installed in the chancel. After another renovation in 1900, stained-glass windows were installed on either side of the sanctuary, but music expressing the glory of God remained a focus in the church. A variety of organs were installed over the years, and the current Allen organ was installed in 1963.

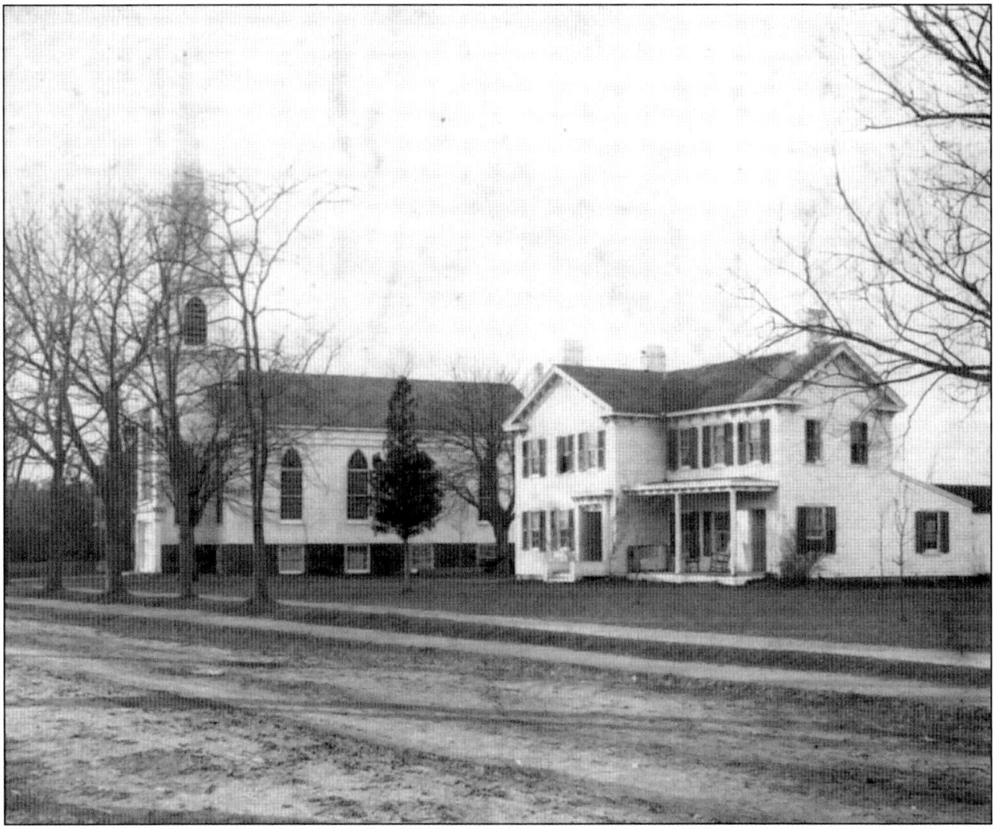

Orient Congregational Church and Parsonage, 1902. Pictured here are the Orient Congregational Church and parsonage. The 19th-century parsonage burned down shortly after this image was taken, in 1908. Rev. Asa Gray, after a violent argument with his wife, was reported in a fit of anger to have smashed a lit oil lamp against the wall of the parlor. Needless to say, after the incident the church needed a new minister.

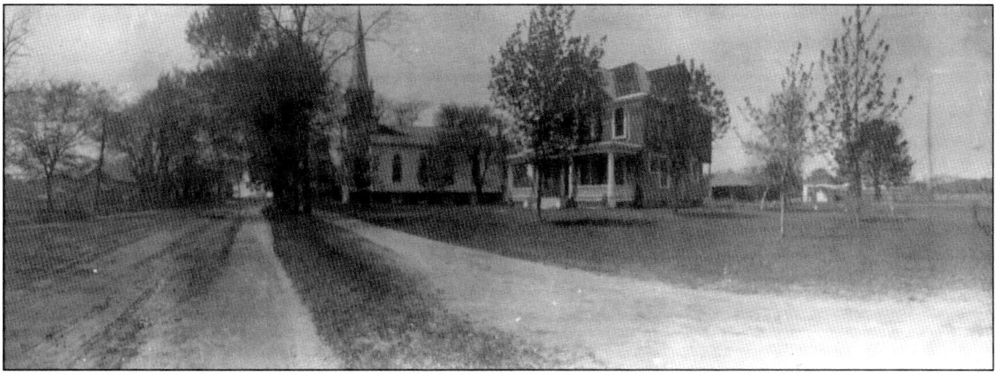

Orient Congregational Church and Parsonage, c. 1930. This is a view westward from Tabor Road showing the Orient Congregational Church and the current parsonage, which was built in 1908. During the 1980s, Rev. Milton Heitzman's wife, Rosamund, a talented artist, added another unique, local landmark to the area when she painted a panorama mural of Orient in the kitchen of the house.

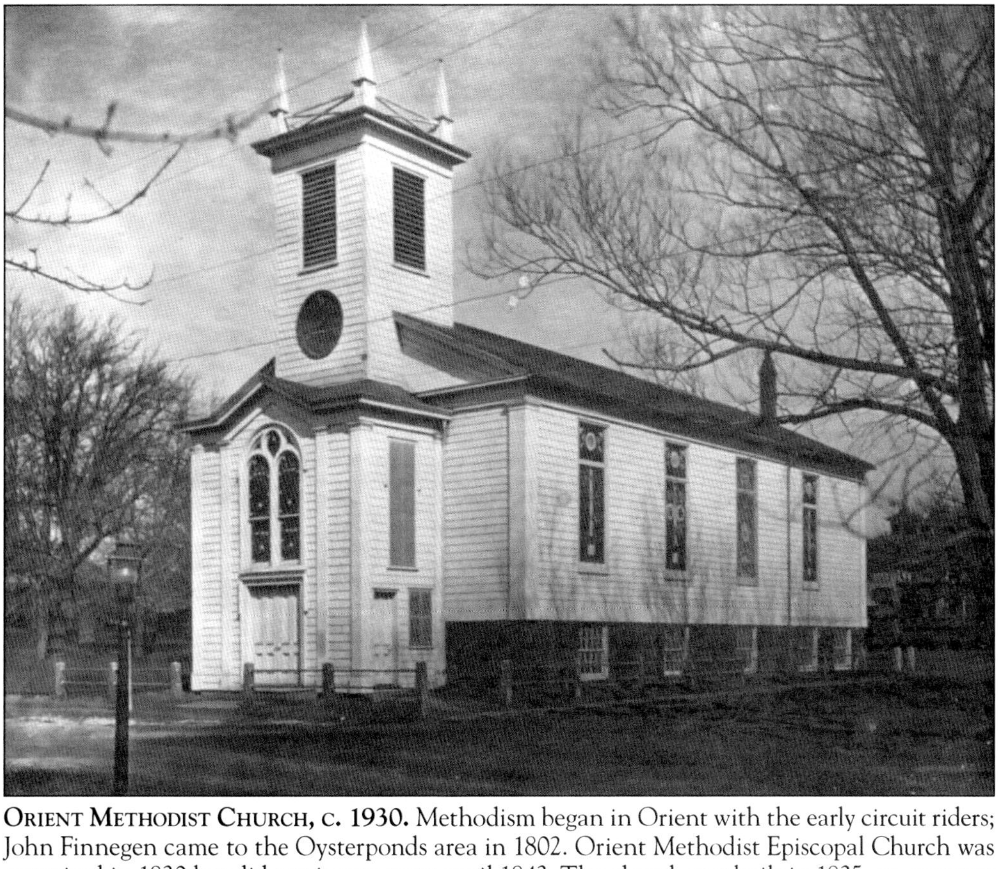

Orient Methodist Church, c. 1930. Methodism began in Orient with the early circuit riders; John Finnegen came to the Oysterponds area in 1802. Orient Methodist Episcopal Church was organized in 1830 but did not incorporate until 1843. The church was built in 1835, on property purchased from Thomas Vincent Young. In 1909, the empty lot next door, which is known as Hallelujah Park, was purchased from the Dyer family, expanding the church's property.

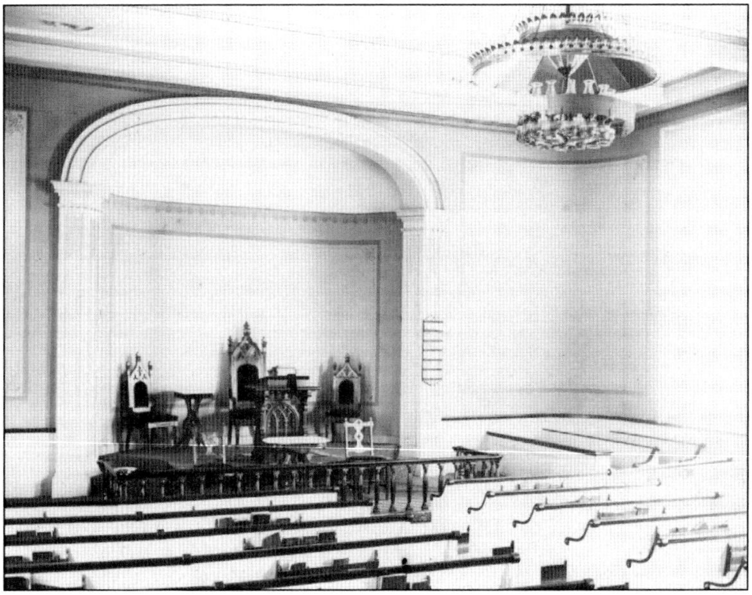

Orient Methodist Church before Renovation, c. 1890. Heated with two wood stoves and six camphene lamps, the interior of the church was austere and laid out in a similar fashion to the Congregational church down the street. The chairs in the front of the church were for the minister and his assistant during the service.

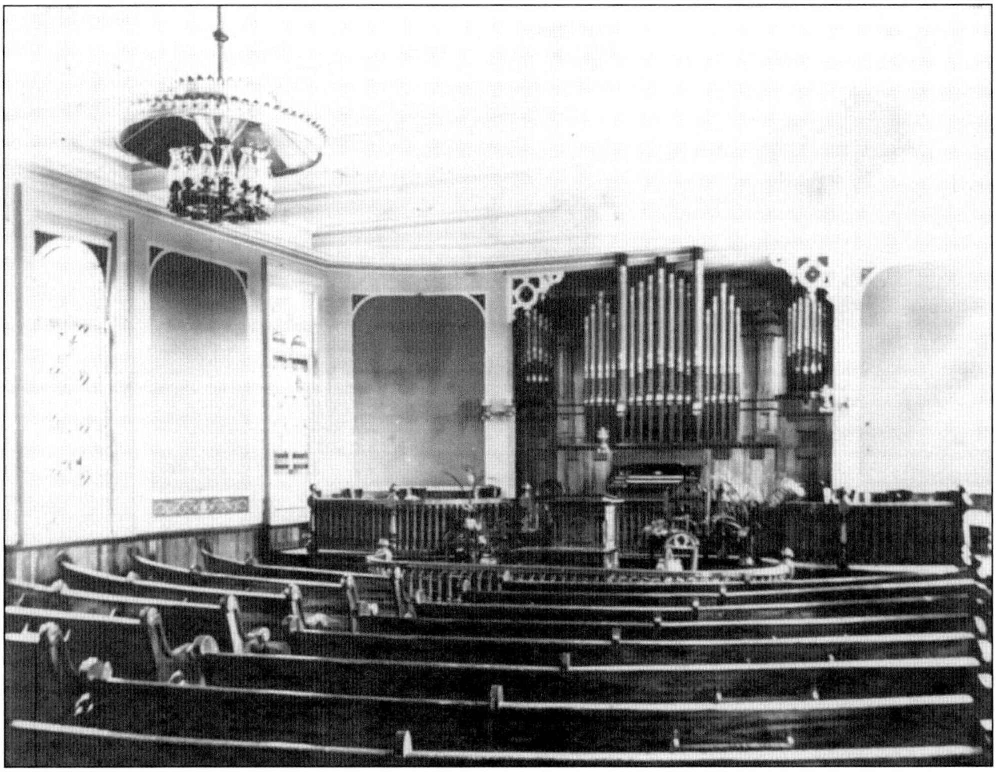

Orient Methodist Church after Renovation, c. 1905. The interior of the church underwent extensive renovations in 1900. The remodeling added 20 feet to the eastern end of the church and allowed the congregation to install a new Hooker and Hastings pipe organ into the former altar space of the church. The movement of the music from the back of the church to the front allowed worshipers to celebrate the central role music plays in the religious services.

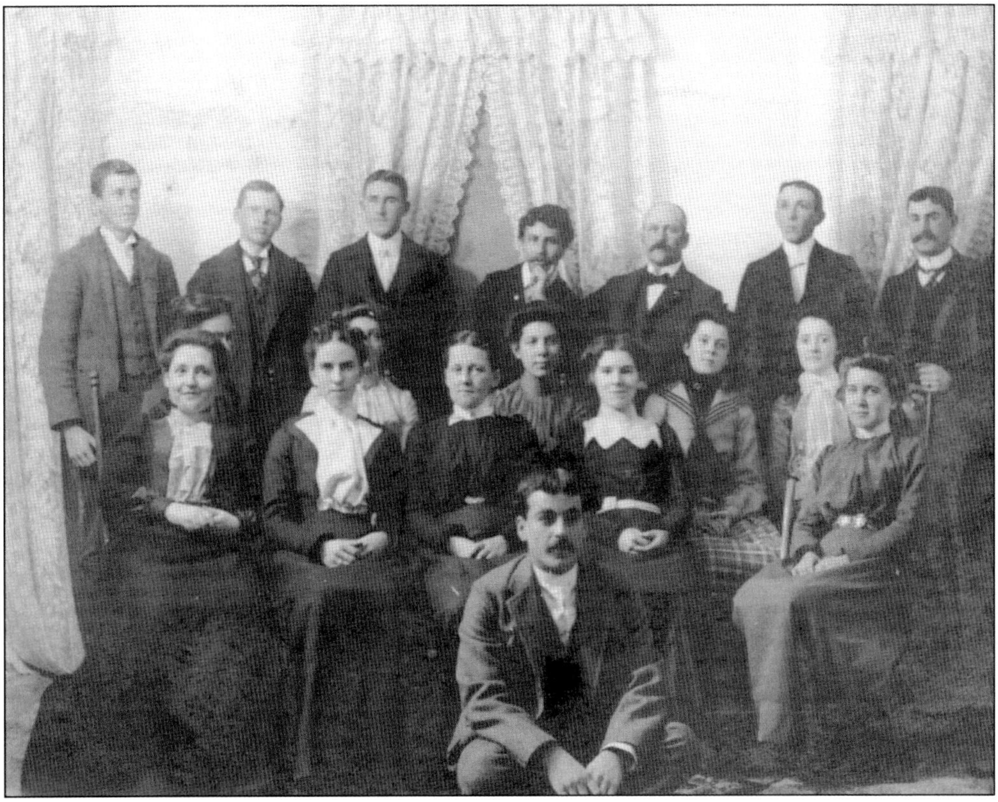

ORIENT METHODIST CHURCH'S EPIWORTH LEAGUE, 1901. The members of the league pose at Ernest Vail's house on Orchard Street in 1901. Pictured here are, from left to right, (first row) Sam Vail; (second row) Effie Potter, Stella Prince Terry, Florence L. Potter, Nellie Berry, and Grace Latham; (third row) Lula Vail, Minnie Russell Frank, Flora Wilcox, Grace Hallock, and Jessie Young; (fourth row): Ellis Hallock, John Jagger, Rufus Petty, Cecil Latham, Philip Taber, Griffing Petty, and John Petty.

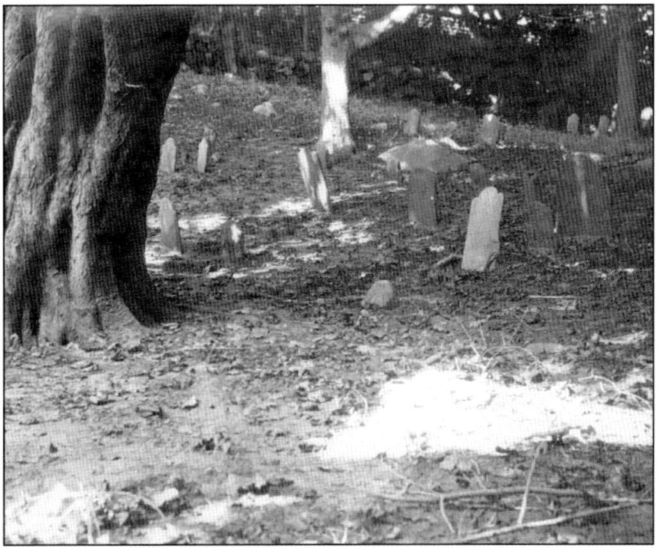

BROWNS HILL CEMETERY, C. 1940. The oldest cemetery in Oysterponds, Browns Hill's earliest occupant is Gideon Youngs, who died in 1699. Cradled in a narrow, rocky valley, the cemetery has only a few stones left standing. Filled by 1800, Browns Hill closed, and a new cemetery along Main Road across from the Orient Congregational Church was opened. Land for the new cemetery, known as Main Road Cemetery, was purchased in 1790 by some local families.

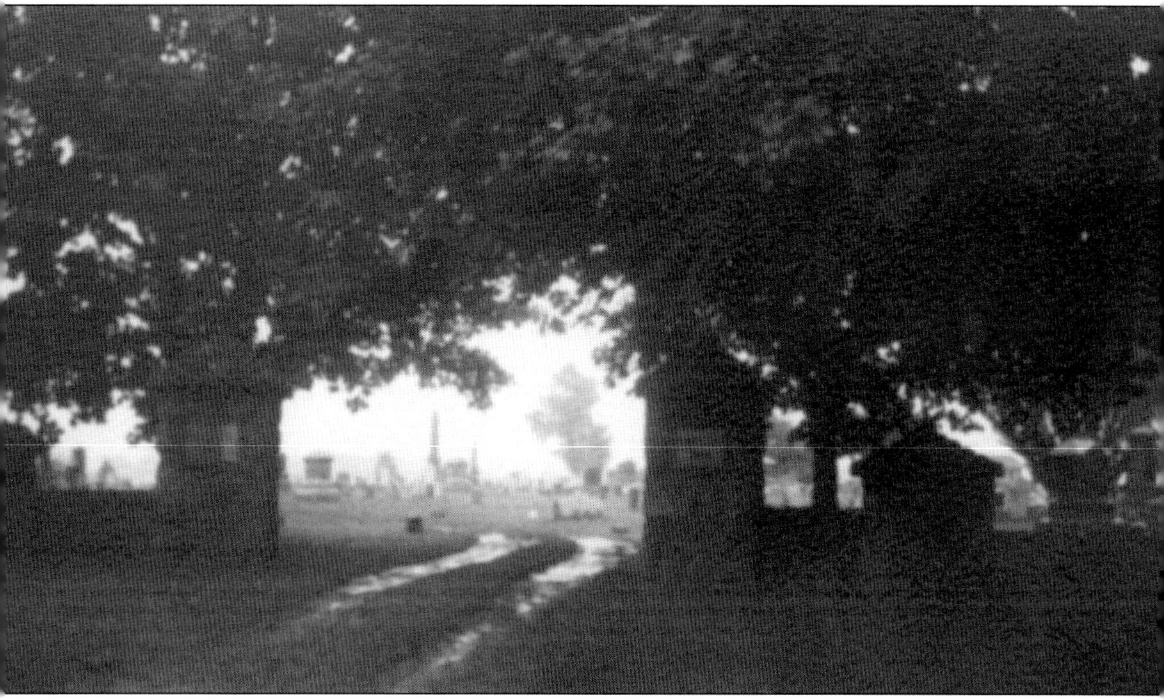

ENTRANCE OF CENTRAL CEMETERY, C. 1935. Opened February 19, 1855, the sprawling Central Cemetery was and is opened to all Orient residents, and many of the old local families are represented among residents of the peaceful resting place on Tabor Road. Of the eight local cemeteries in the Oysterponds area, only this cemetery and the East Marion cemetery, which was started in 1864 on a parcel of land along the shores of Lake Marion, are still in regular use.

Three

BUSINESSES

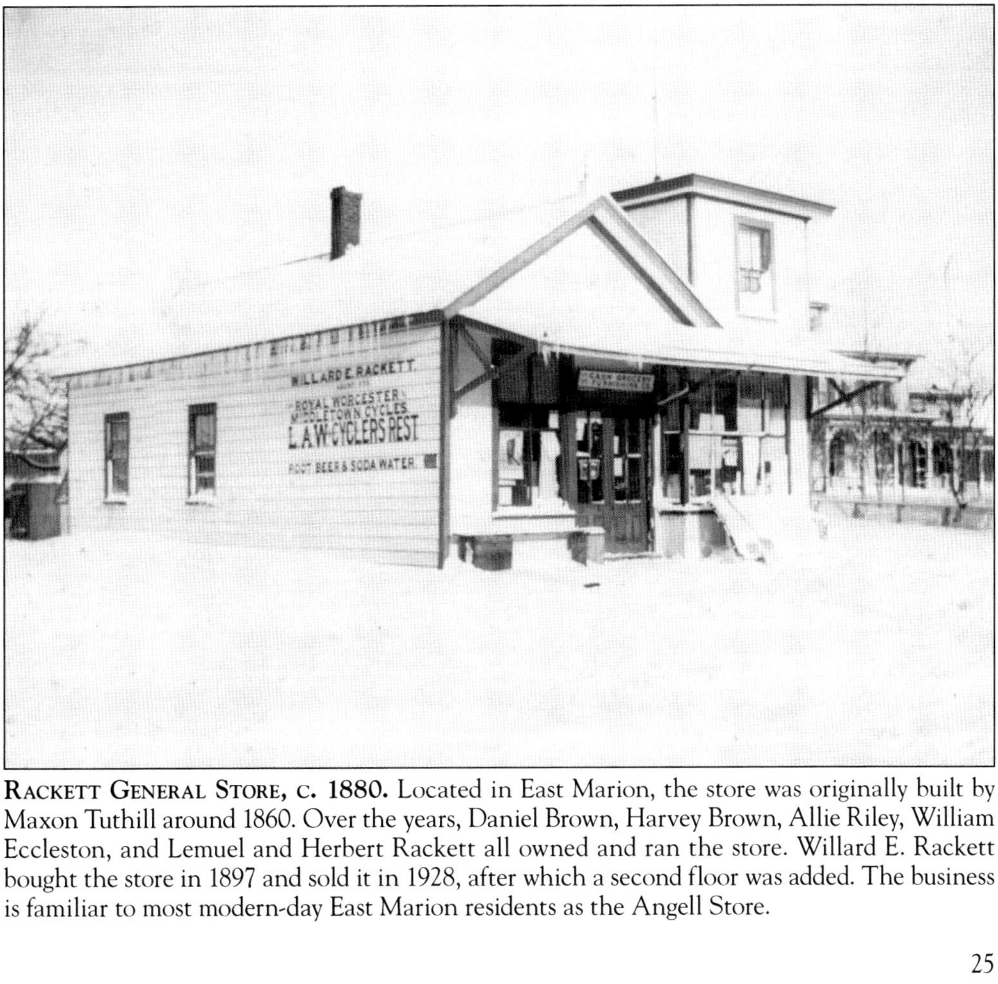

RACKETT GENERAL STORE, C. 1880. Located in East Marion, the store was originally built by Maxon Tuthill around 1860. Over the years, Daniel Brown, Harvey Brown, Allie Riley, William Eccleston, and Lemuel and Herbert Rackett all owned and ran the store. Willard E. Rackett bought the store in 1897 and sold it in 1928, after which a second floor was added. The business is familiar to most modern-day East Marion residents as the Angell Store.

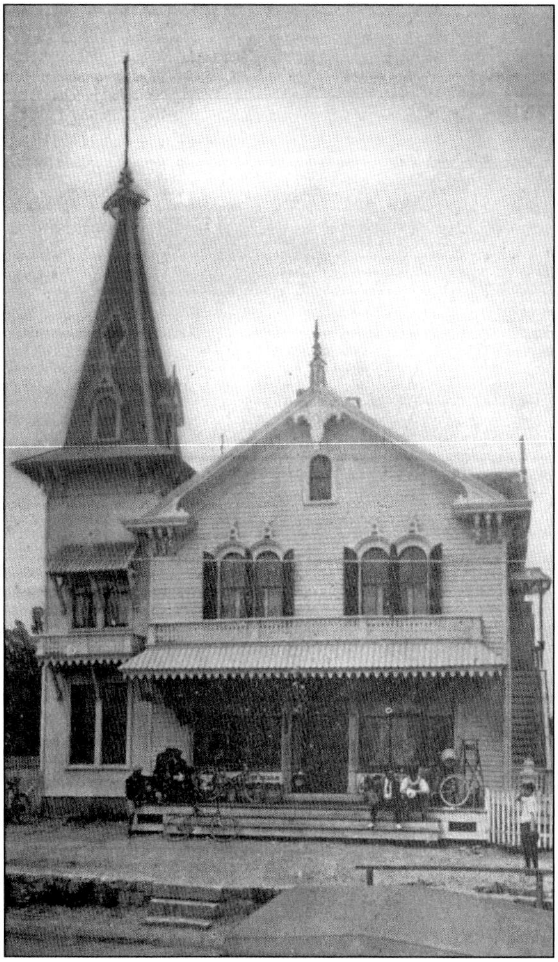

ANKER'S GENERAL STORE, C. 1890. Formerly known as the Benjamin Clark Tuthill store, this building was erected in 1880 and replaced an earlier building. Clarence Ankers, from Rockville Center, bought the business from Tuthill. In 1923, he thrilled the hamlet by installing electric lights in the store. In 1930, Ankers retired, and the business was rented out for a short time to J.R. Vaughn. The building was badly damaged by the 1938 hurricane and was demolished.

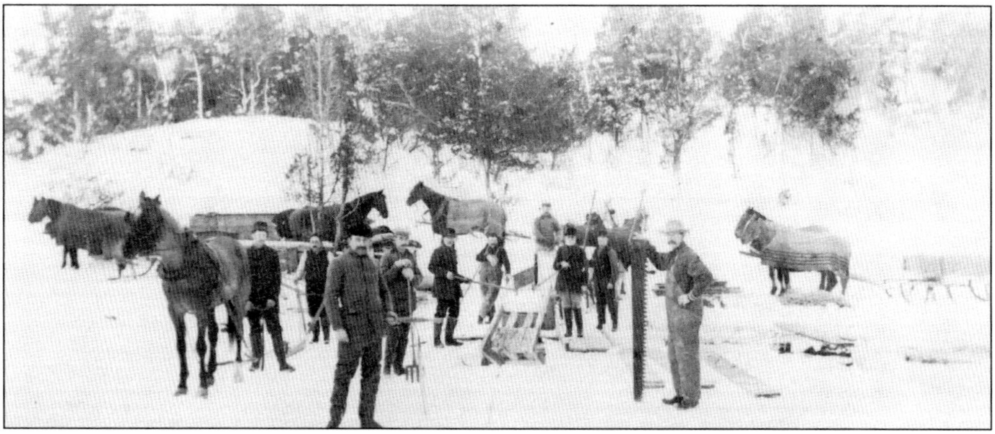

ICE CUTTING ON LAKE MARION, C. 1890. The ice harvest was an annual event in which the whole community participated. Each winter, men would gather at Lake Marion to pack the community icehouses with blocks of ice for the upcoming warmer seasons. The ice was used over the course of the year to pack and ship fish to New York City using either local ships or the Long Island Rail Road.

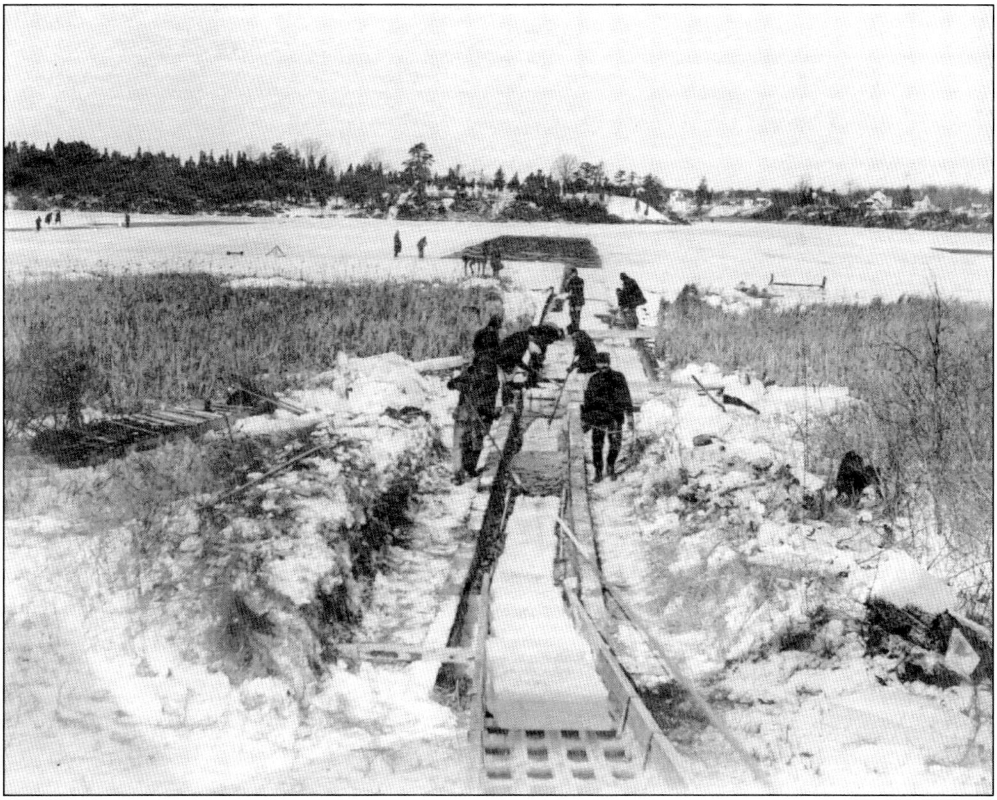

ICE CUTTING RAMP ON LAKE MARION, C. 1900. Pictured here is the ramp from the lake to the icehouses on the shore between Lake Marion and Peconic Bay. Lake Marion, a freshwater lake, sits protected from the salty Peconic Bay by a narrow strip of beach. After each block was cut, it was dragged by hand along a narrow channel towards the icehouse.

HAULING THE ICE, C. 1900. The blocks were moved along the sluiceway to the icehouse; at the shoreline, the cakes of ice were then slid along an icy ramp to the building where they would be stacked with layers of sawdust and straw, which would insulate the ice long into the summer and fall.

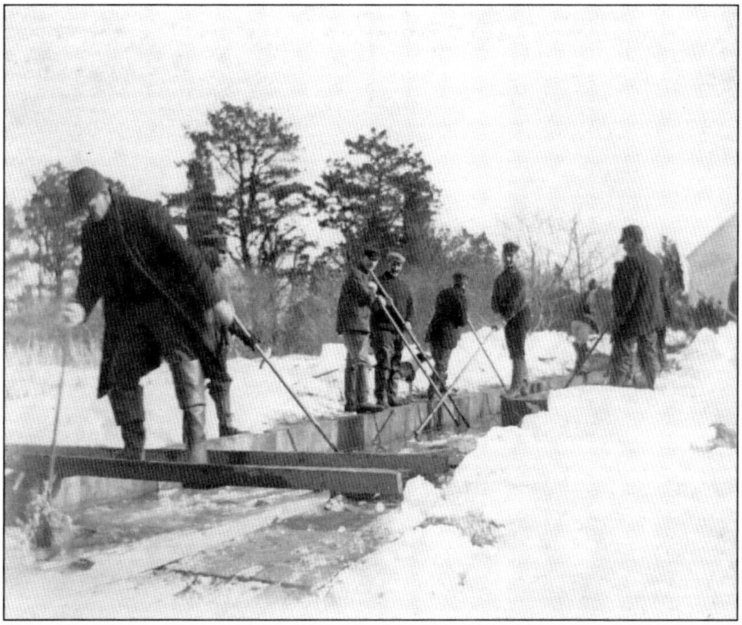

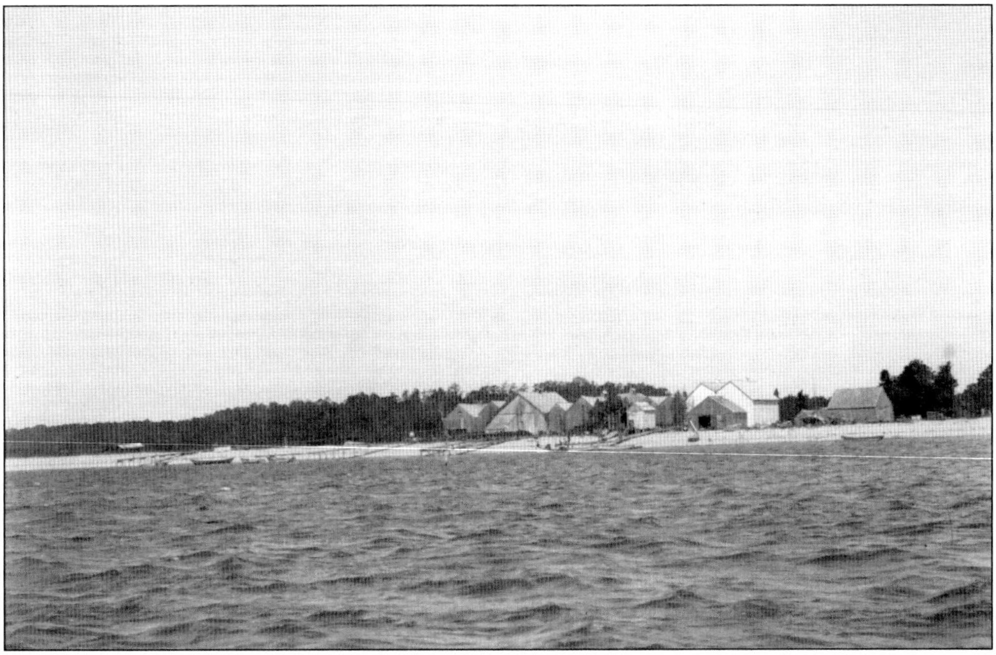

Ice Houses, 1898. Pictured here is the row of icehouses between Peconic Bay and Lake Marion. Starting with one icehouse, as the fishing industry in the area grew so did the number of icehouses. These houses were situated at the foot of Rabbits Lane, and the smaller buildings were boat and storage sheds for some of the local fishermen.

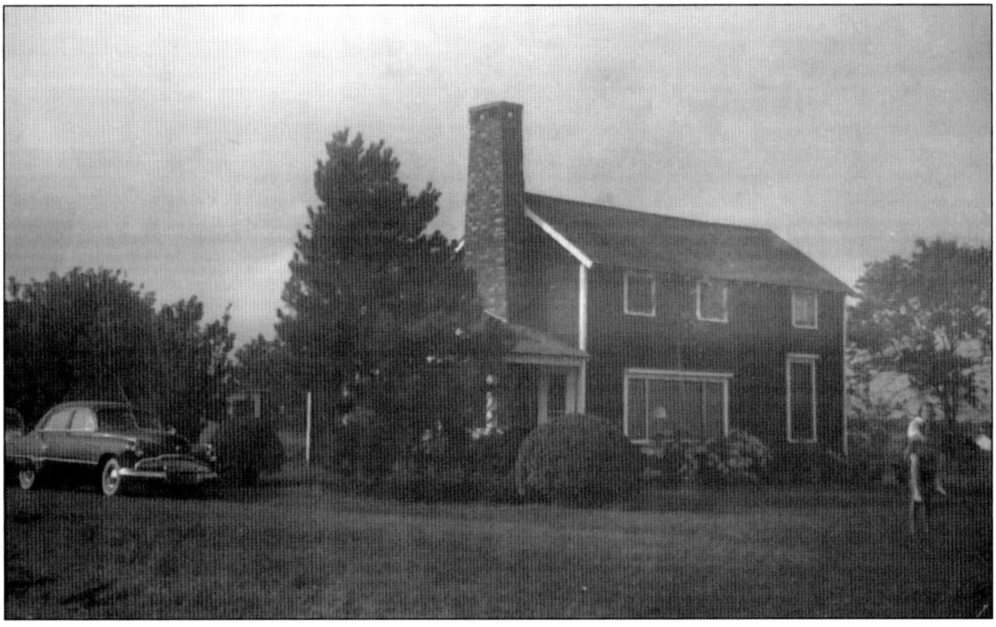

Mosback Summer Cabins, c. 1950. East Marion had several summer colonies that rented small cabins to tourists, and many residents of the area also owned and rented out houses to families who returned to the area every summer. This house owned by the Mosback family was originally part of the St. Thomas Summer Camp. It was purchased for $100 after the camp closed, to replace the house that had burned down. (Courtesy of Ruthann Bramson.)

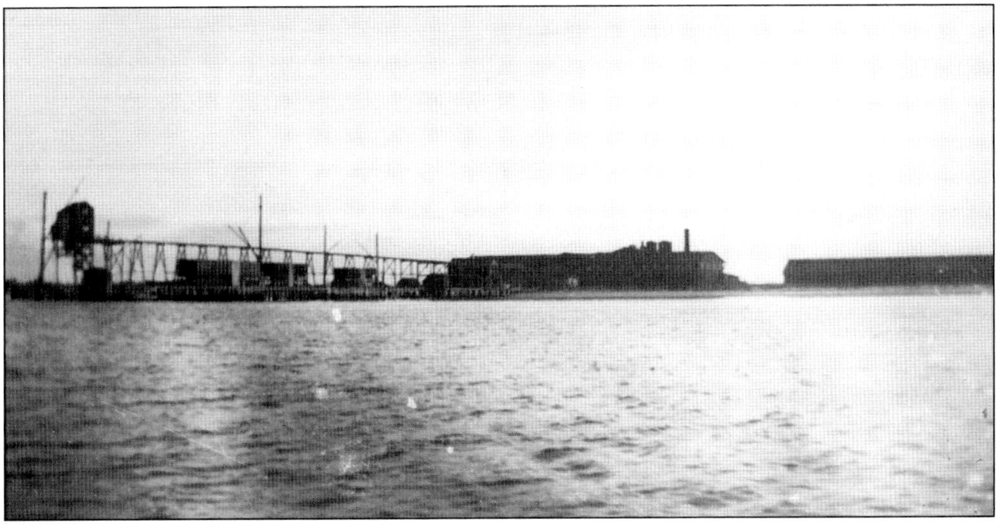

The Atlantic Oil and Guano Company, c. 1935. In 1865, Lewis A. Edwards and the Waterbury and Marshall Company of Brooklyn leased land on Long Beach to establish a factory to turn a very oily fish, menhaden, into fertilizer and oil. Originally called the Atlantic Oil and Guano Company, later the Atlantic and Virginia Fertilizer Company, the factory caught fire in 1880 and again in 1881. After the second fire, the factory was abandoned.

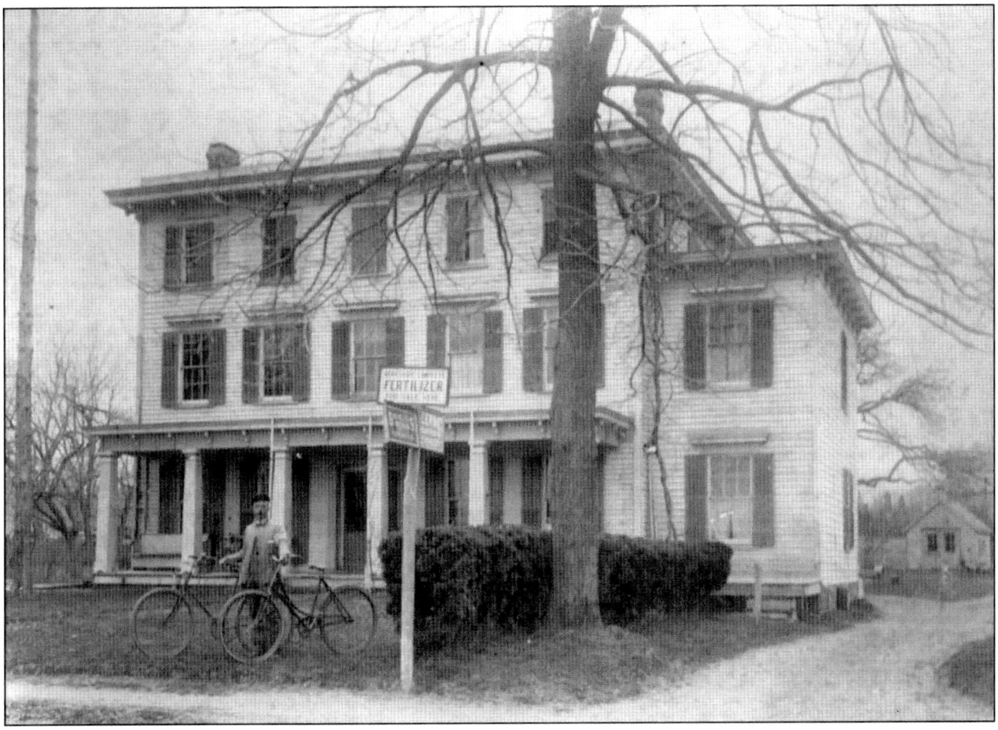

The Brown House, c. 1870. This home was built by Orient's only whaling captain, Edwin Peter Brown (1813–1892). Brown was the master of the *Lucy Ann*, the *Amelia*, and the *Franklin*. In 1843, he married Martha S. Brewer (1820–1911), whom he had met in Brooklyn. The couple needed a large house to accommodate their 10 children. After Brown died in 1892, his wife turned the home into a boardinghouse for tourists who flocked to the area in the summers.

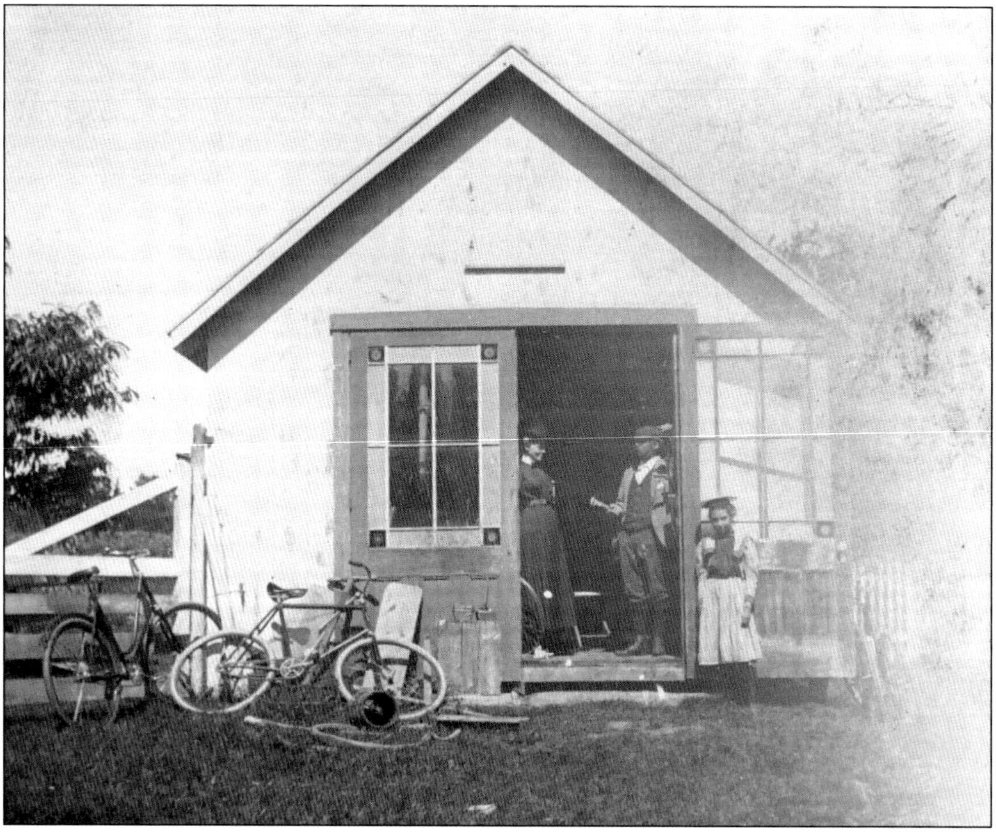

William E. Brown's Bicycle Shop, c. 1890. The shop was located in the backyard of the Brown House. During the 1890s, bicycling was a fashionable craze. A number of bicycle clubs abounded on Long Island, and the East End was a popular destination for long rides. Brown, capitalizing on the craze, was one of two bicycle shops in the Oysterponds area. Standing with Brown in the photograph are his sister Minnie (left) and his niece Madeline (right).

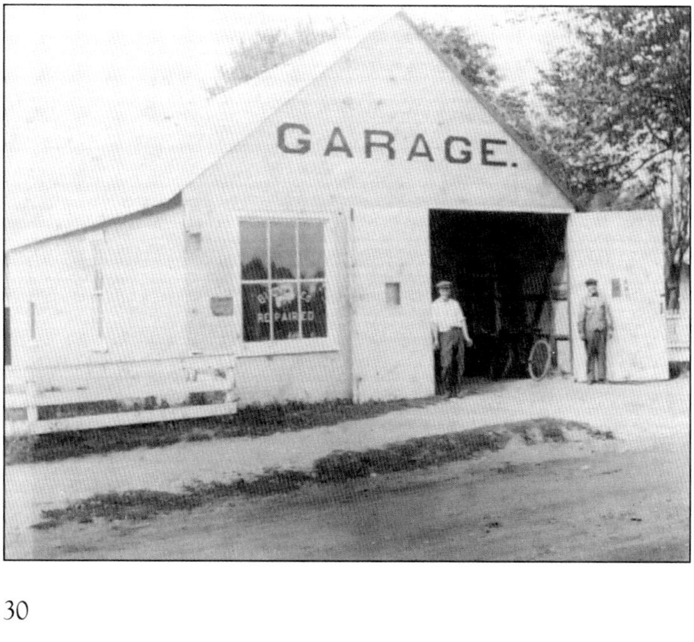

Alfred Luce's Garage, c. 1925. One of the early automobile repair shops in the Orient area, Luce's garage was located on Village Lane next to the Country Store. The building, which was metal sided, was not up to the punishing winds of the 1938 hurricane and collapsed during the storm. In this image, Elbert and Alfred Luce stand outside the building.

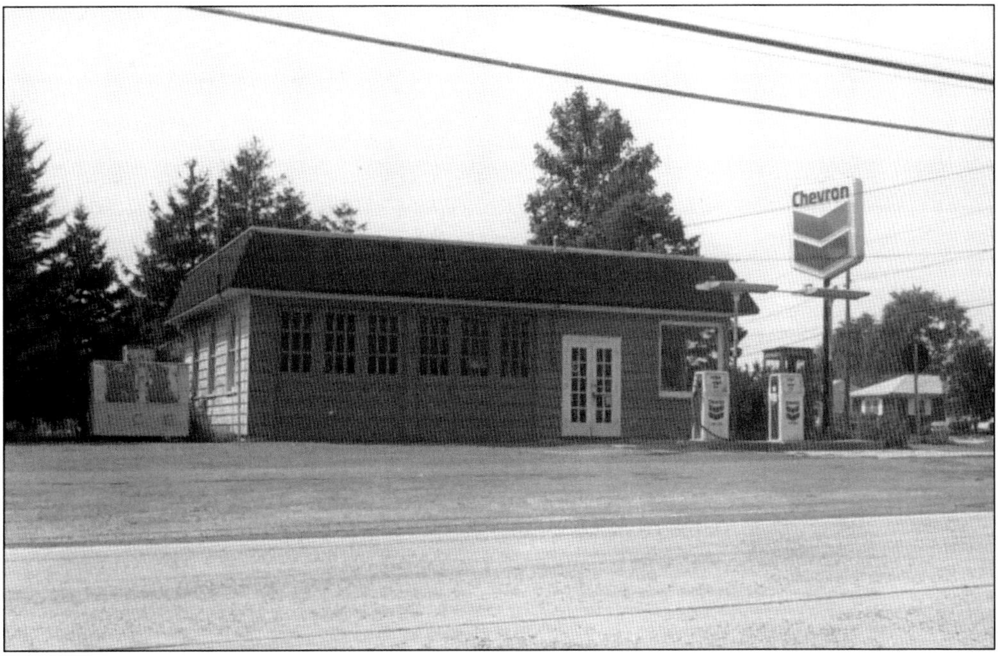

CHEVRON SERVICE STATION, C. 1960. After losing his garage, Alfred Luce decided to build a Tydol gas station on Main Road. He purchased a strip of land that ran from Main Road to Skippers Lane, subdivided the property into housing parcels, and built Oysterponds Lane. Eventually, Ted Rackett bought the gas station, which had changed to Chevron. In 1980, the station was renovated to house Bill Heins's candy business, the Candyman.

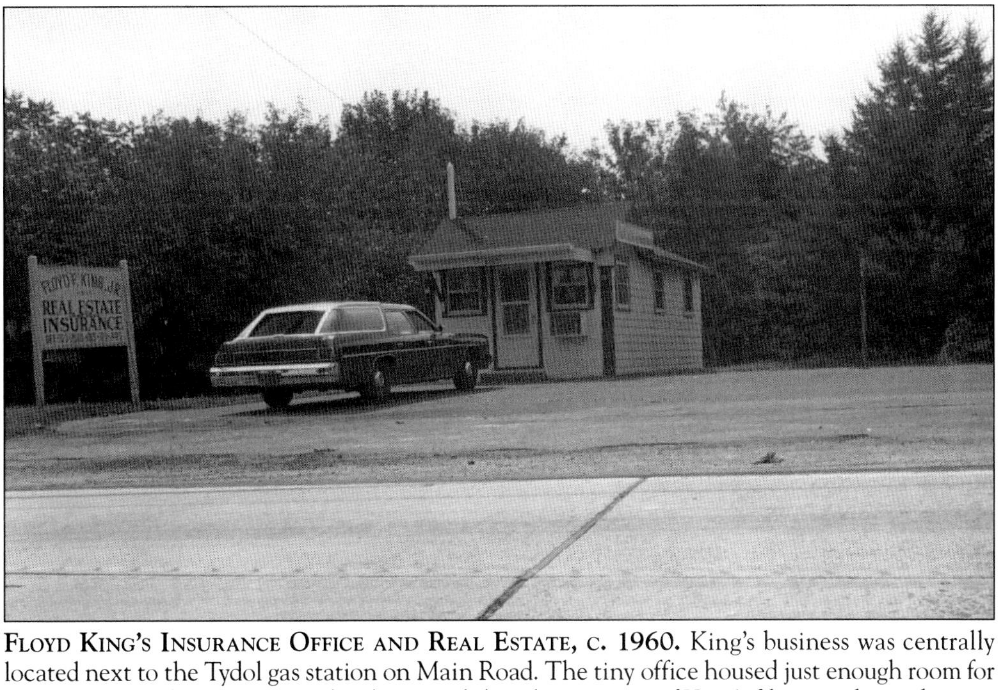

FLOYD KING'S INSURANCE OFFICE AND REAL ESTATE, C. 1960. King's business was centrally located next to the Tydol gas station on Main Road. The tiny office housed just enough room for King's desk and his assistant. It has been said that the majority of King's files were housed not in this office but in the trunk of his car.

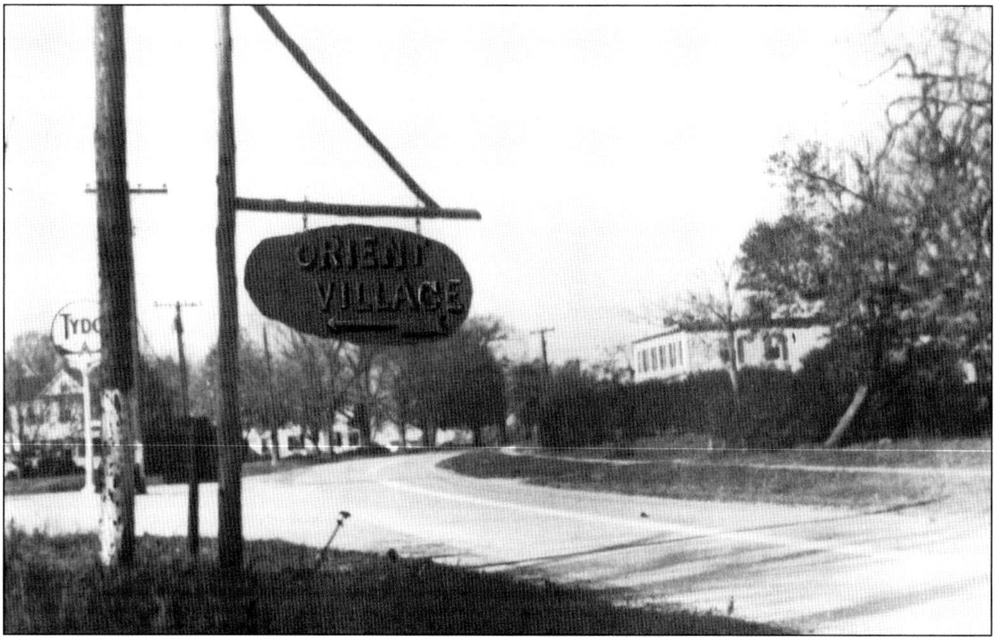

The Intersection of Main Road and Village Lane, c. 1950. Originally, this intersection was Main Road and Main Street. In 1946, in an effort made to again make Orient more attractive to tourists, residents decided to change the name of the main thoroughfare through Orient Village. The street sign, pictured here, points south towards Orient Village and the former business section of Orient.

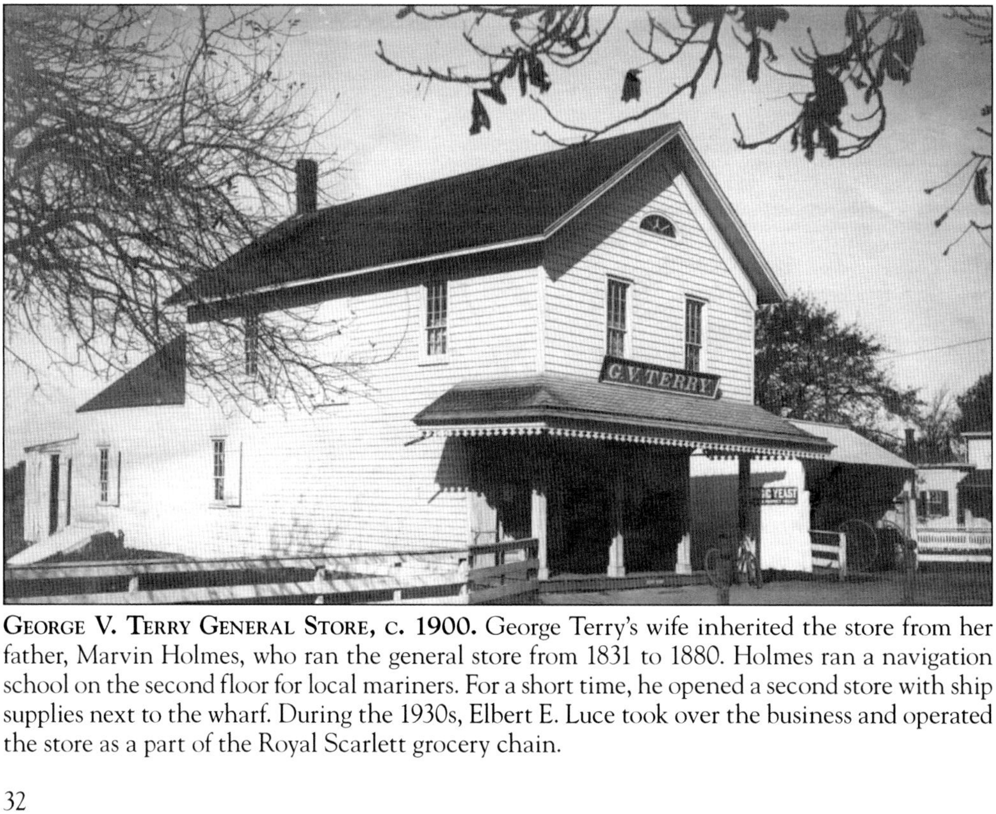

George V. Terry General Store, c. 1900. George Terry's wife inherited the store from her father, Marvin Holmes, who ran the general store from 1831 to 1880. Holmes ran a navigation school on the second floor for local mariners. For a short time, he opened a second store with ship supplies next to the wharf. During the 1930s, Elbert E. Luce took over the business and operated the store as a part of the Royal Scarlett grocery chain.

BEEBE ICE CREAM PARLOR, C. 1890. On State Street, today known as Skippers Lane, Ann Beebe sold ice cream from her home on the north side of the street. Identified by the small square sign mounted next to the door, the frozen treat was offered to customers who were welcome to enjoy their purchase on the wide front porch of the house. In this image, Jessie Young (right) and a young companion enjoy a refreshing break.

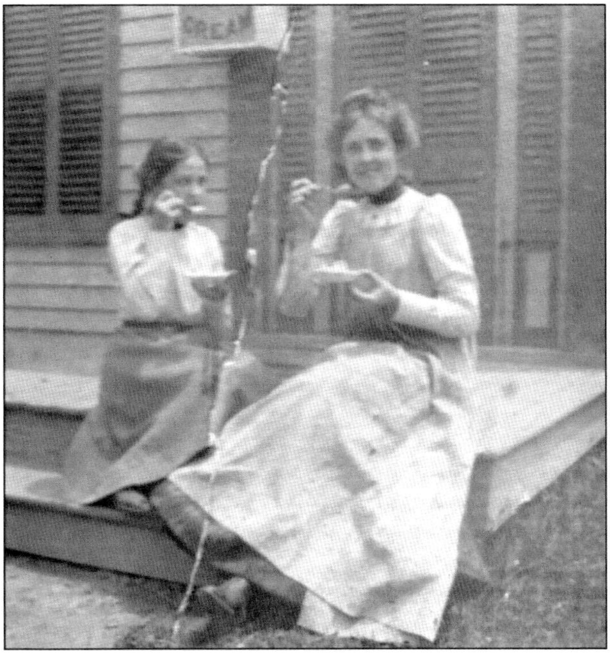

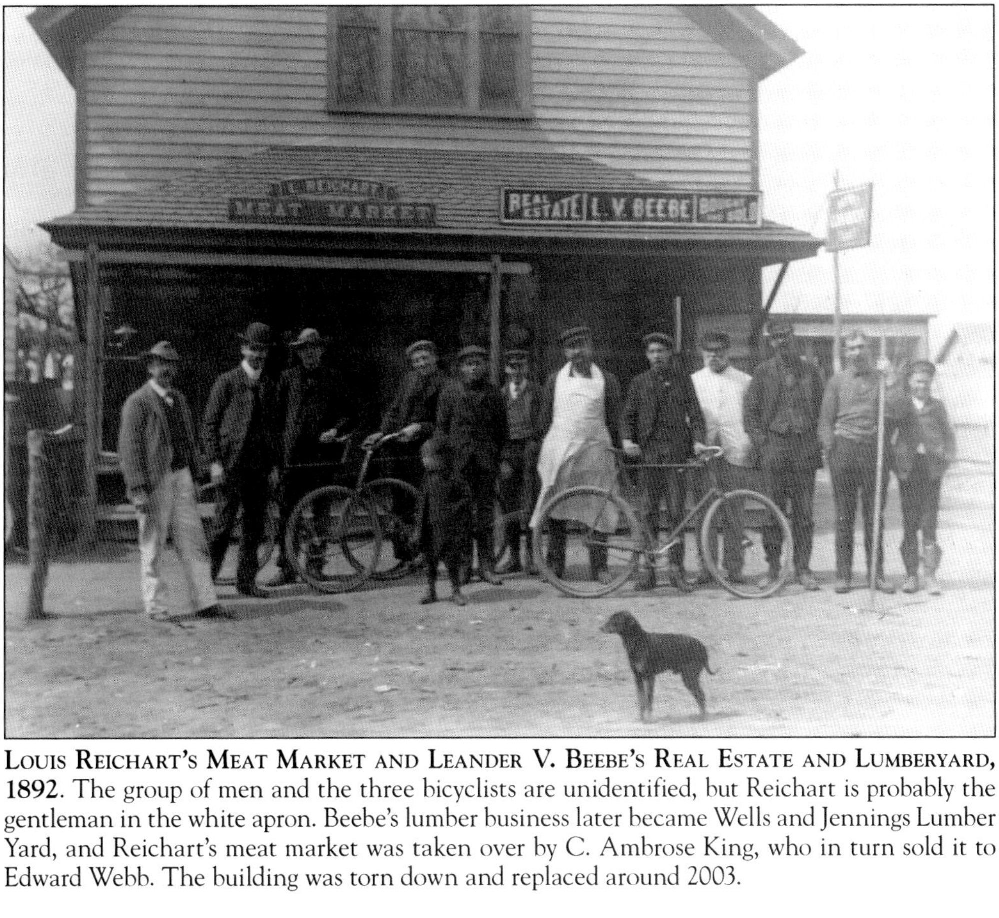

LOUIS REICHART'S MEAT MARKET AND LEANDER V. BEEBE'S REAL ESTATE AND LUMBERYARD, 1892. The group of men and the three bicyclists are unidentified, but Reichart is probably the gentleman in the white apron. Beebe's lumber business later became Wells and Jennings Lumber Yard, and Reichart's meat market was taken over by C. Ambrose King, who in turn sold it to Edward Webb. The building was torn down and replaced around 2003.

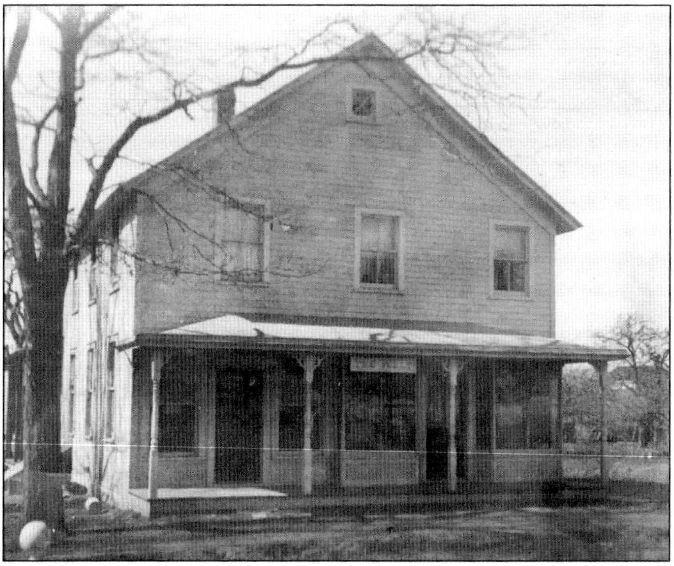

The Folly, c. 1890. Built by Abram D. Latham, the Folly sold cigars, cigarettes, tobacco and an assortment of snacks aimed at passing tourists. Located south of the Webb House driveway on Village Lane, in 1921 the Folly became the Wigwam tea room, which served lunch as well as ice cream and candy. The Wigwam advertised having a pool room, which could be rented by women. The building burned down shortly after it opened.

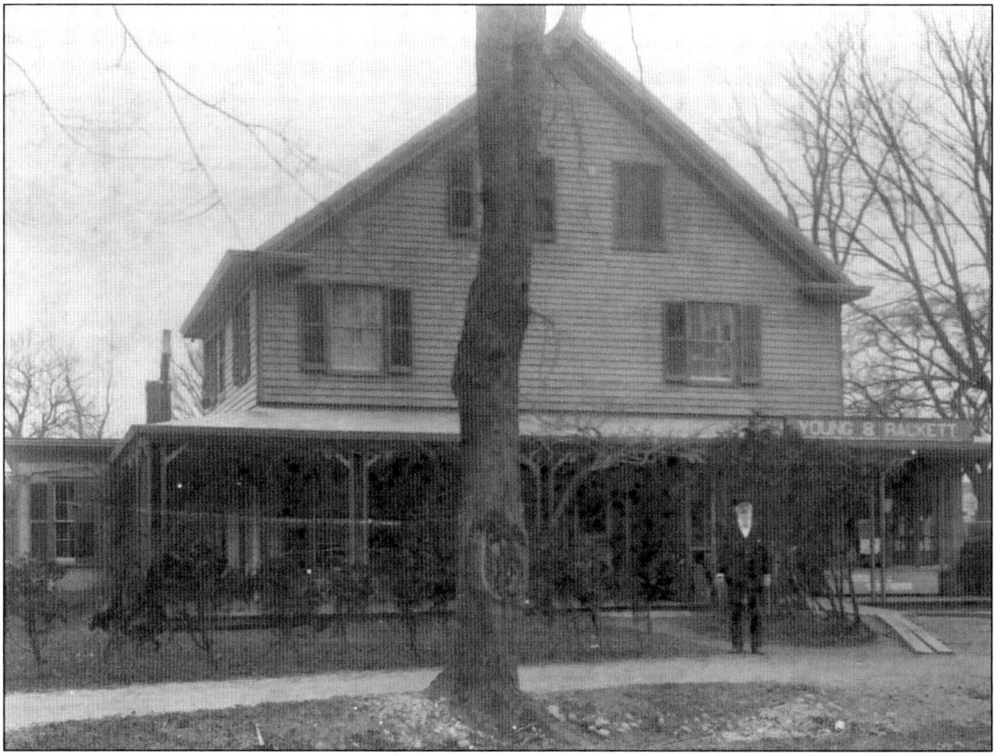

Young and Rackett General Store, c. 1880. Built by Capt. Frederick King, the building was purchased in 1853 by John Brown Young. Young, with his partner, Elisha Rackett, turned it into a general store. The building was later rented by C. Ambrose and H. Cortland King, who operated a meat market. The King Brothers' market later moved to another location down the street. Sometime in the 1920s, it was converted into a medical recovery center and senior citizen nursing home.

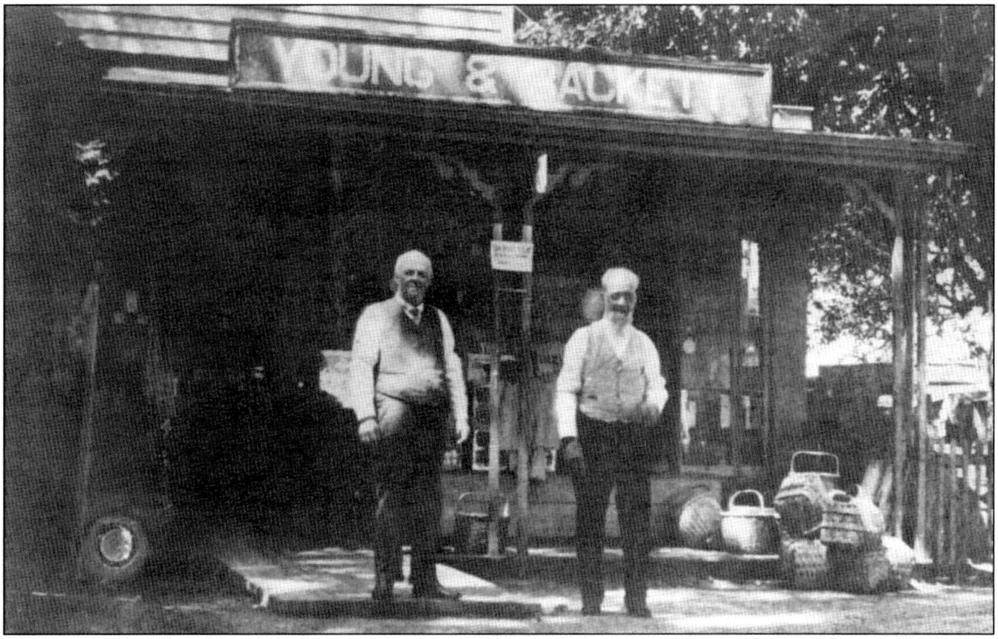

Young and Rackett Owners, c. 1880. Business partners John B. Young and Elisha Rackett pose in front of their establishment. Elizabeth F. Young used a wing in the building to capture wild yeast, which the partners sold in the store. Located directly across from the Oysterponds Historical Society's Village House in the heart of downtown Orient, today the building is a private home.

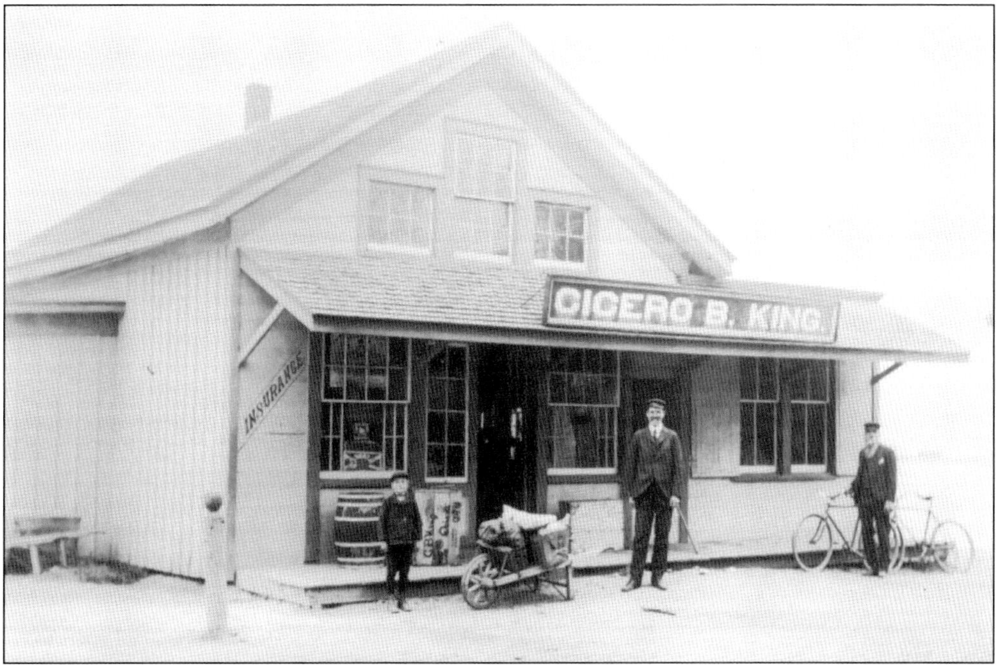

Cicero B. King's General Store, c. 1900. The King store was situated at the end of the Orient Wharf on the north side. Known for his sharp business acumen, King was not a man to let a good business deal go past. King also had a reputation for being careful with his financial dealings and would weigh out a customer's order to the ounce.

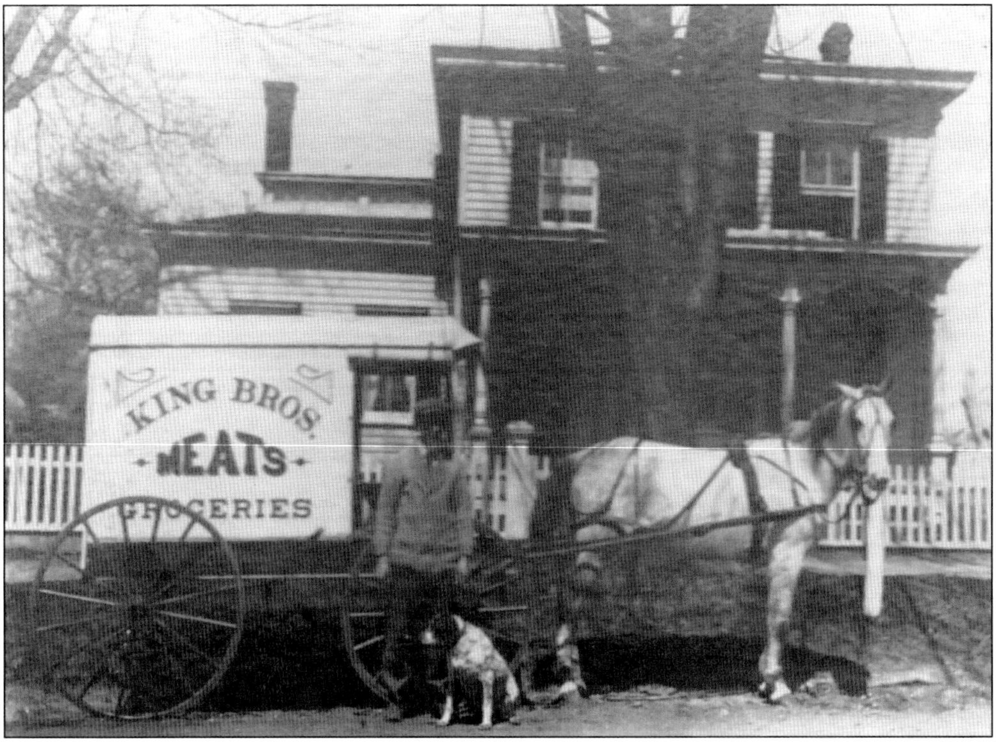

KING BROS. MEAT WAGON, C. 1910. The King brothers' delivery wagon pauses in front of James Douglass's house on King Street in Orient. King Bros. was C. Ambrose King and H. Cortland King's meat market business, which operated out of the Young and Rackett store and later in a small building down near Orient wharf. The man and dog posed in front of the wagon are not identified.

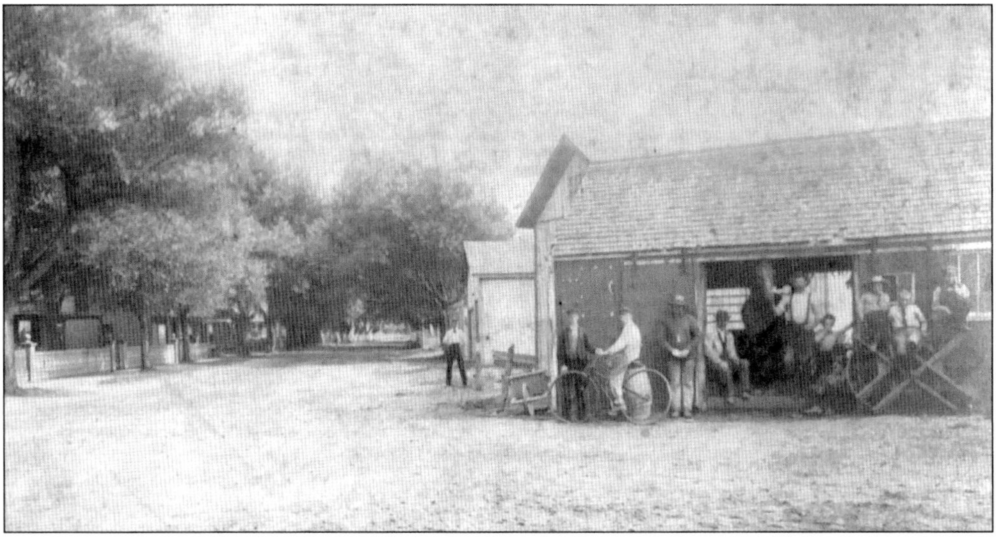

THE JOHN CLEVELAND BLACKSMITH SHOP, C. 1870. The shop was located on the southern corner of the foot of the Orient Wharf. John Cleveland was from Southold and moved to the Orient area after the Civil War. Like most blacksmiths, he worked on a variety of metal objects, including the repair of maritime equipment for the many ships that tied up to the Orient Wharf. The shop was later moved to Skipper Lane and became a carpenter shop.

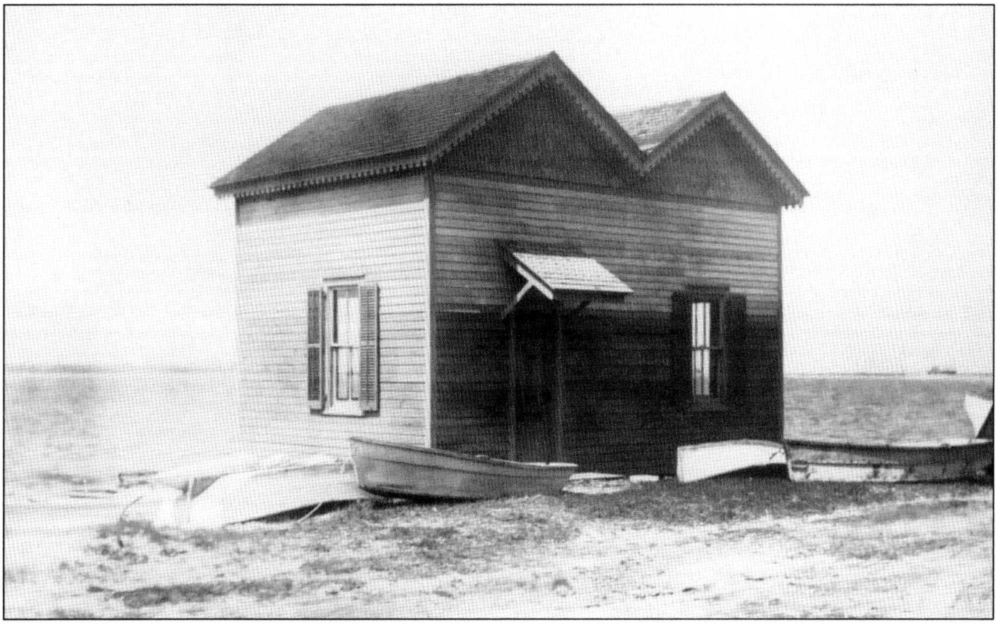

The Orient Cornet Band Hall, c. 1880. Local bands were very popular during the 19th century, when most communities had musicians who performed at dances and concerts. Orient's band featured the brass cornet. Band members built and practiced in this small structure at the edge of Orient Harbor, north of the wharf. The building was later sold to Edward F. Dewey, who used the building as a cigar store, confectionery, and hairdressing shop in the 1890s.

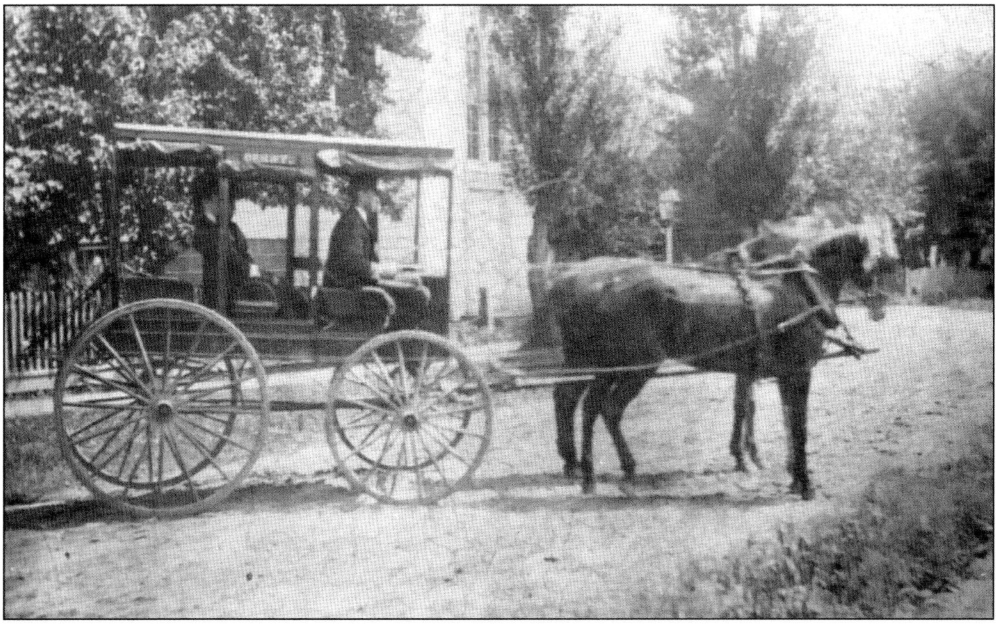

Elbert W. Tabor's Taxi Service, c. 1870. Tabor's taxi is momentarily poised in front of the Orient Methodist Church. During the summers, he transported tourists around Orient and from the train station in Greenport. Tabor also carried the mail to the local post offices. In addition to his taxi and livery stable service, he worked as the local constable, road inspector, and overseer of the poor. Tabor was also a founding member of the Orient Band.

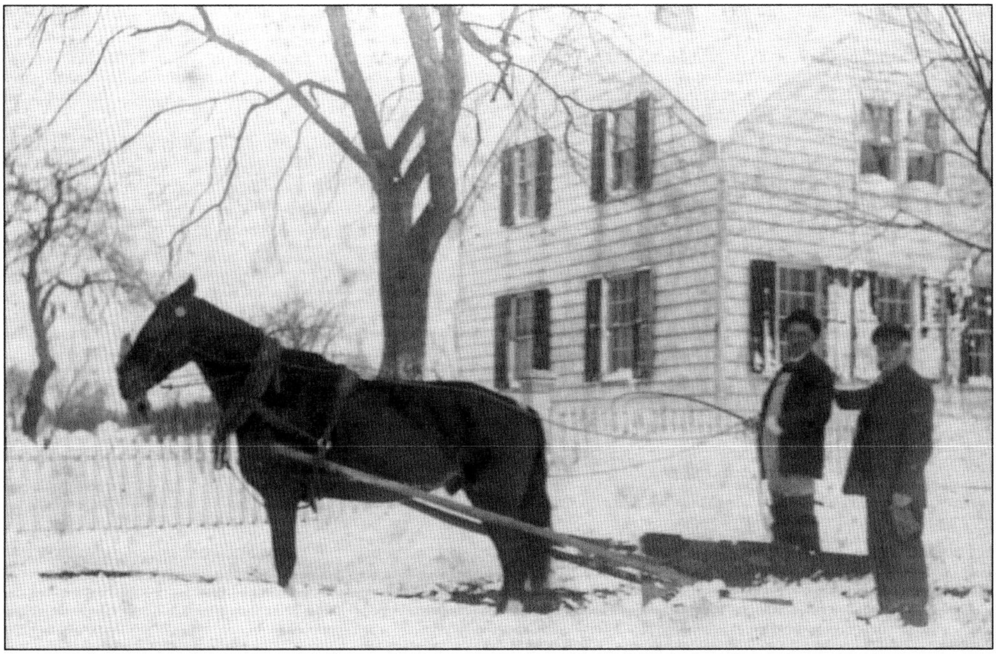

Orient Road Crew, c. 1870. Joseph Miller (left) pauses to chat in front of Hollis Vail's house on King Street while clearing snow. Clearing the streets in the past was the responsibility of homeowners. Eventually, people began to hire others to clear the area in front of their houses. The snow was usually pushed to the sides, with a layer left on the ground packed firmly down to support sleighs and sleds.

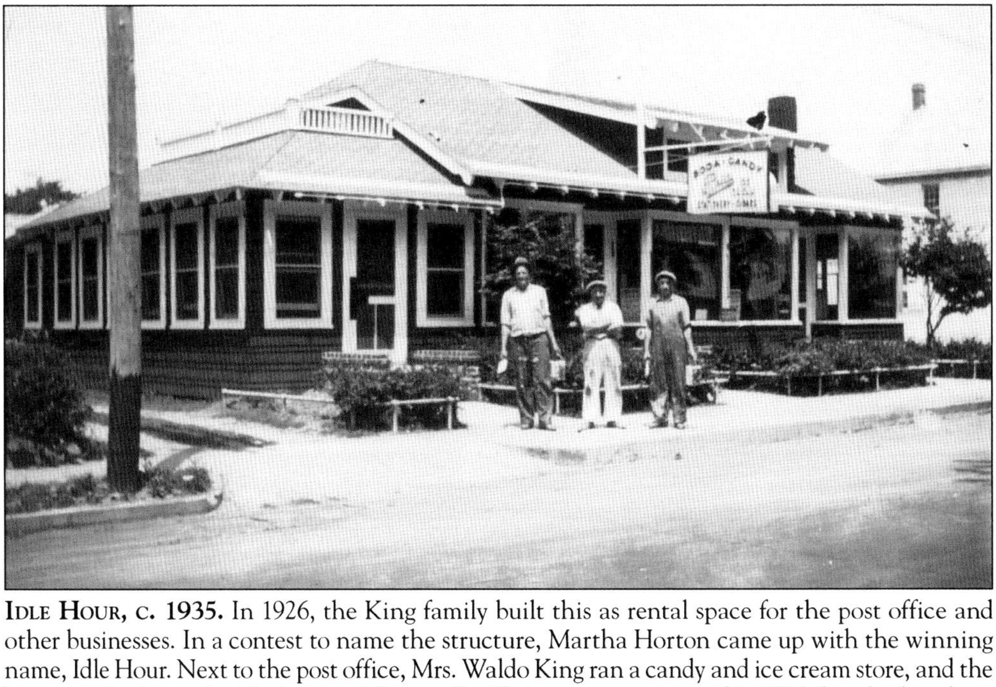

Idle Hour, c. 1935. In 1926, the King family built this as rental space for the post office and other businesses. In a contest to name the structure, Martha Horton came up with the winning name, Idle Hour. Next to the post office, Mrs. Waldo King ran a candy and ice cream store, and the basement had a pool table for rent. The small addition was constructed in 1931 for a barber shop. Standing in front are, from left to right, Frank Andrade, Robert Biggers, and Edwin H. King.

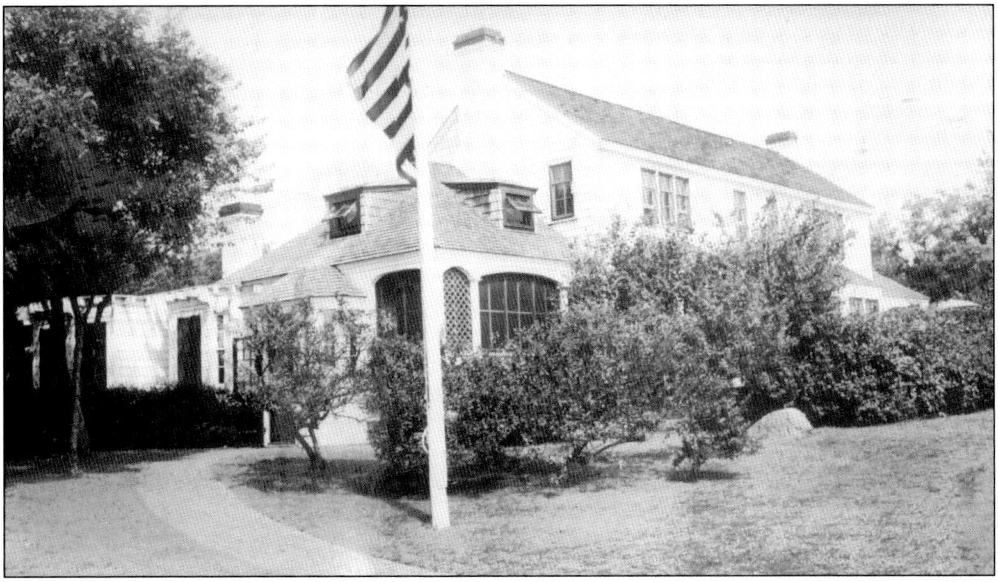

White Shingles Boardinghouse and Tea Room, c. 1930. Located on Main Road not far from the causeway, White Shingles was owned and operated by Hortense Knox, a local artist. The boardinghouse had six or seven rooms for rent by visitors, and the house next door was Knox's home and the dining room for travelers. The business closed down around 1953 when Knox died.

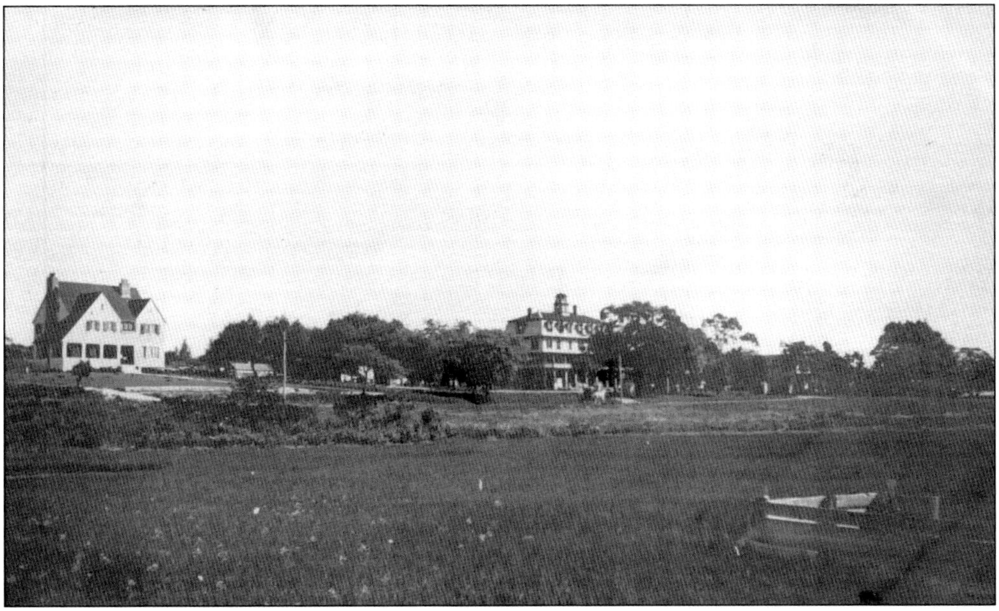

Mount Pleasant House, c. 1890. In 1879, the Mount Pleasant House was built by William and Samuel Young, who sold it to John and Joseph Miller in 1882. John Miller became the sole owner in 1883 and expanded the building. Five years after hotel was leased to Eugene McDonnell during the 1920s, Jenny Medeiros took over the management. In 1937, William Charlton of Riverhead bought the hotel. Dissatisfied with profits, he demolished the house in the 1940s.

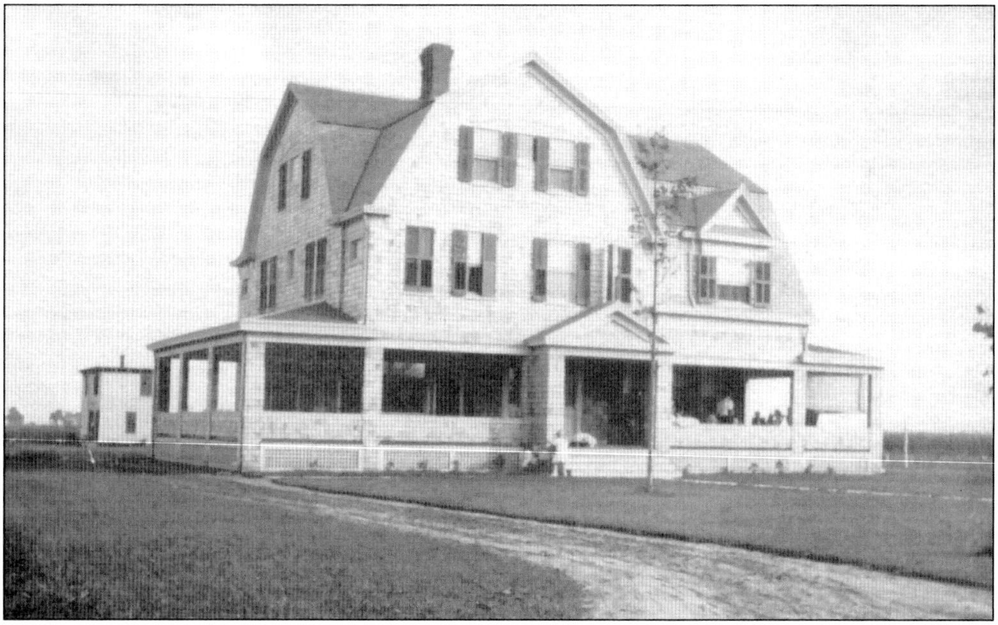

REST-A-WHYLE, C. 1905. Edward Edwards's house on Main Road in Orient was known as Rest-a-Whyle. Edwards built the house on property left to him by his father, Issac Edwards. Originally a private house, the building was turned into an adult home during the 1980s. Later, the house was converted into a bed and breakfast known as the Oysterponds Manor. It is currently known as the Orient Inn. (Courtesy of Joan Turturro.)

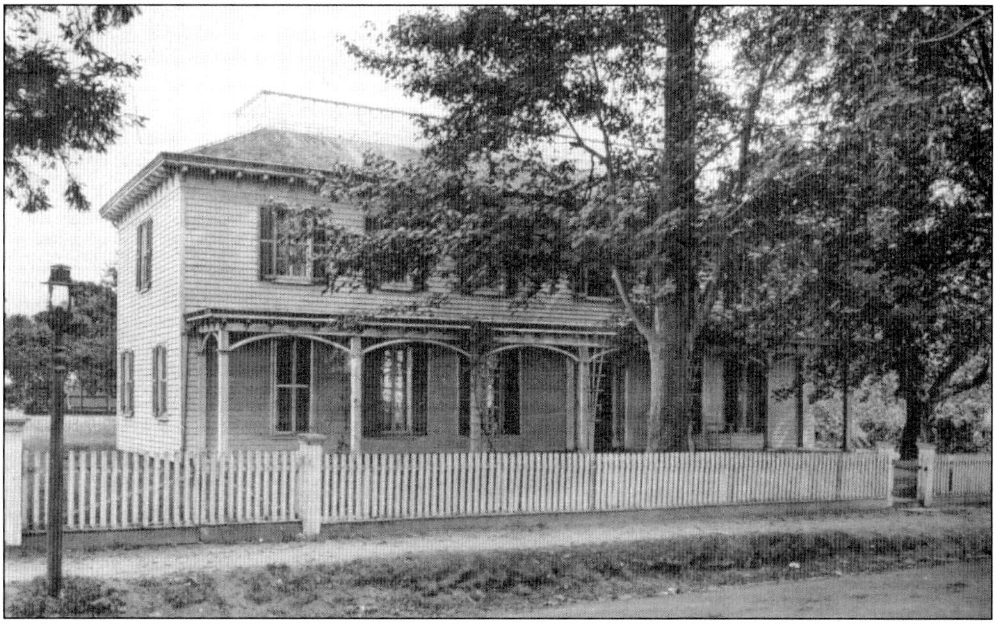

VILLAGE HOUSE, C. 1905. The home of the Oysterponds Historical Society, Village House was originally constructed by Augustus Griffin, Orient's locally famous historian. The building was eventually sold to Jeremiah and Nancy Vail, who expanded the structure (pictured). Nancy Vail, like many Orient residents, rented rooms to summer visitors while her husband was away running their fishing business.

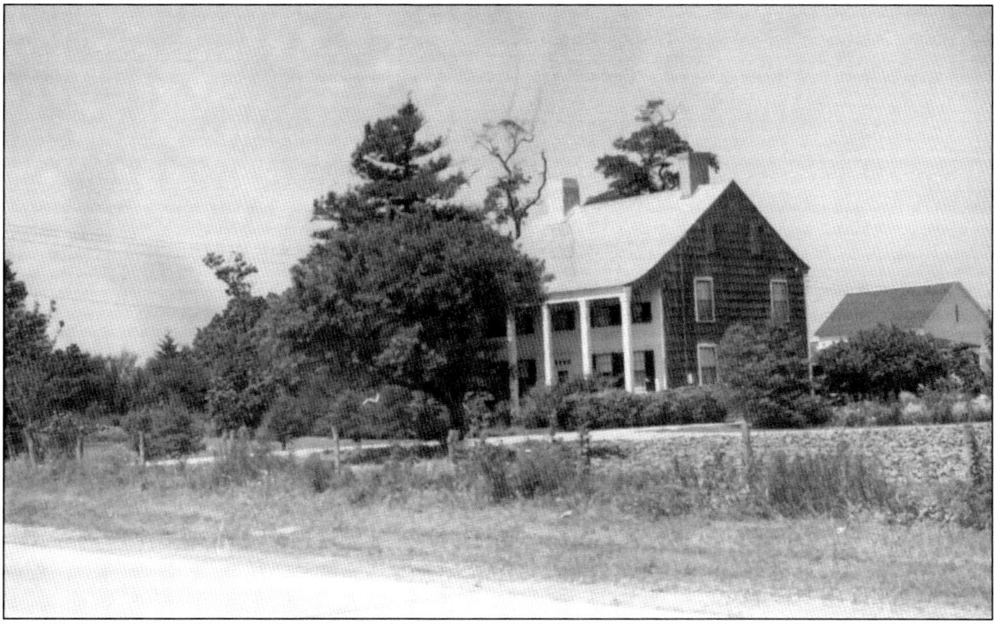

WEBB HOUSE, C. 1950. Originally located in Greenport, this building was the Constant Booth tavern and inn. In the 1840s, Orange Webb bought and moved the structure just east of Route 48 on Route 25. In 1954, it was on the verge of demolition, as seen here, when George Latham purchased and moved the house by barge to Orient to be his private museum. In 1983, Latham gave the structure to the Oysterponds Historical Society.

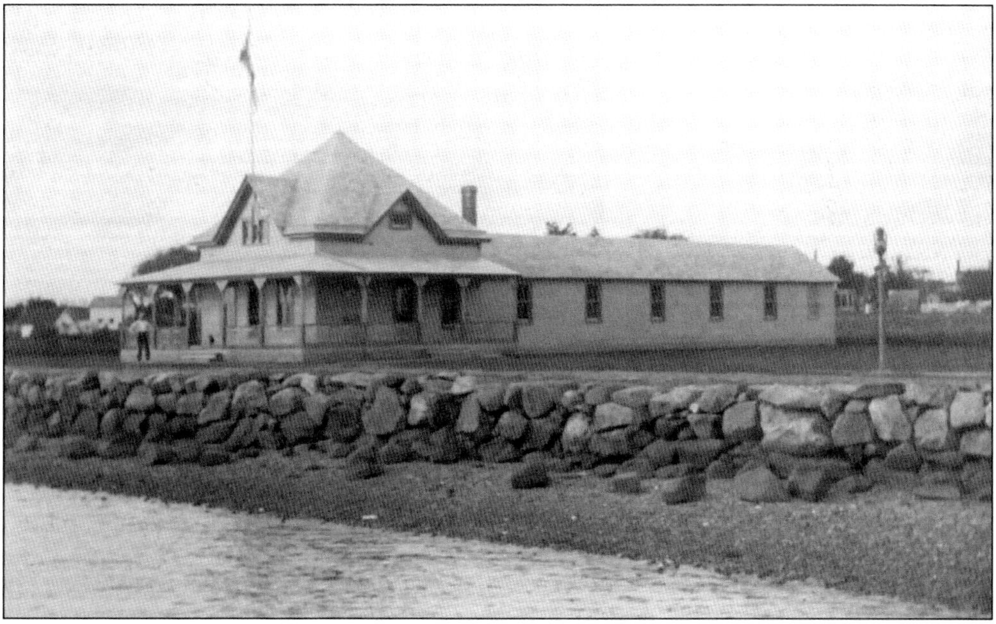

BOWLING ALLEY, C. 1900. Located on Bay Avenue, the bowling alley was built by James A. Coffin. The lanes stretched out in the wing behind the main building. Damaged during the 1938 hurricane, it was divided into three parts and converted into houses. The rear wing was detached and moved across Poquatuck Park, while the wing on the west side was picked up and moved slightly to the west.

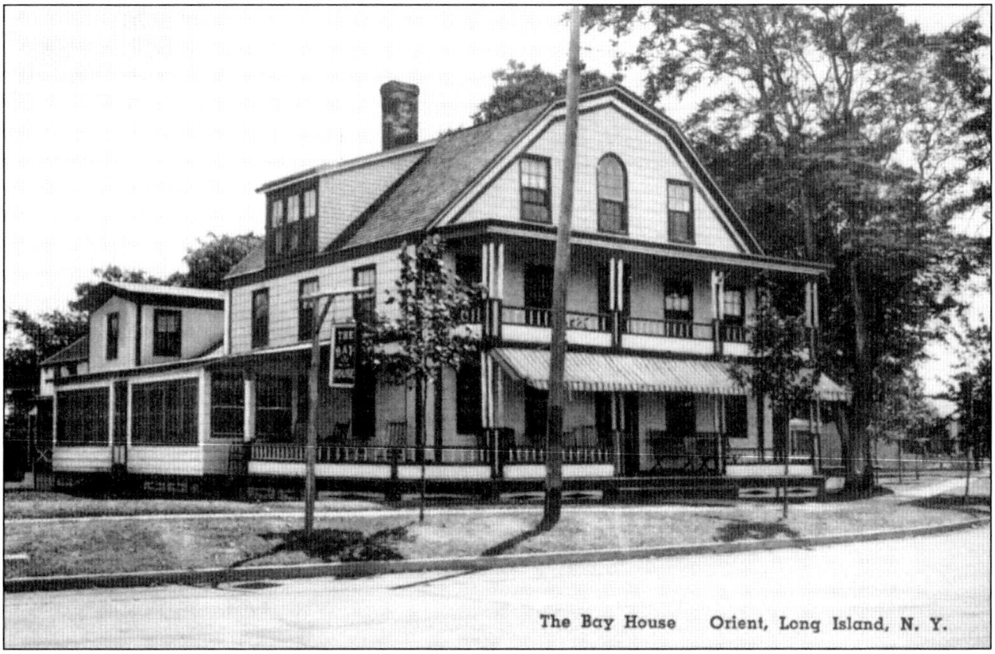

Bay House, c. 1950. Owned by Maria R. Merriman, the Bay House was a temperance hotel. In 1896, when Merriman passed away, the inn was sold to a consortium of local businessmen who wanted to maintain its no alcoholic beverages policy. Cicero B. King eventually bought out his partners and gained sole ownership of Bay House. The business was passed down in the family and remained a hotel until the 1970s.

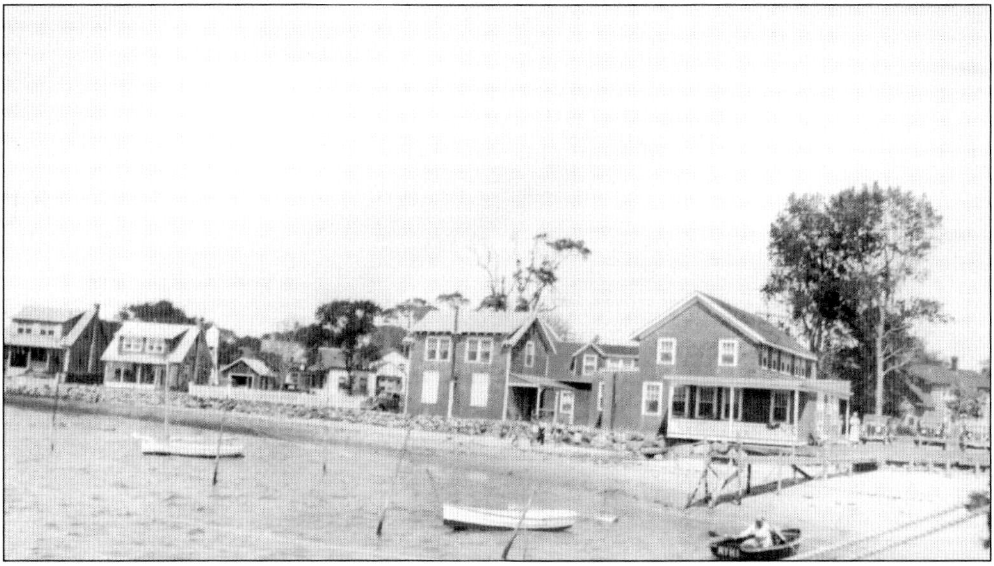

Bay House Cottages, c. 1940. After C.B. King retired and closed his general store near the wharf, he converted the building to one of the small rental cottages offered by Bay House. King also purchased several other small buildings in the vicinity. The family maintained the small houses along the shore and rented them through the hotel up until the closing of the business.

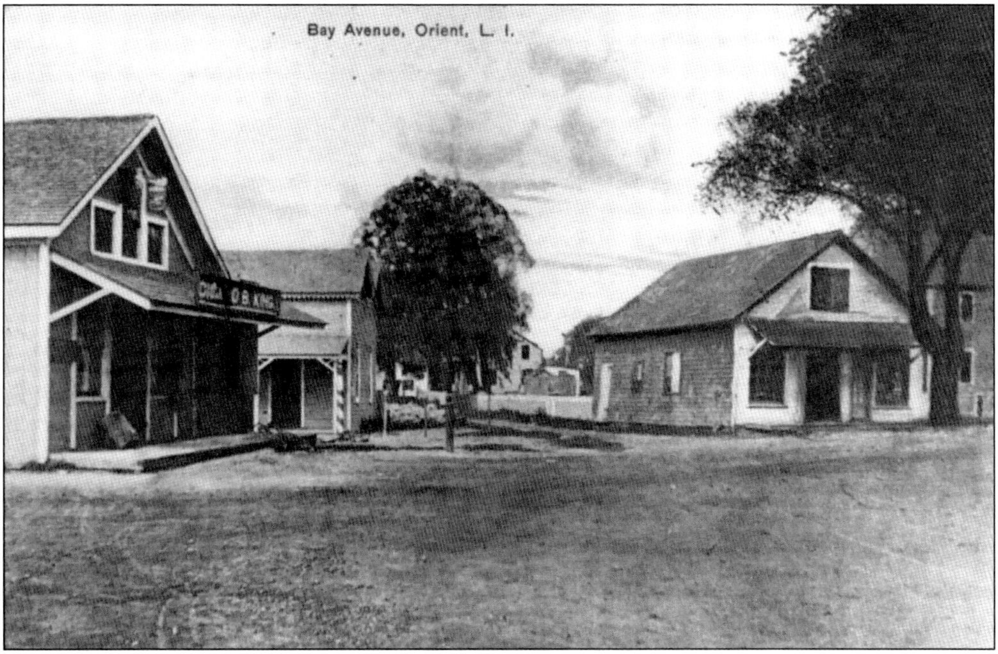

INTERSECTION OF VILLAGE LANE AND BAY AVENUE, c. 1907. This popular postcard shows the commercial area around the wharf. Next to C.B. King's store on the left side is Dewey's barbershop and candy store, and King Brothers butcher shop stands across Bay Street on the right. Cleveland's blacksmith shop is behind the photographer.

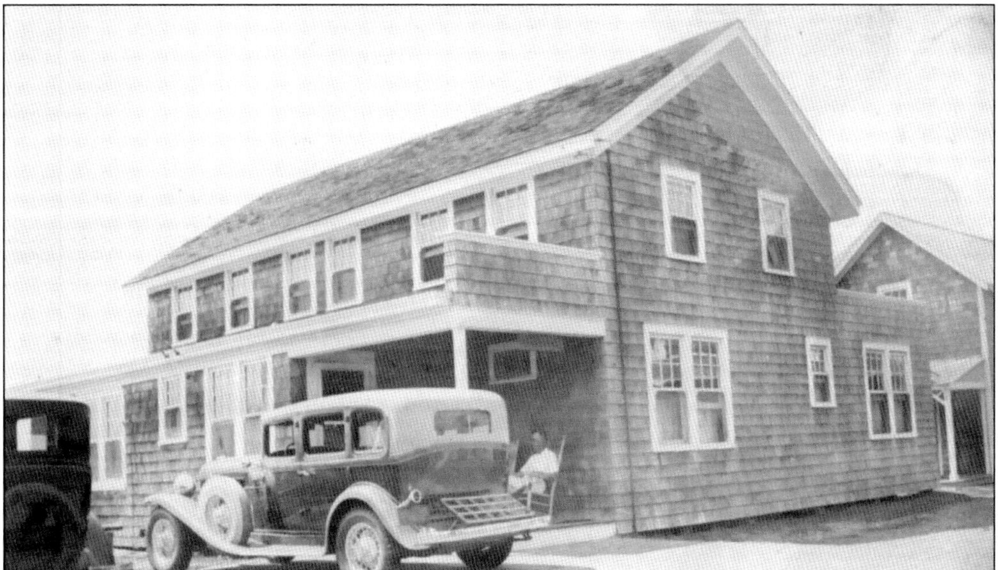

EDGEWATER COTTAGE, c. 1930. At the foot of wharf, next to where C.B. King's store stood, Edgewater Cottage was Charles Herman's barbershop. Herman, from Bavaria, immigrated in 1889 and moved to Orient by 1900. Like many other businessmen in the area, Herman ran his business from his home. The building eventually was purchased by the King family and incorporated into the Bay House Hotel as a stand-alone cottage that could be rented.

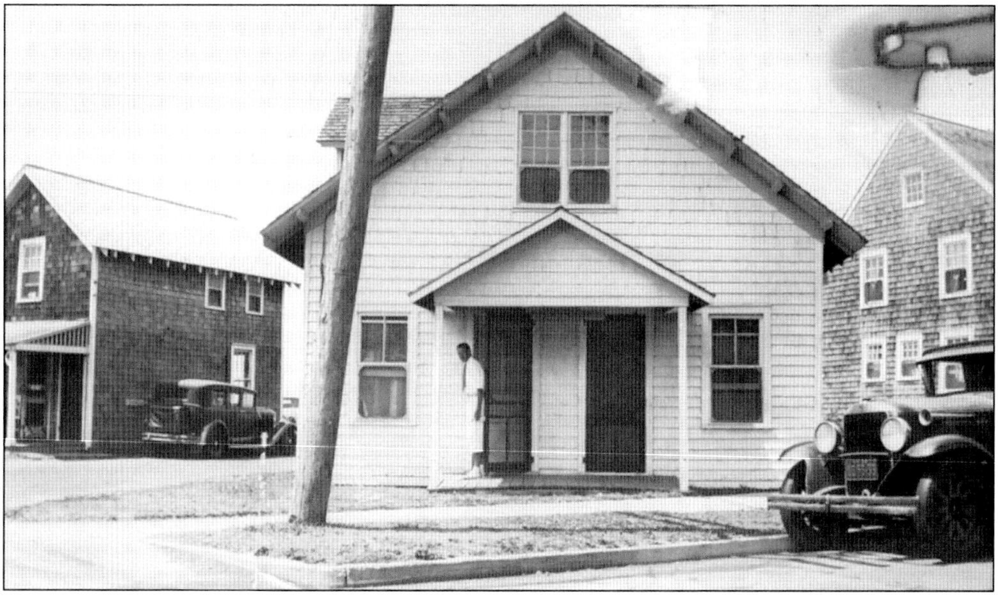

Bay House Cottage, c. 1929. This building was where the King Brothers Meat Market moved after they left Young and Rackett. In 1910, brothers C. Ambrose King and H. Courtland King were partners for a short time in a butcher shop. By 1920, C. Ambrose had moved to Albany, New York, and became a policeman. H. Courtland moved to Orient Point to farm, and the cottage then became part of the Bay House. Sometime after 1970, the building was demolished.

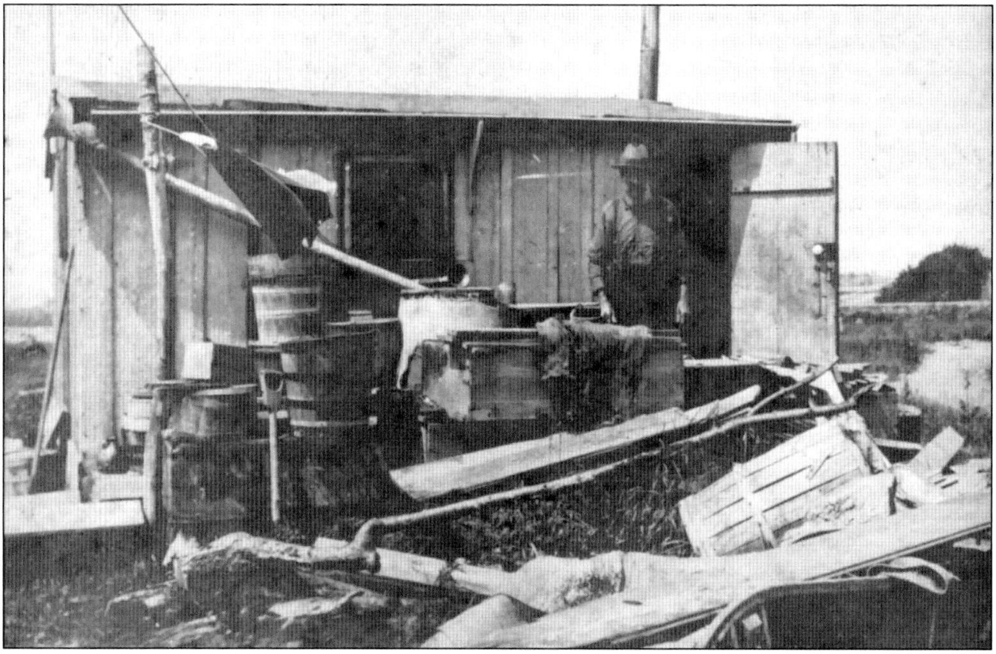

Shack, 1904. Scattered along the shoreline in the south of Orient were several shacks like this one, captured on film by Ernest Thompson in 1904. Colorful hermits who eked out a living doing odd jobs and selling whatever they caught lived in these shacks. Men like Kid Allen, who arrived in Orient to live on Gids Island from Alaska, or Pete's Neck Jim and Augi lived along the shoreline.

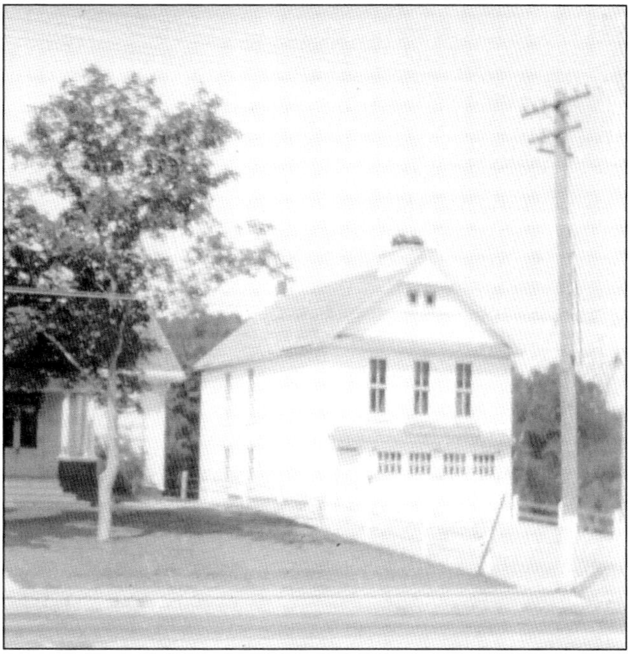

East Marion Fire Department, c. 1935. The East Marion Fire Department was founded in 1899 by 11 men from the East Marion Literary Union. In 1902, the group purchased their first hook and ladder wagon, which was pulled by the firemen to emergencies around the hamlet. In 1907, the East Marion Literary Union sold their clubhouse on Main Road for $1 to become the fire department's first building. Today's firehouse is still located on the 1907 site.

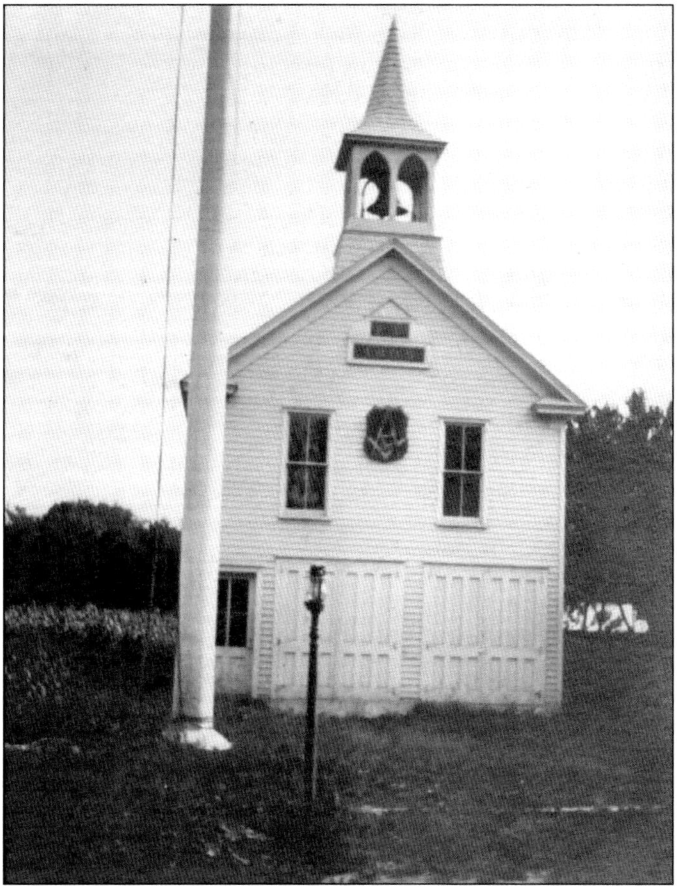

Orient Fire Department, c. 1900. The Orient firehouse was built in 1895 when it was incorporated. Located on Orchard Street, the building housed firefighting equipment on the first floor and a dance hall and lodge for the local Masons on the second floor. For a while, Orient was divided on whether or not a fire department was a good idea. After several fires, objections to the department disappeared. Ironically, in 1938, the firehouse burned down.

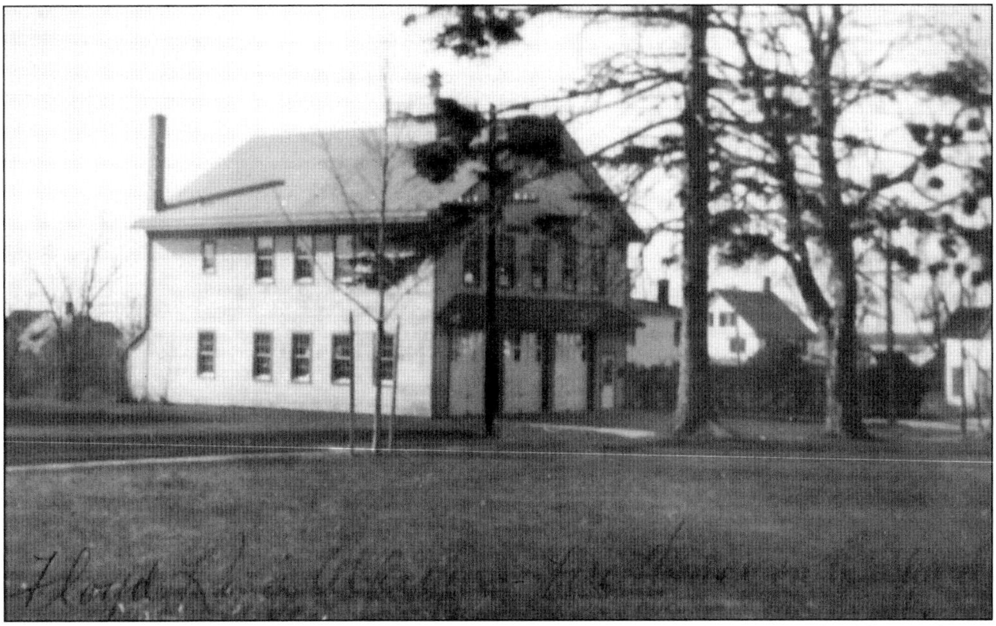

ORIENT FIRE DEPARTMENT, C. 1939. Out of the ashes of the lost fire department building, a larger structure was erected. The new building was better designed to handle the modern equipment that the department had acquired. In 1916, the fire department changed its name to the Oysterponds Chemical Company, then sometime prior to 1920 changed it back to the Poquatuck Hook and Ladder Company.

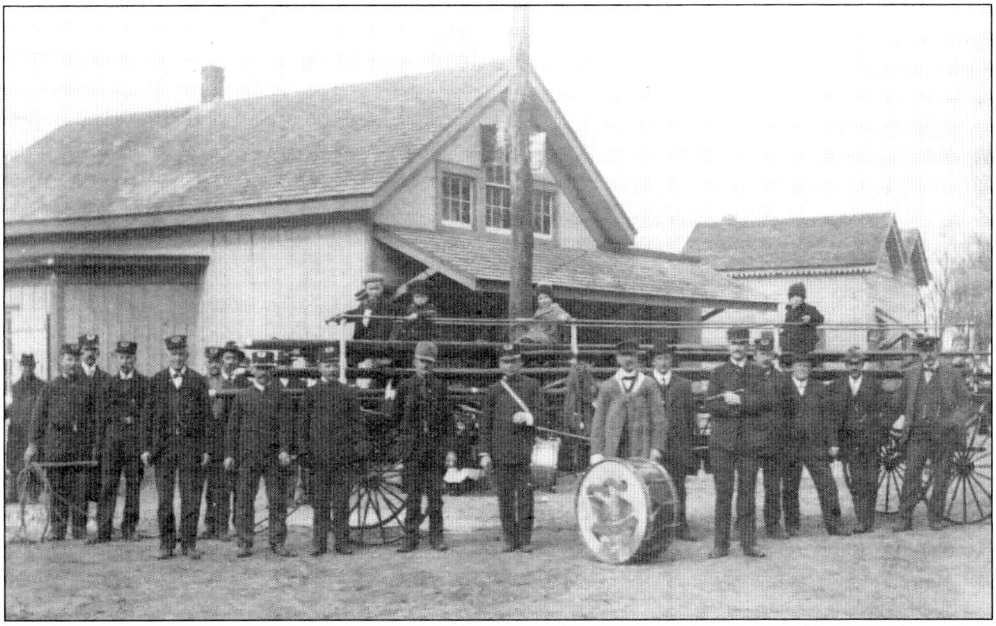

ORIENT FIRE DEPARTMENT, C. 1900. Formally known as the Poquatuck Hook and Ladder Company, members are lining up for a parade by the Orient wharf. Pictured here are, from left to right, Henry Terry, Gene Conklin, E.F. Dewey, Abram Latham, James S. Dewey, Greely Tabor, Joseph Miller, John Bower, James Fox, Cook Petty, W. Sing Young, Bill Terry, Fred Hommel, Bryant Young, Eldridge Latham, E.M. Rackett, Edward Coffin, and William Haberman.

EAST MARION MEMORIAL POST OFFICE, 1949. The East Marion post office, the only war memorial post office in New York, was built in 1945. The post office began in B.C. Tuthill's store in the 1850s. His son-in-law W. Halsey Wiggins inherited the job. In 1927, Wiggins retired, and eventually Hattie Udell took over and ran the post office from her home. In 1937, Udell turned it over to Helen Vail, who moved it to F.L.R. Francisco's apartment house.

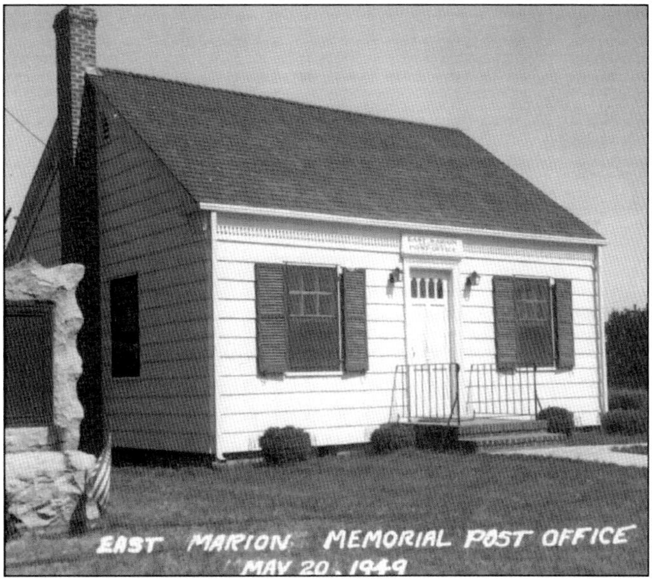

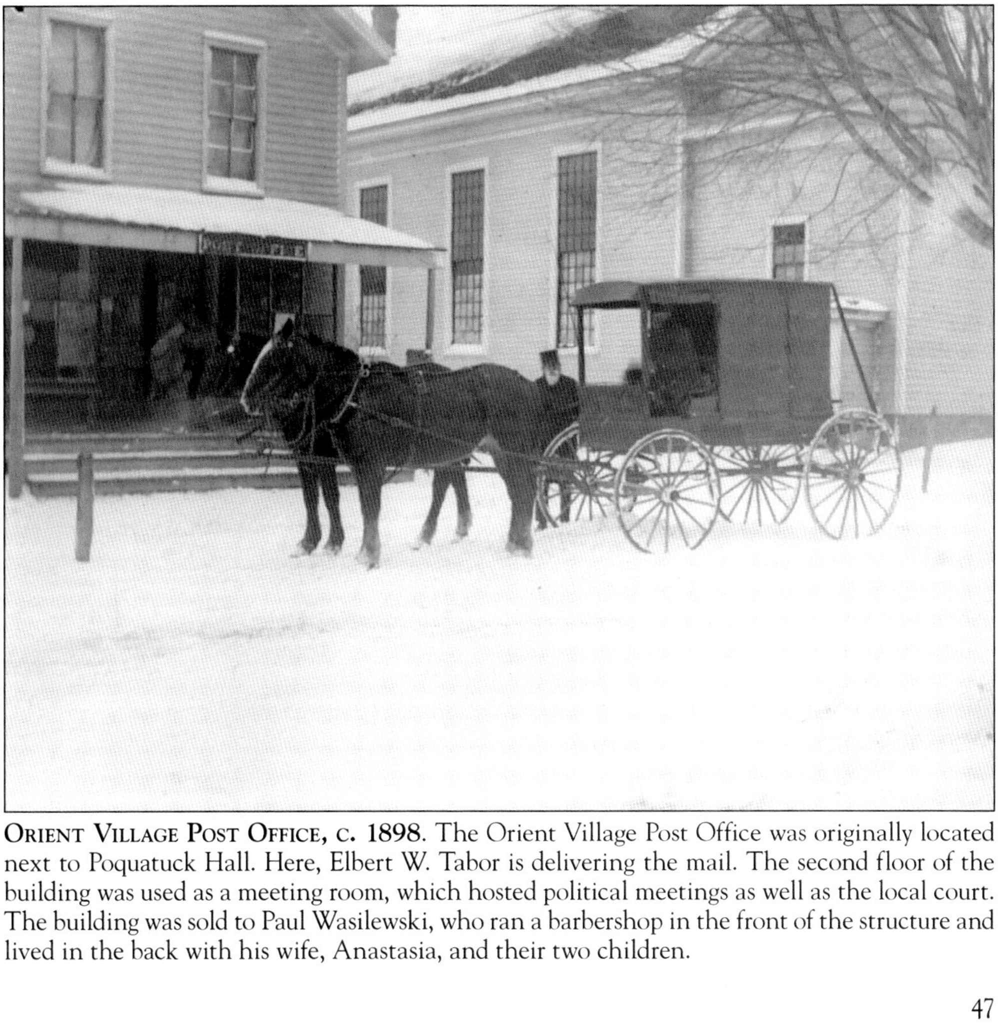

ORIENT VILLAGE POST OFFICE, c. 1898. The Orient Village Post Office was originally located next to Poquatuck Hall. Here, Elbert W. Tabor is delivering the mail. The second floor of the building was used as a meeting room, which hosted political meetings as well as the local court. The building was sold to Paul Wasilewski, who ran a barbershop in the front of the structure and lived in the back with his wife, Anastasia, and their two children.

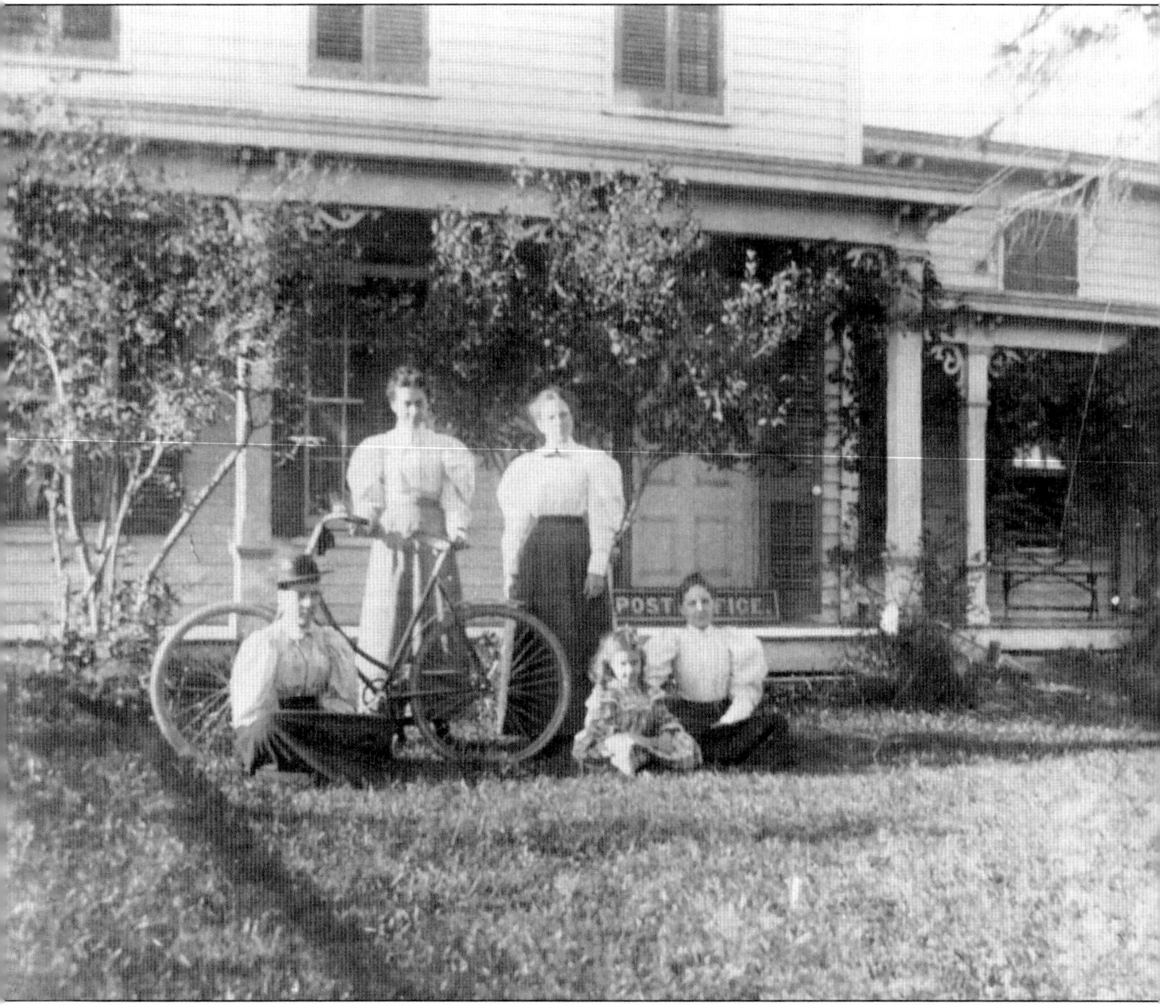

Orient Point Post Office, c. 1900. In the days before the automobile, the residents of Orient Point did not have to travel far to collect their mail. The post office was located in Marcus Terry's house on the north side of Main Road. The sign can just be seen behind the woman seated on the right. Terry held the post of postmaster for Orient Point from July 1, 1890, to November 15, 1913.

Four

SCHOOLS

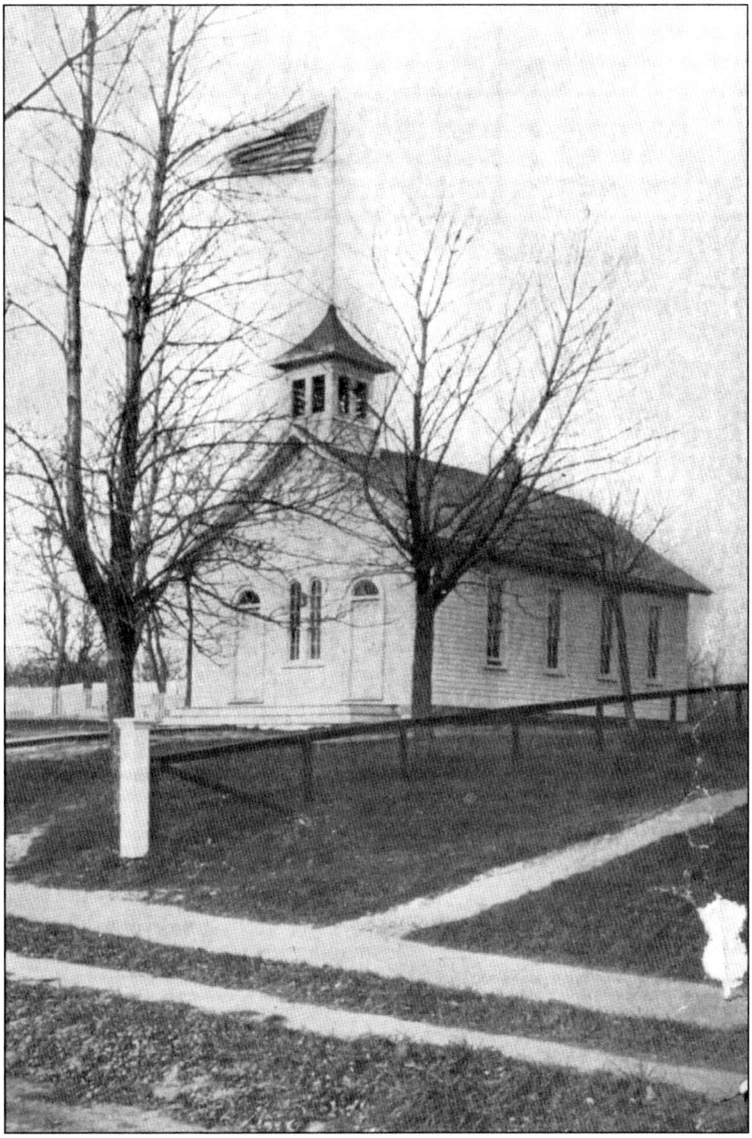

DISTRICT NO. 3, EAST MARION SCHOOLHOUSE, C. 1868. Located on Main Road and Gillette Drive, this is the second schoolhouse in East Marion. In 1812, the building was rented, but residents purchased it by 1815. In 1839, the school was moved east to Old Schoolhouse Park. When the building grew too small for the number of students, it was moved across the street and raised to become the second floor of the house on the eastern side of the chapel.

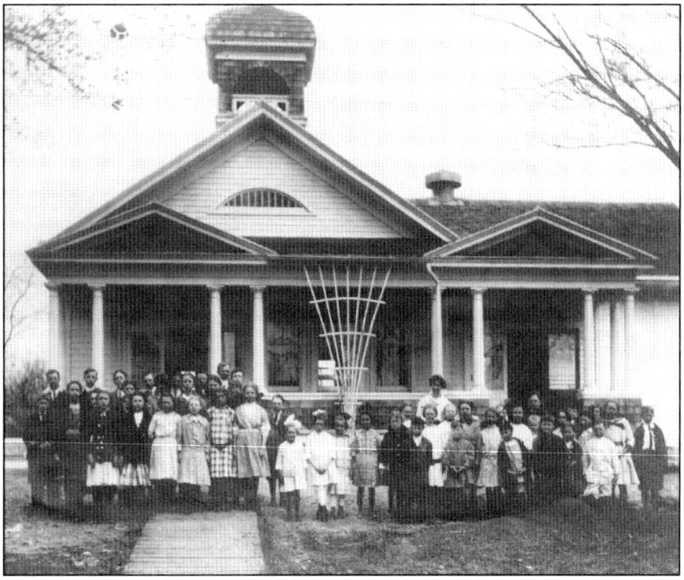

EAST MARION SCHOOLHOUSE, c. 1930. The new schoolhouse was built in 1869 on the same site. The new structure featured two classrooms and a small library. In 1908, an adjacent lot was used to lengthened the building on the western side. The school was decommissioned when the district was combined with Orient, and the schoolhouse was sold, moved up towards the sound, and the grounds were turned into a park.

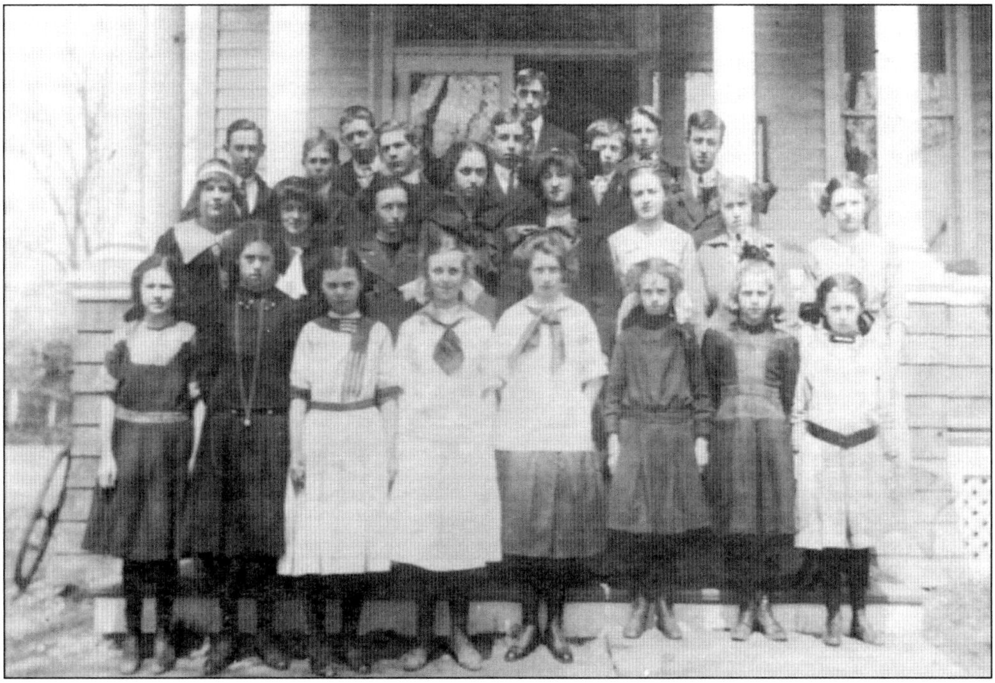

STUDENTS OF DISTRICT NO. 3, 1913. Students pose on the front steps. Pictured are, from left to right, (first row) Caroline Downs, Vera Adams, Clara Rackett, Eunice Redmond, Esther Tuthill, Minnie Udell, Lillian Thieringer, and Hazel Rackett; (second row) Louisa Thieringer, Emma Tuthill, Mabel Wiggins, Emily Edwards, Mildred King, Marion Gardiner, Irma Redmond, and Estelle Downs; (third row) A. Halsey Brown, Elbert Udell, Leland King, Otis Thieringer, Linwood Rackett, Forrest Brown, Albert Vail, Elwood Rackett. A Mr. Brooks, teacher, stands at back.

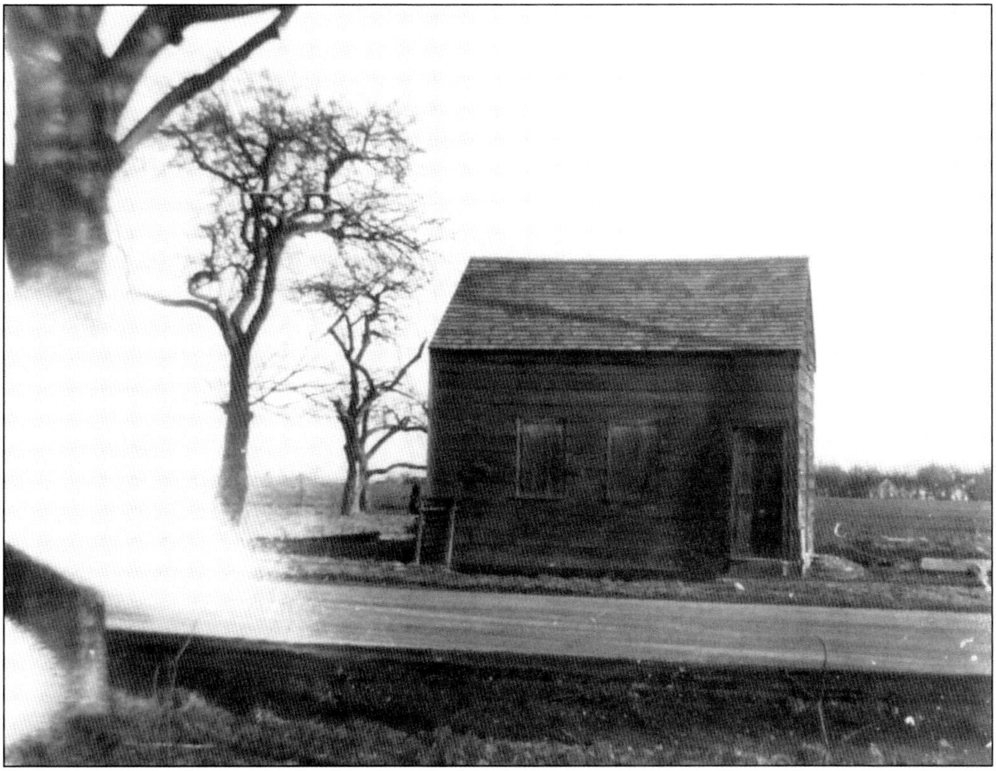

The Amanda Brown Schoolhouse, c. 1940. This was originally part of Amanda Brown's house on Main Road. During the early 1800s, Brown's sisters taught children from the surrounding farms the basics in education. The wing was detached from the main house during the early 20th century and was moved east to the Orient Point Inn, where it served as a tearoom and gift shop, before going to the historical society.

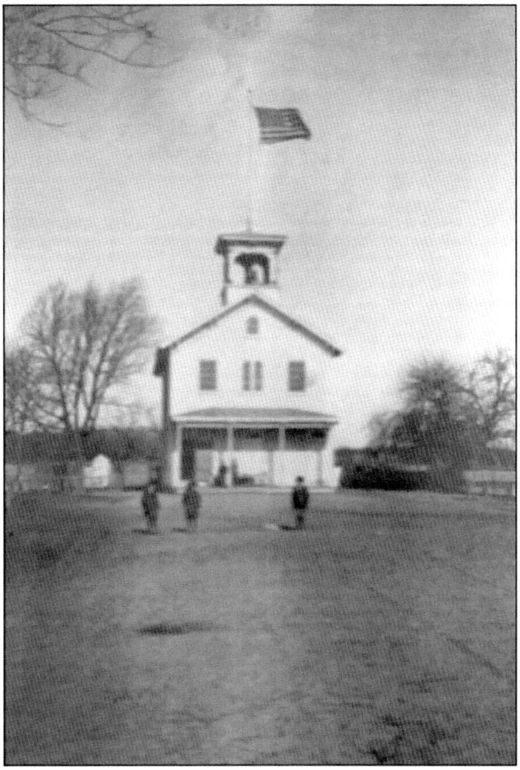

District No. 2 Schoolhouse, c. 1880. Orient Village School was built in 1820 on Main Road, not far from the present school. The building, which is almost identical to the school constructed at Orient Point, can be identified not only by the three windows that lined the space above the porch, but by the large flagpole that surmounted the roof.

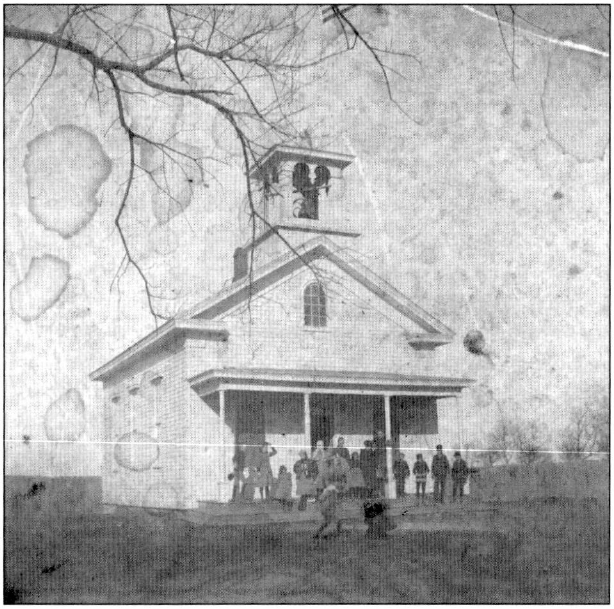

DISTRICT NO. 1 SCHOOLHOUSE, C. 1875. Known as the Down Neck School, it originally stood on Main Road in Orient Point. This one-room schoolhouse was built in 1873 and replaced an 1846 schoolhouse. The earlier building was sold to Fred Latham, who moved it and incorporated it into his house. In 1930, this spacious, single-room building was decommissioned, and the children of Orient Point were sent to District No. 2.

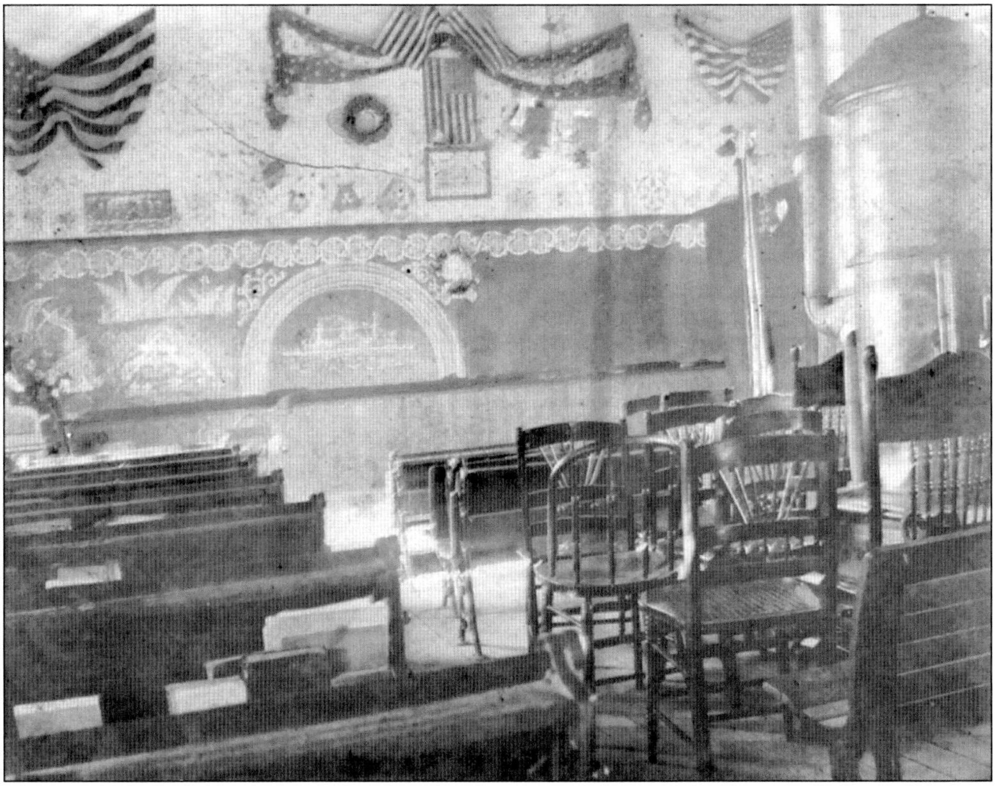

INTERIOR OF DISTRICT NO. 1 SCHOOLHOUSE, C. 1885. The interior of the schoolhouse shows it decorated for an event, with chairs lined up to accommodate guests. The large furnace used to heat the room, seen at right in this image, was installed in the same space where the wood stove had been. Schoolhouses often were used as community centers. District No. 1 was used several times a week for an evening Bible study class by the adults of the area.

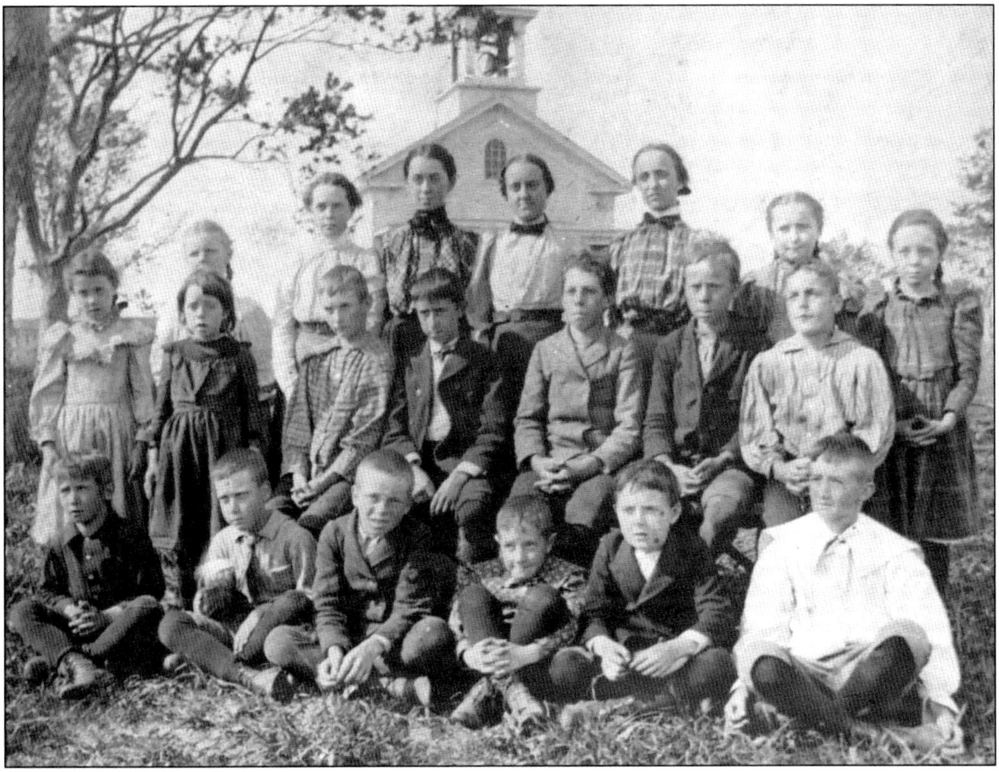

STUDENTS OF DISTRICT NO. 1 SCHOOL, 1898. Orient Point students line up for a photograph. From left to right are (first row) Harrison Demarest, George Latham, Frank Latham, Louis Tuthill, Bruyn Hambler, and Lonnie Latham; (second row) Ruth Latham, Pearl Latham, Harold Latham, Dan Latham, Spencer Terry, Moses Latham, and Edgar Beebe; (third row) Bertha Latham, Ethel Tuthill, Agnes Terry, Cora Petty, Rose Latham, Teresa Hambler, and Allie Latham.

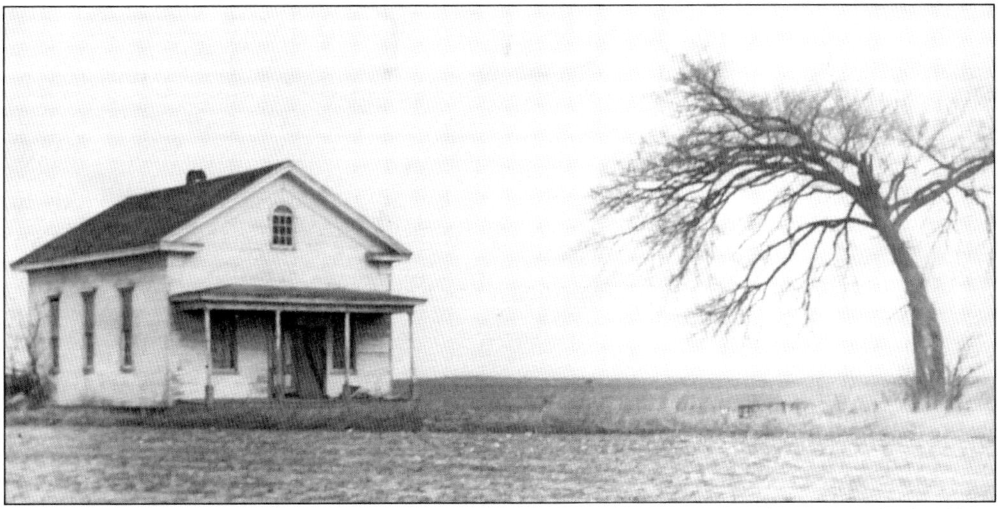

DISTRICT NO. 1 OR DOWN NECK SCHOOL, C. 1935. Last used as a school in 1929, the building was abandoned in 1930. It was then moved to the King Farm and used as a dormitory for migrant farm workers. The structure lost its cupola in the 1938 hurricane. In 1949, it was donated to the historical society. Today, the building is an exhibit space and lecture hall.

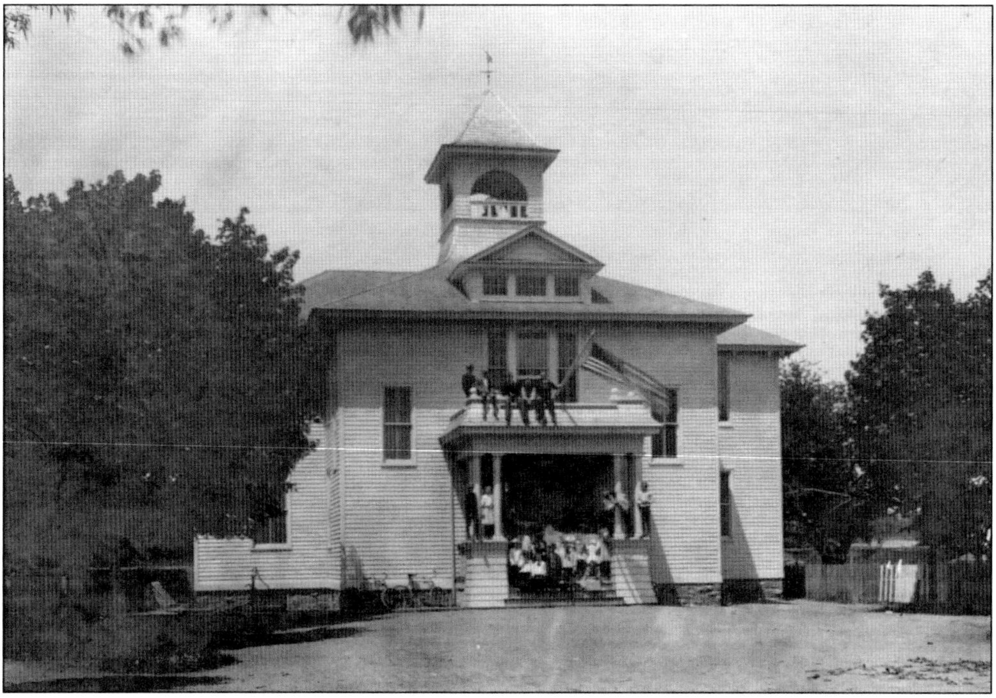

DISTRICT NO. 2 OR UNION SCHOOLHOUSE, C. 1930S. In 1872, the 1820 school building had grown too small to accommodate the number of students in the area. The school board decided to expand the one-room schoolhouse into a larger building. The single-room structure was expanded into a two-story building with eight classrooms, which were used by students ranging from first grade to high school.

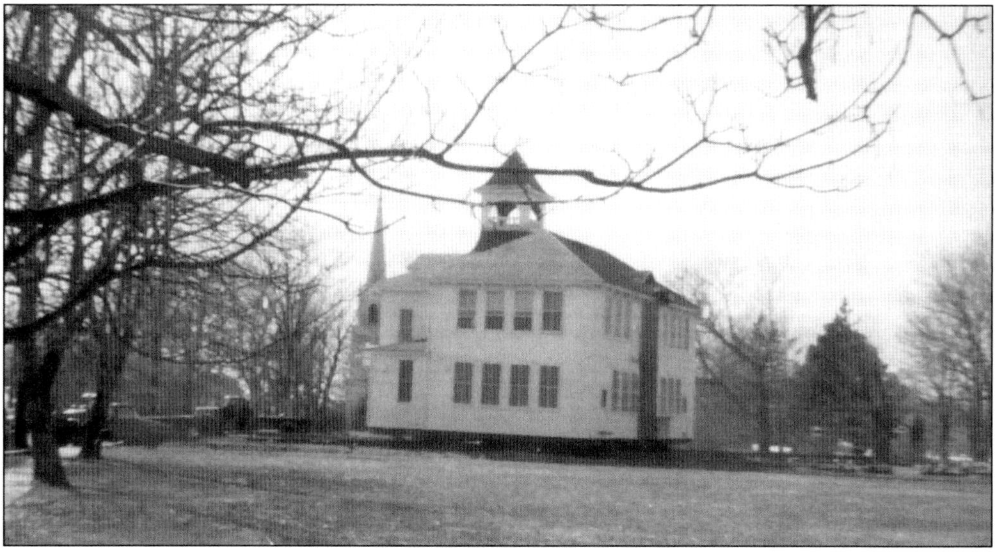

MOVING DISTRICT NO. 2 SCHOOLHOUSE, 1966. In 1966, the school district, which had been consolidated with District No. 1 Orient Point and with District No. 3, was in dire need for space to handle the students of the area. The old District No. 2 school was sold with the condition that the new owners move the building to a new site. Here, the building has been lifted off its foundation in preparation for the move.

Moving District No. 2 Schoolhouse, 1966. The old school building was moved by truck to a new location south of Main Road on the eastern edge of Orient Village. Its new owner, famous sculptor Robert Berks, renovated the building to become his sculpture studio. Berks worked there up until his death in 2011.

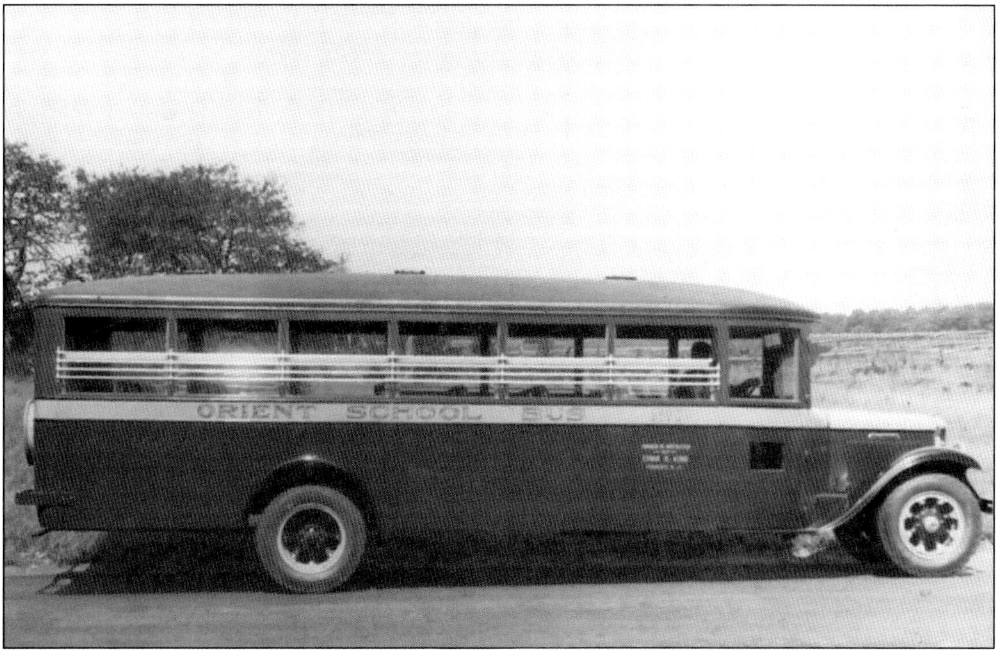

Orient School Bus, 1936. Edwin King owned the official Orient school bus, which served the Orient Village and Orient Point area. His daughter Gertrude King Reeves drove the bus for many years, and she used to keep a wash basket by her driver seat where she could keep an eye her children as babies.

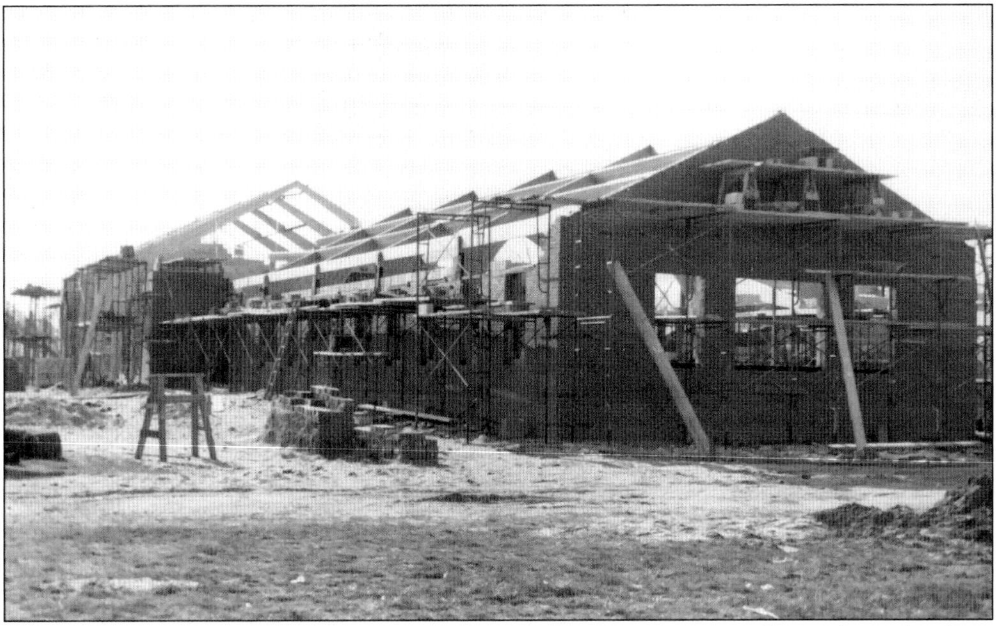

CONSTRUCTION OF THE NEW OYSTERPONDS ELEMENTARY SCHOOL, 1966. This modern school was the replacement for the old one- and two-room schoolhouses built in Orient Point, Orient Village, and East Marion. The motivating force behind the construction of the new building was not the need for a modern learning environment. Donald Boerum, the new school superintendent, made the building one of the conditions of his acceptance of the job.

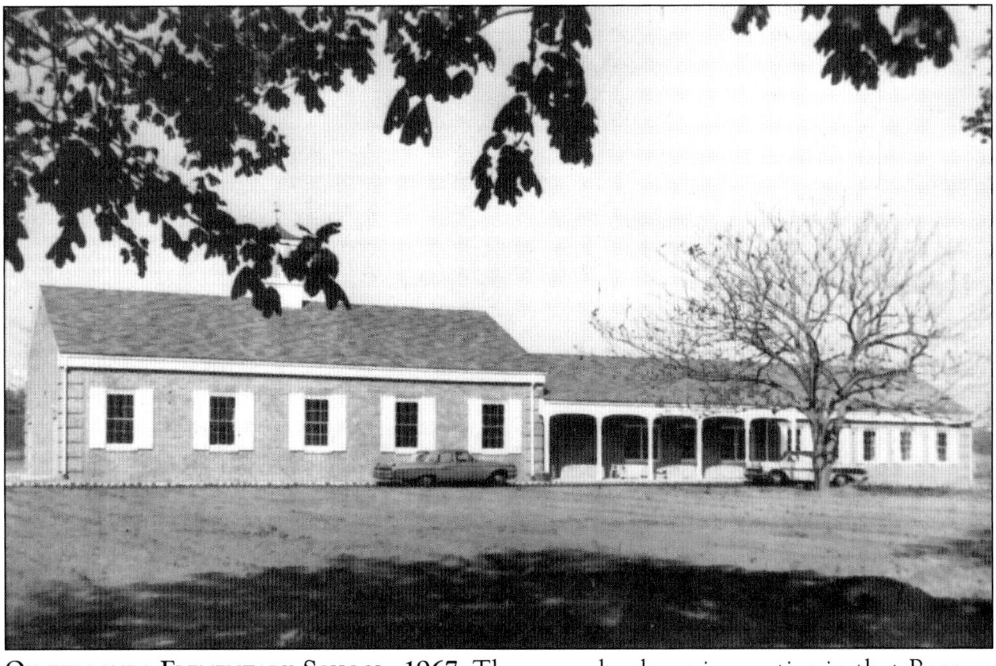

OYSTERPONDS ELEMENTARY SCHOOL, 1967. The new school was innovative in that Boerum insisted that skylights be installed to let in natural light not only in the hallways, but also in the large and spacious kindergarten room. Over time, the school has been expanded twice since its original construction, adding extensions on the rear of the building.

Five

FARMING AND FISHING

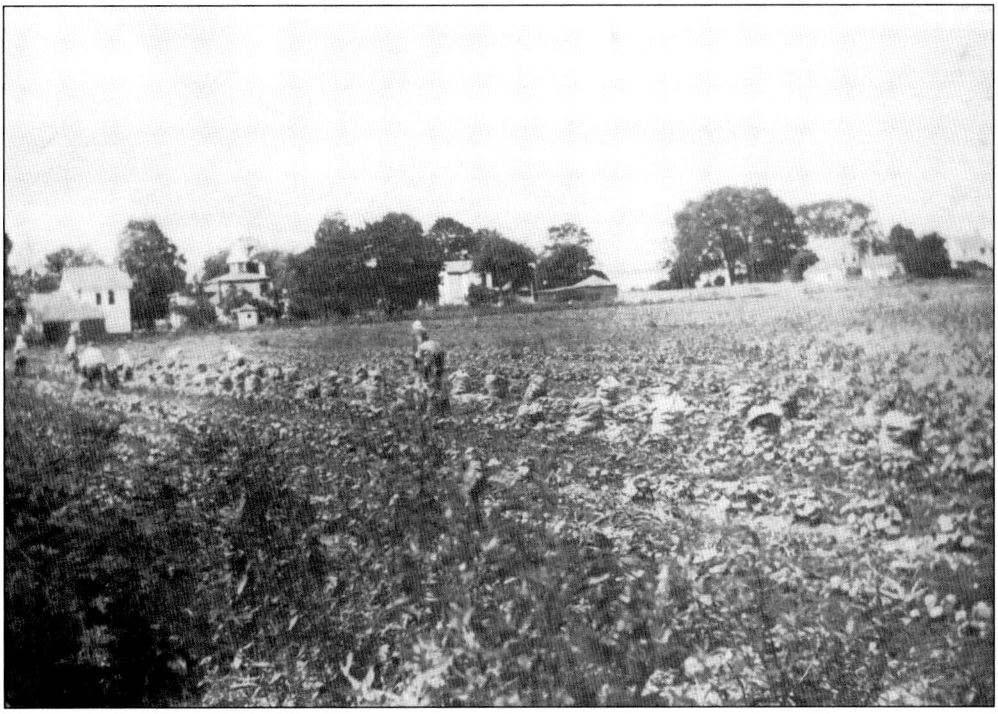

DYER FARM, C. 1930. The Dyer farm was located between the eastern edge of the causeway and the western end of Orient Village, bounded by Main Road and Peconic Bay. In this image, workers are harvesting and bagging for market one of the primary crops that the East End of Long Island is known for—potatoes. Until mechanical innovations in the 1950s, potatoes were gathered by hand after the plant was uprooted.

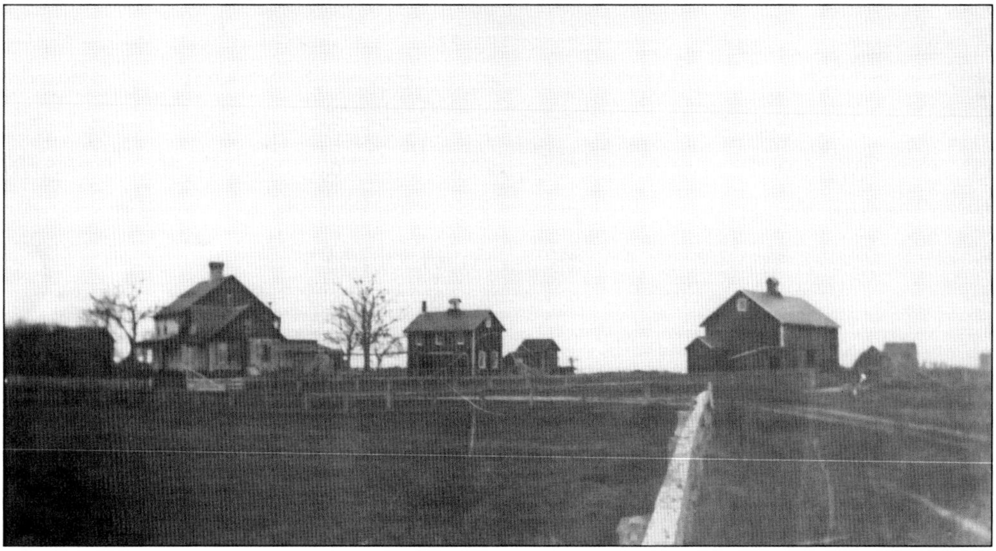

HOG POND FARM, C. 1890. Hog Pond Farm, owned by the Tuthill family, was first settled by John Tuthill, one of the original settlers of Orient, and it remained in the family until the mid-20th century. The farm encompassed two landmarks of the Orient area: Major's Pond, named after Maj. Nathaniel King, who was reputed to be seven feet tall, and Slave Cemetery, in which Dr. Seth H. Tuthill and his wife, Maria, are buried.

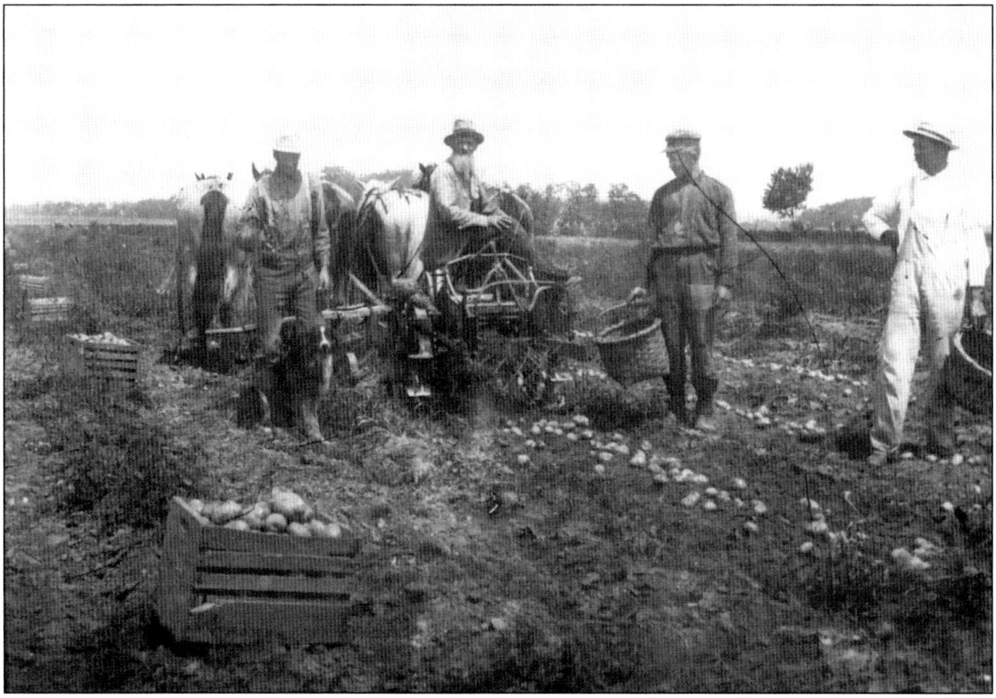

EAGLE NECK FARM, 1904. The Eagle Neck Farm was located on one of the peninsulas that juts into Hallock Bay. The farm was worked by another branch of the Tuthill family. Roy Latham recalled the area got its name from the ospreys that would nest in the trees. From left to right are Rufus Tuthill, uprooting potatoes; Daniel Tuthill, on a hoover digger; an unidentified Polish farmhand; and Walter Tuthill.

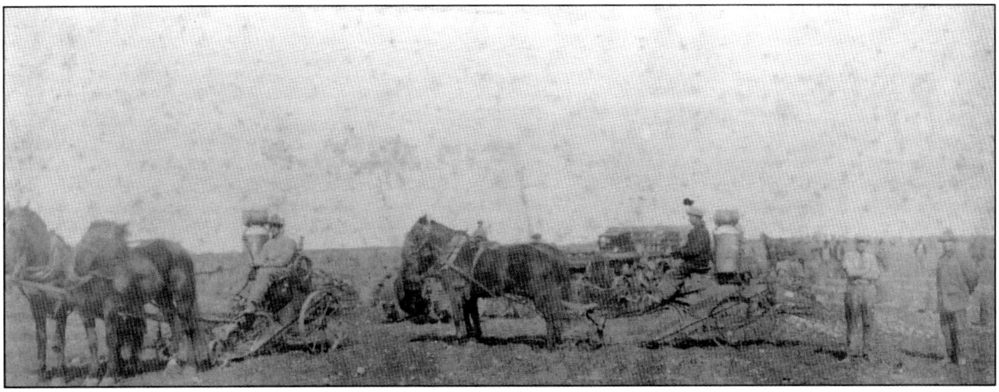

Edwin H. King's Farm Field, 1921. Also out at Orient Point, King's Farm encompassed much of the land on the north and south sides of Main Road and was located just west of the Orient Point Inn. In this panorama image, King shows off some of his newest farm equipment, driven by Steve and Stanley Koroleski. Edwin King is standing at left, with Brown Tabor at far right.

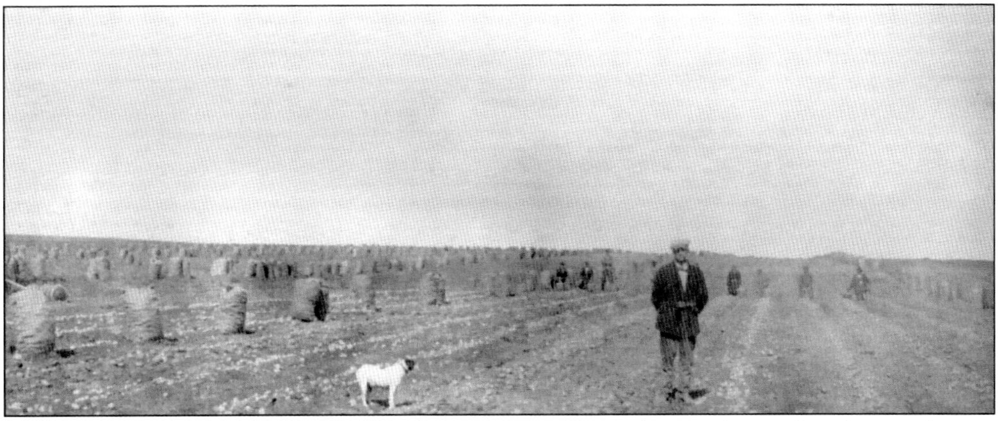

King's Farm, 1921. Ed King and his dog Buttons are standing in front of workers gathering potatoes. King was one of the few farmers who turned the concept of commercial farming into a year-round endeavor. During the winter months in New York, instead of spending the time relaxing and preparing his equipment for the upcoming season, King invested in farmland in Florida and spent the winter months farming large tracts of land down south.

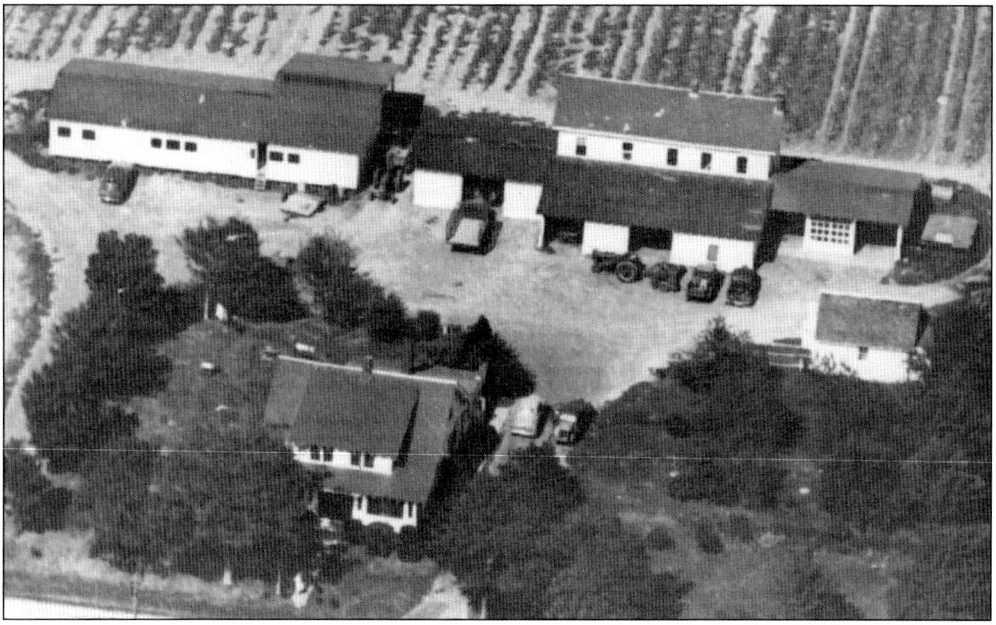

Ariel View of the King House and Farm Buildings, c. 1930. The King family lived in the snug bungalow in the foreground. Behind the house are a corn crib, pig pen, cow shed, and barn. The two-story building just to the right of center was the game room from the Orient Point Inn, moved by King and used as a cookhouse. The second floor housed rooms for the 30 workers that he employed. The shed attached to the front housed machinery.

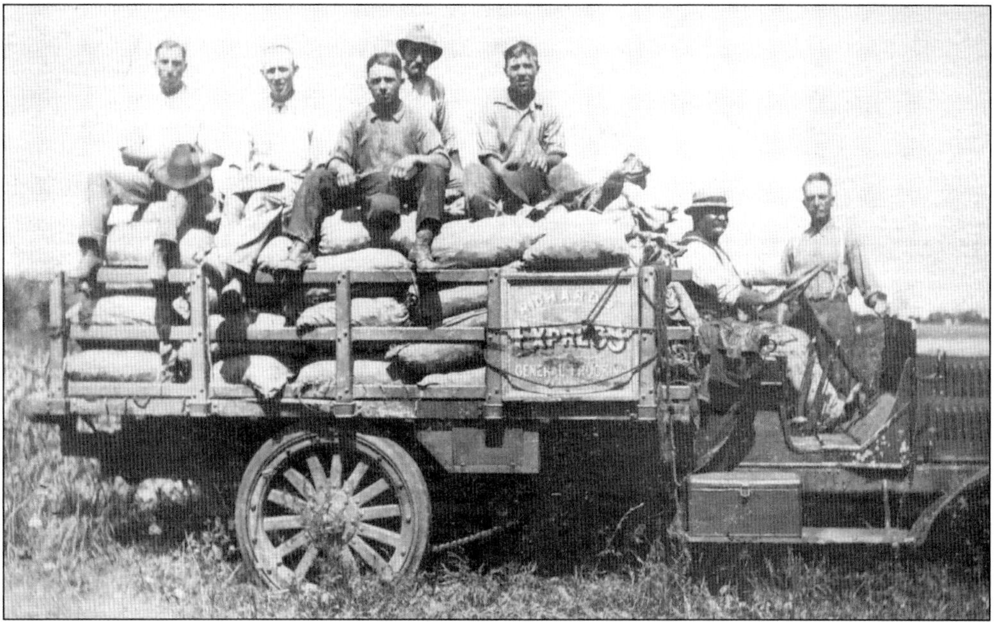

H.H. Richard's Trucking, 1918. Crops and workers are being transported to the ferry by Henry H. Richard, sitting in the driver's seat. Eugene Price stands on the far side of the truck in front. The chain-drive truck is loaded with sacks of lima beans being shipped to market. Richard advertised that "trucking of all descriptions would be attended to." Taken by Henry M. King, the image was printed and sent as a postcard.

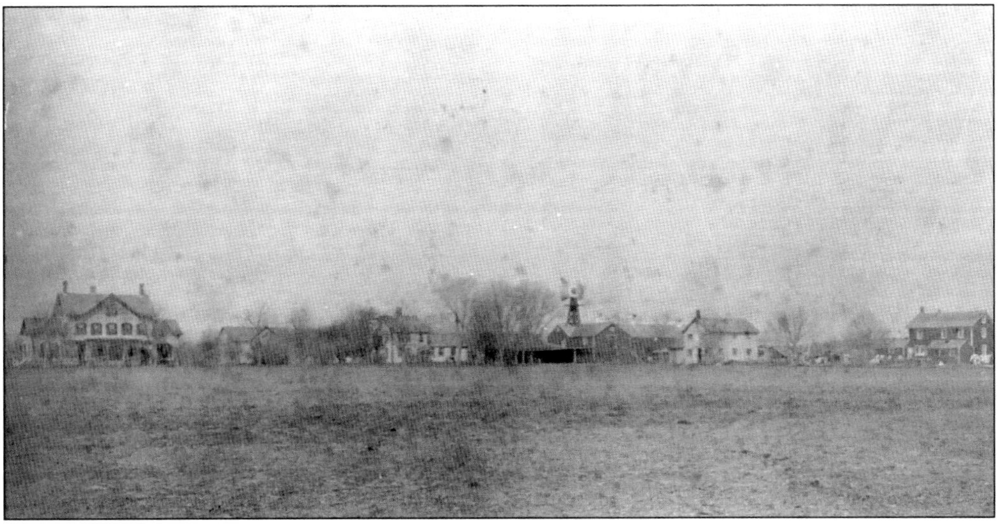

HALLOCK FARM, C. 1880. The Hallock farm was founded by George Hallock, who moved from Franklinville (now known as Laurel) in 1870. Purchasing a run-down farm, Hallock turned it into one of the most profitable enterprises in Orient. Dubbed the "Long Island Vegetable Factory," the farm expanded to encompass a large section of eastern Orient. Lucius Hallock, George's son, an engineer at heart, pioneered a number of projects to improve and diversify the business.

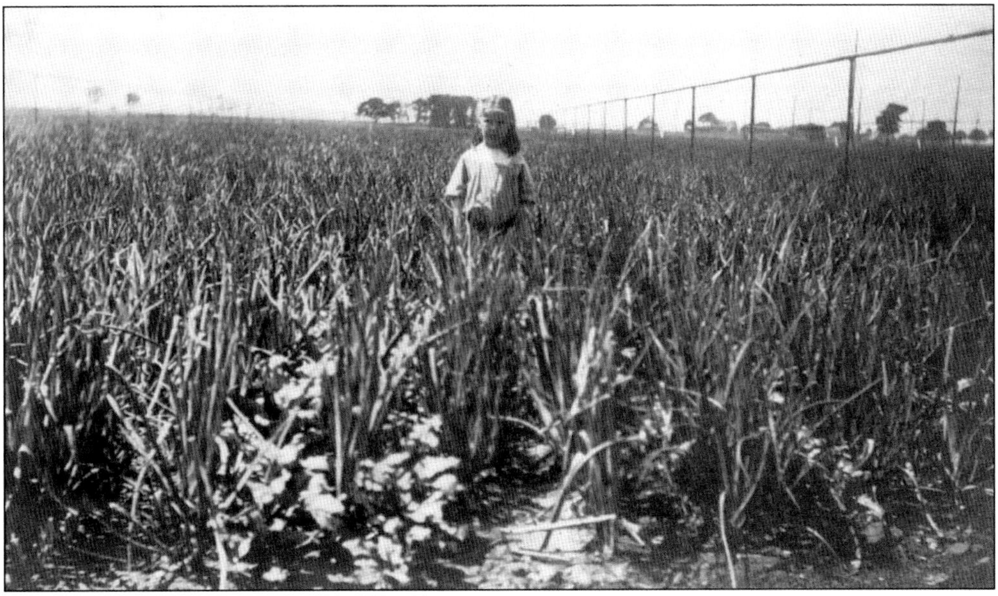

HALLOCK FARM FIELD, C. 1905. Katharine Latham is pictured here standing in a field of onions and beets. Lucius Hallock was constantly tinkering with new farming innovations. Part of Hallock's overhead irrigation system can be seen, created when most farmers either watered their fields by hand or dry farmed—leaving the watering of the fields to nature. Hallock kept careful track of what was planted in his fields, experimenting with growing multiple crops together to increase yield.

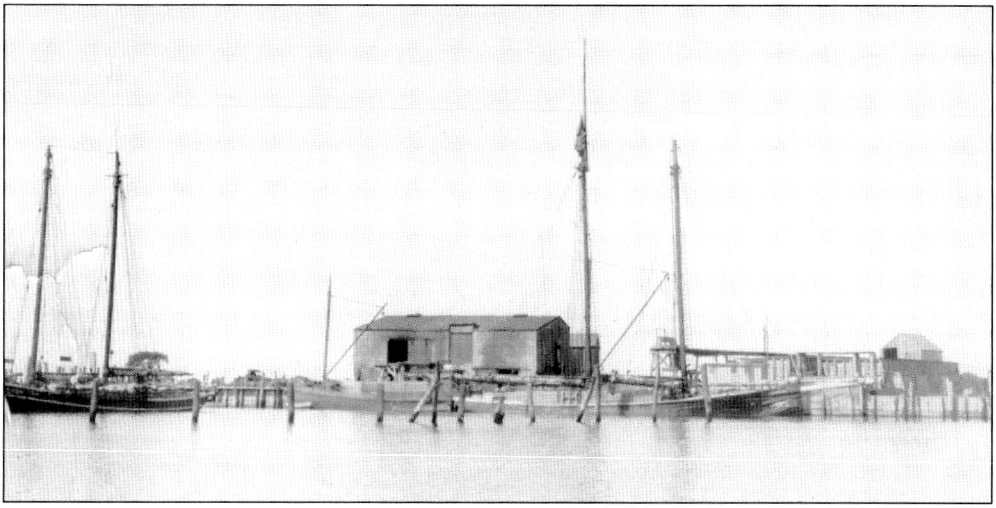

Hallock Dock and Coal Storage Shed, c. 1912. The Hallocks, in an attempt to control their overhead shipping costs, approached the shareholders of the Orient Wharf and asked for discount based on volume. When their request was denied, the Hallocks decided in 1879 they would build a dock to ship their crops to market. After opening the dock to other farmers in the area, the family diversified and increased the profitability of the dock by selling coal for home heating.

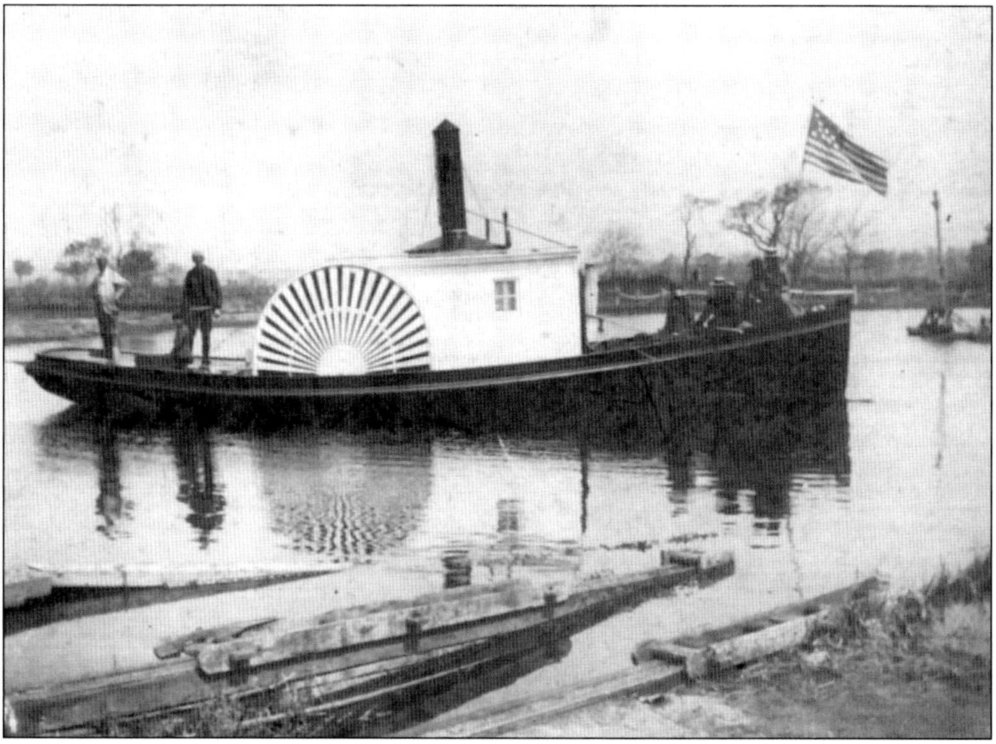

***Walter Royale*, c. 1900.** The small, all-purpose, steam-driven work boat *Walter Royale* was designed and built by Lucius Hallock in a barn near the Hallock dock. The ship was named after Hallock's son Walter, who died at age 11 of kidney disease. The family needed work boats to keep the channel they had cut to their dock through Hallock's Bay to Orient Harbor clear for shipping.

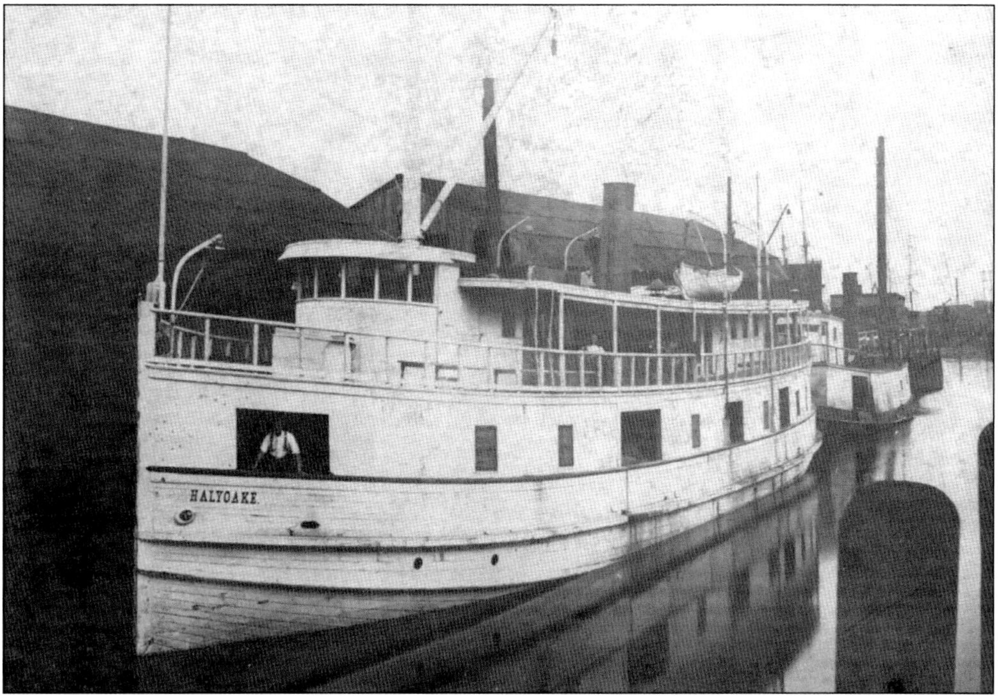

HALYOAKE, C. 1925. The ship pictured here is the second ship bearing the name *Halyoake*. This ship was in service by the Hallock farm during the 1920s, and it was used mainly to carry coal and produce. In 1939, Ned Adams, who worked on the ship, bought it from the Hallocks and continued to run the *Halyoake*, shipping produce and goods from the East End to various markets along the East Coast.

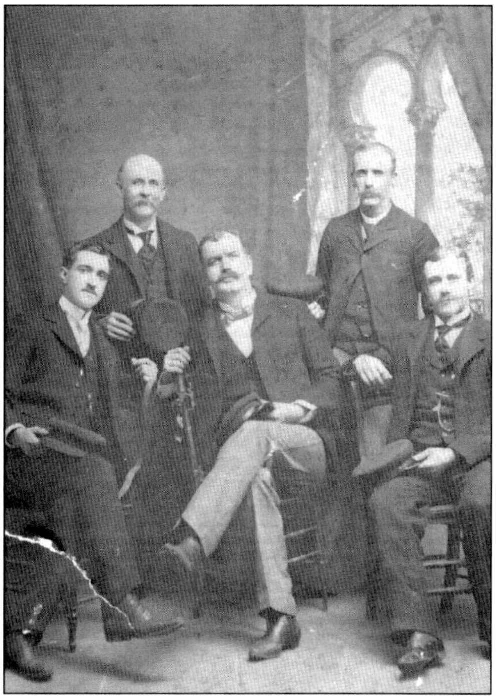

CREW OF THE *HALYOAKE* AND *JUDD FIELD*, C. 1885. Posed at a photographer's studio are, from left to right, Percy Latham, Capt. Johnny Latham, Clarence Babbidge, Capt. Abram Latham, and Eldridge P. Latham. Steam-powered ships needed not only a captain and sailors, but also an engineer to watch the pressure-driven engine. Percy and John Latham handled the *Halyoake*, and Babbidge was the engineer. On the *Judd Field*, Abram Latham navigated while Eldridge Latham was both sailor and engineer.

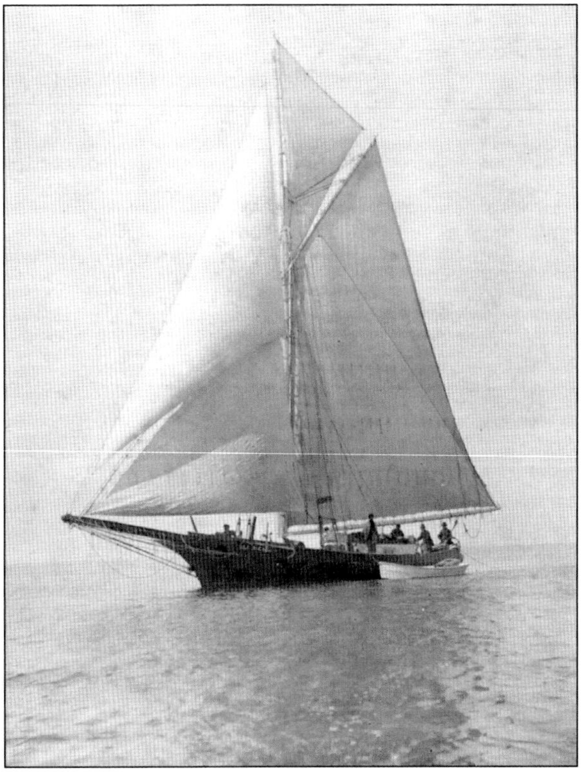

BLACK EAGLE, C. 1900. The *Black Eagle* was a former yacht, purchased by George Maxon Vail and turned into one of the more graceful commercial fishing ships of the area. Specializing in trap fishing and trawling, the *Black Eagle* had a crew of nine men, members of the Vail family or close neighbors. Most commercial fishing boats of the area were manned with closely interrelated crewmembers.

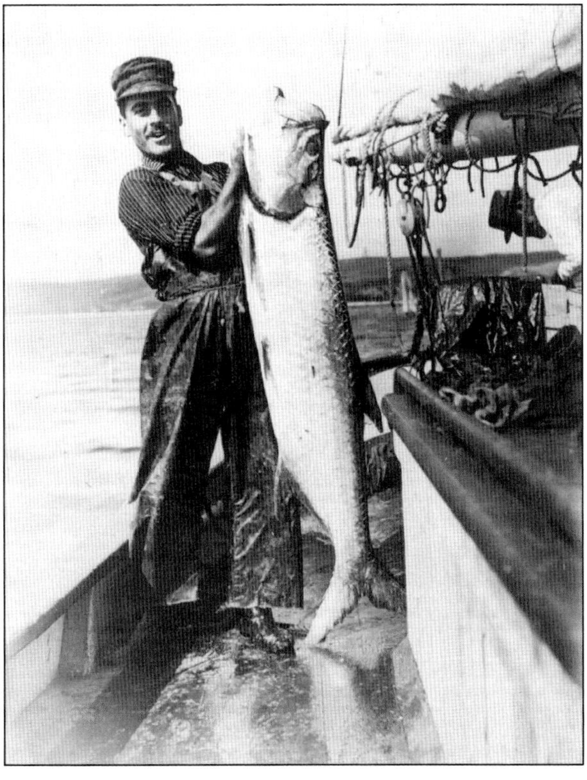

SAM VAIL HOLDING A TARPON, C. 1895. In the background, Capt. George Maxon Vail can be seen ducking under the boom. Generally found from Virginia to Brazil, tarpons grow up to four to eight feet in length. This tarpon was an unusual catch for the *Black Eagle* in the Peconic Bay area. William Hollis Vail, who took the photograph, was another member of the crew and occasionally brought along his camera.

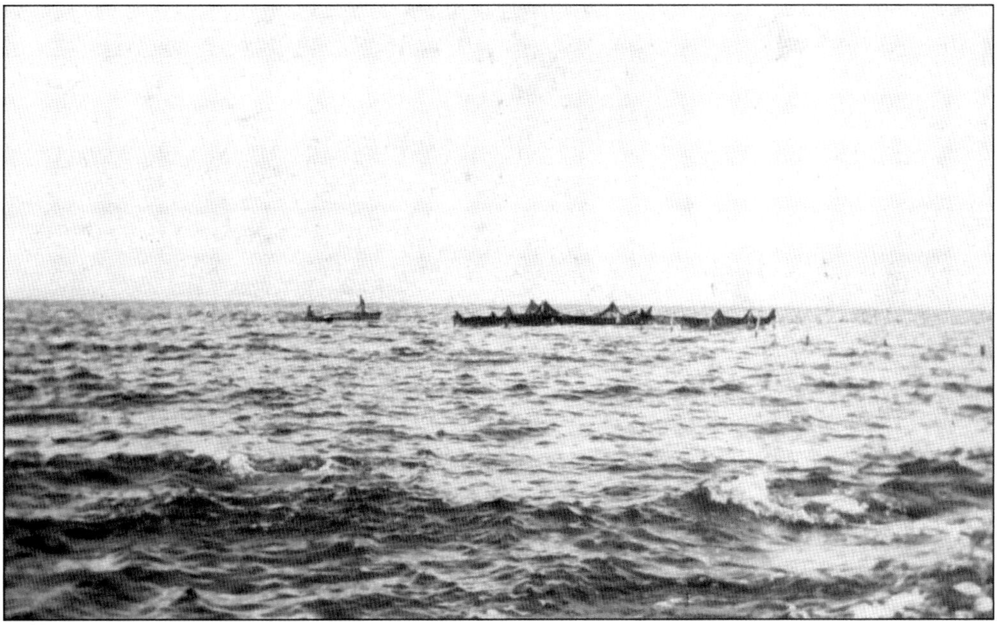

Fishing Trap as Seen From a Distance, c. 1900. Once dotting Peconic Bay, trap designs were a zealously kept secret, each fishing crew believing they had the configuration that would capture the largest schools of fish. Fishermen set posts in Peconic Bay and strung a maze of nets that lead fish into an enclosed trap or "pound" area. Periodically, the trap was checked, and any fish that was caught could be scooped up and taken to market.

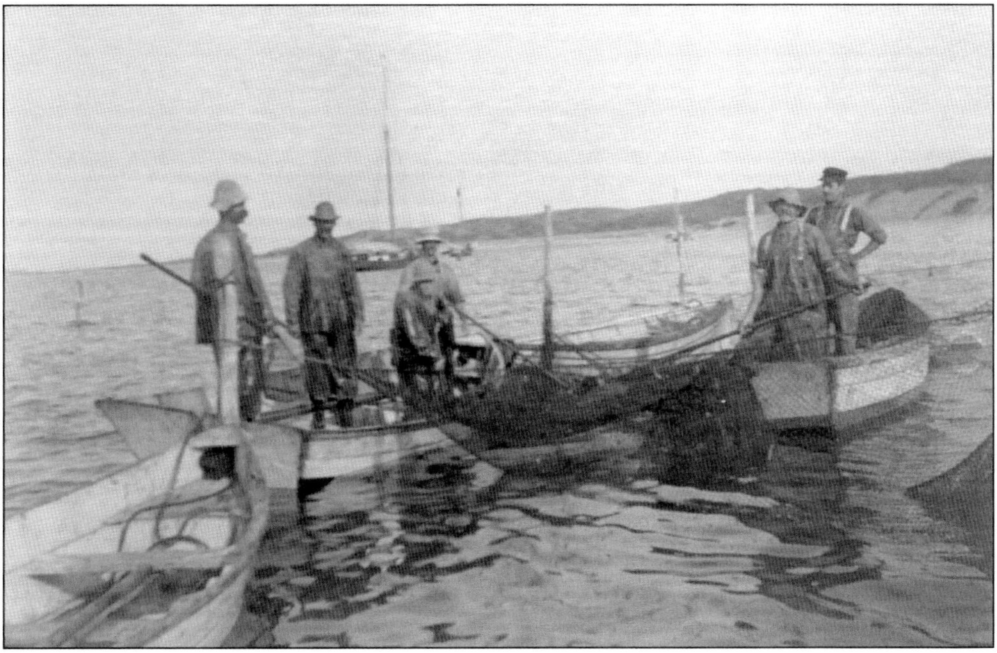

Hauling in the Catch from the Trap, c. 1895. A labor-intensive job, men with nets on long poles would scoop up fish from inside the trap. It was not unlike trying to catch fish in a fish tank. In this photograph, men from two ships owned by the Vail family, the *Black Eagle* and the *New York*, pause in the task of clearing one of the traps in Peconic Bay.

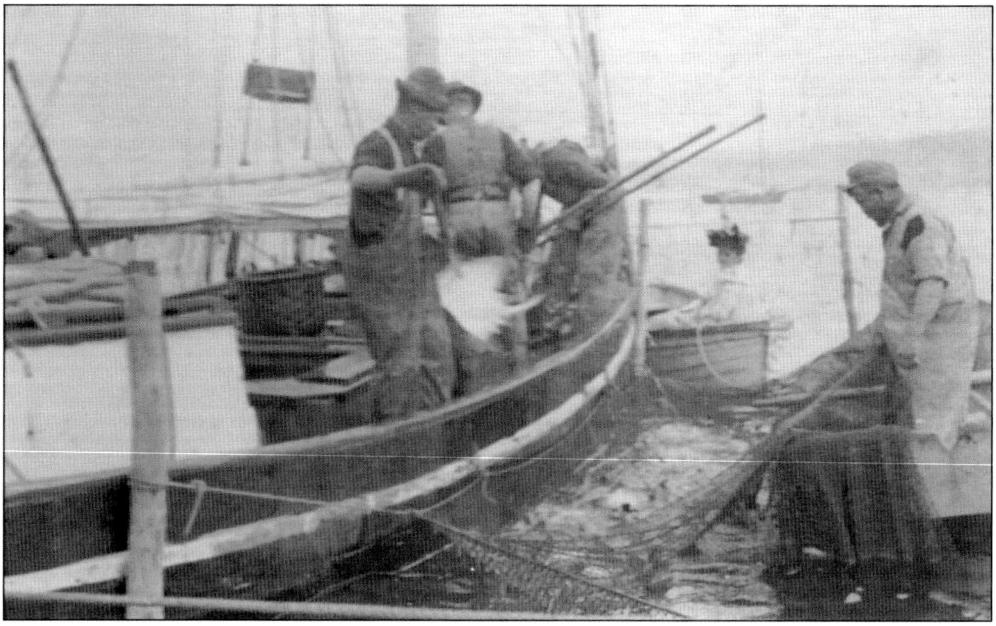

MOVING THE CATCH FROM THE NET ON BOARD THE *BLACK EAGLE*, C. 1900. The fish then had to be transferred to the ship for transportation to shore. Peconic Bay on the East End of Long Island was a very popular tourist destination for city dwellers seeking relief from the sweltering heat of the summer. Probably considered picturesque, if not a bit smelly, a female tourist (background) watches the *Black Eagle* crew work.

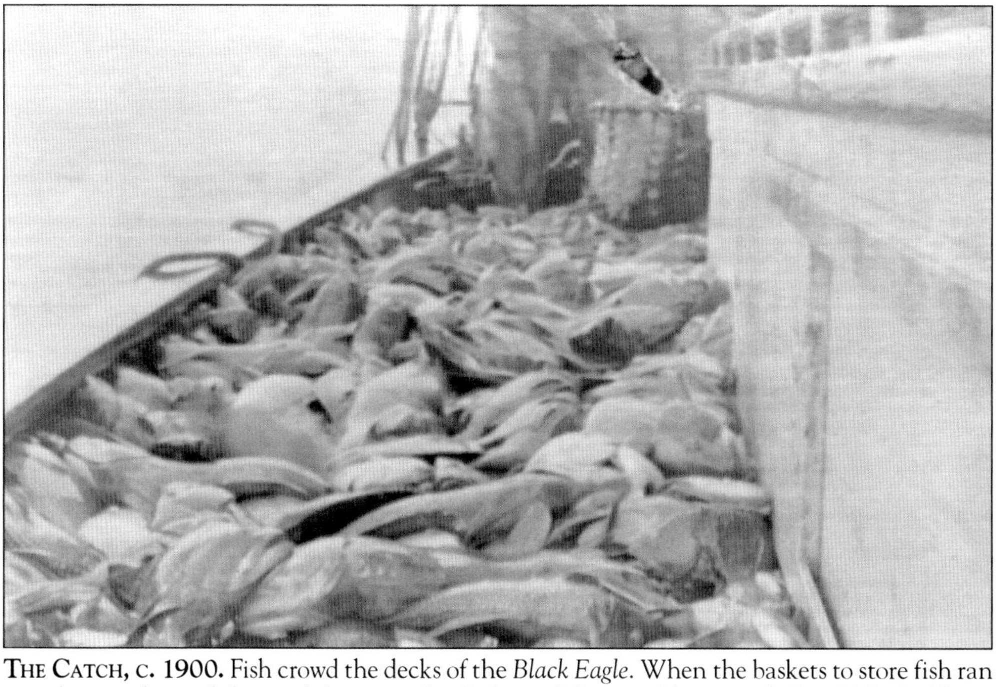

THE CATCH, C. 1900. Fish crowd the decks of the *Black Eagle*. When the baskets to store fish ran out, the crew heaped the catch loose on the deck until they could move it below. If the hold was filled, the catch remained on deck until the crew docked and unloaded. When the ship docked, the fish were then packed on ice and sent by either railroad or coastermen to market.

Moving the Catch to the Ship, c. 1900. Up to his knees in sea bass, Lem Rackett begins to load the fish onto the *Black Eagle*, set off Montauk, by shoveling the fish taken from a trap onto the deck. Rackett is garbed in rain gear to protect his clothes from the fish and the water.

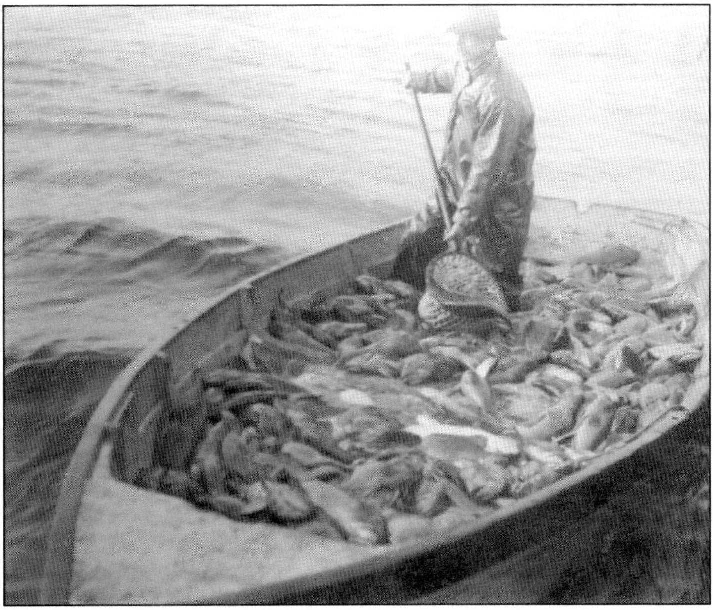

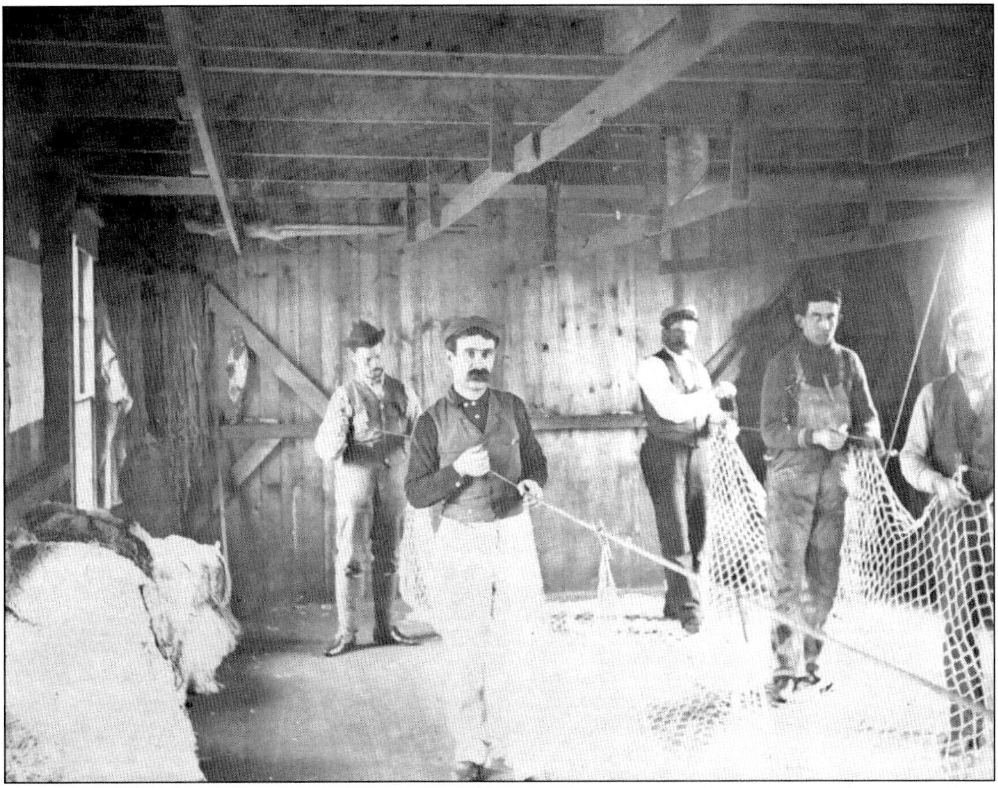

Repairing the Nets, c. 1880. The *Black Eagle* crew repairs nets at the Vail seine house on Navy Street. Fishermen had a building to store, hang dry, and repair their nets, which were periodically inspected for wear and tears. Larger, carnivorous fish, such as sharks, attracted to the schools of fish trapped inside the fish pounds, often ripped holes in the nets. Crews gathered to repair the nets during the off season.

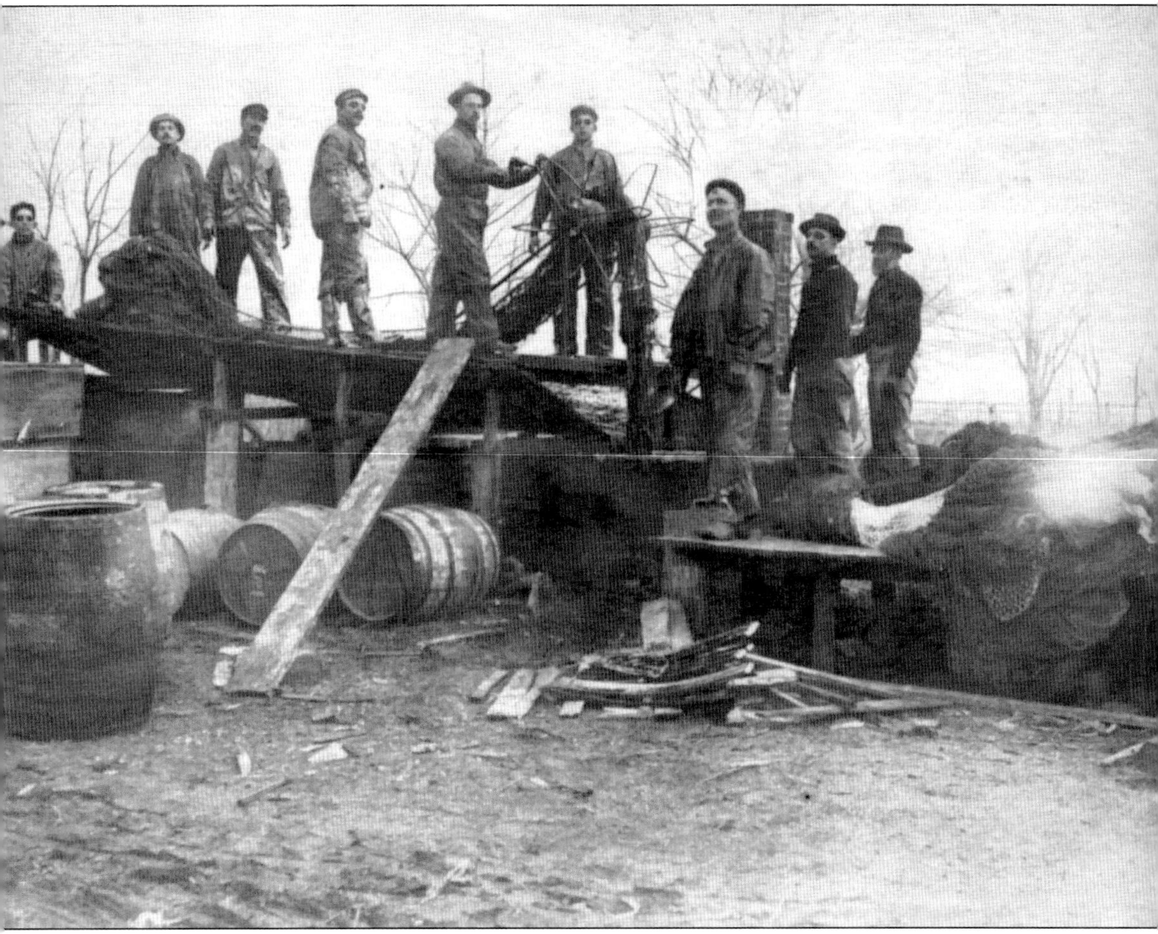

BLACK *EAGLE* CREW TARRING NETS, C. 1900. To make nets last longer, fishing crews gathered at the beginning of the season to coat the nets in tar. The nets were laid out and pulled into the hot tar pot by a hand-cranked roller. At least three of these tar pots were located in the Oysterponds area. The tar pots were community owned, and any residents that needed to tar nets could use them.

Six

Hamlets and Homes

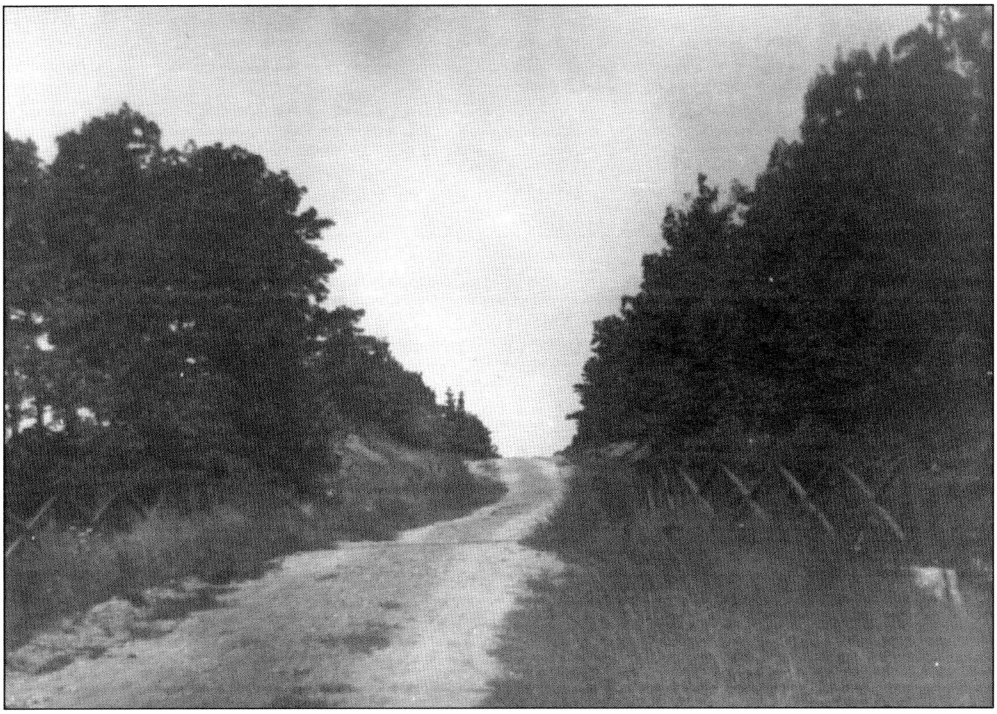

Bay Avenue, East Marion, c. 1890. Although it is hard to believe, most of the side roads leading off Main Road once looked like this view of Bay Avenue in East Marion. Roads were generally unpaved, sandy paths until sometime after 1920. Bay Avenue was a main thoroughfare leading to not only Peconic Bay, but also to Marion Lake and the icehouses.

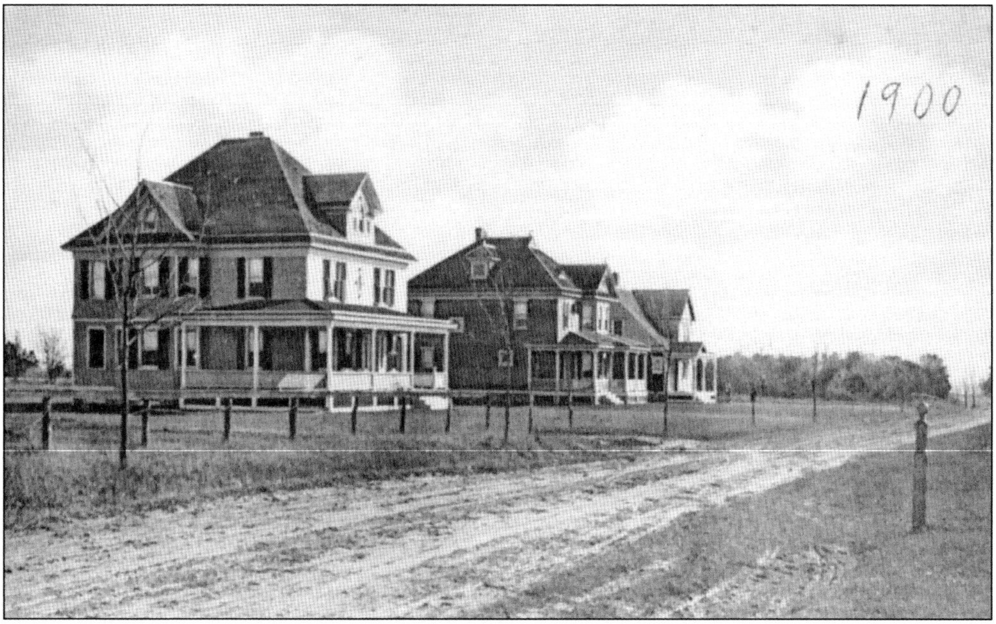

Bay Avenue, East Marion, c. 1900. Houses began appearing on the sandy, tree-lined path of Bay Avenue. These roomy houses were the precursor of a row of homes that attracted new residents. The advent of the automobile helped to end the tourist boom to the East End, where average citizens rented rooms for the season, but the same phenomenon began to encourage wealthy businessmen from New York to invest in larger summer houses, particularly in East Marion.

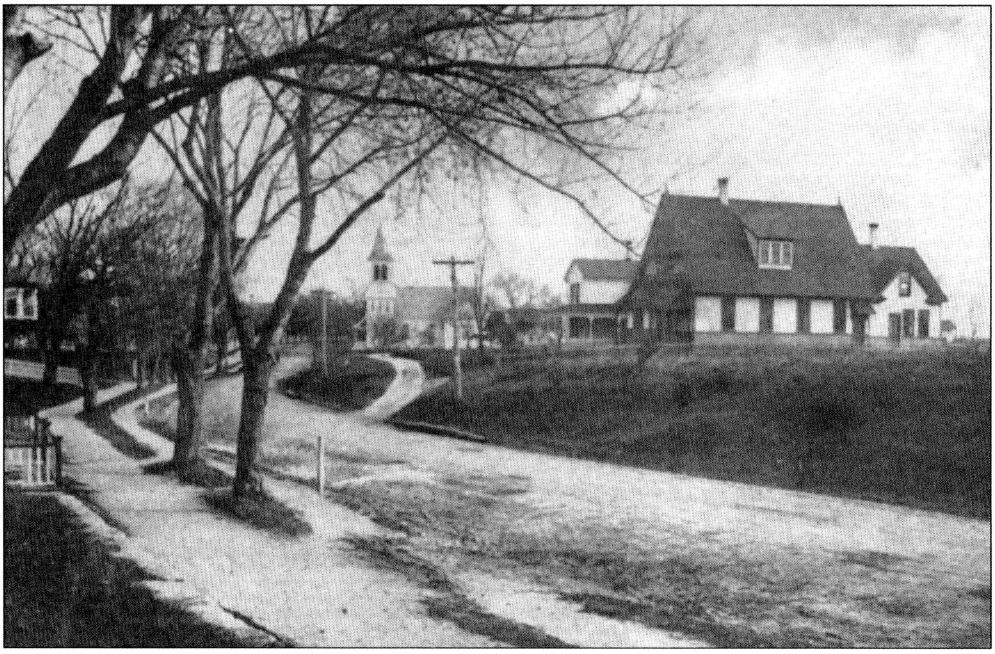

Main Road in East Marion, c. 1900. This photograph captures Main Road looking east from just before Cemetery Lane. The image is one of many taken by Loren Rowley and shows the newly built chapel with the church in the distance. The image also clearly shows the old East Marion schoolhouse, which was raised to become the second story of the house next to the chapel.

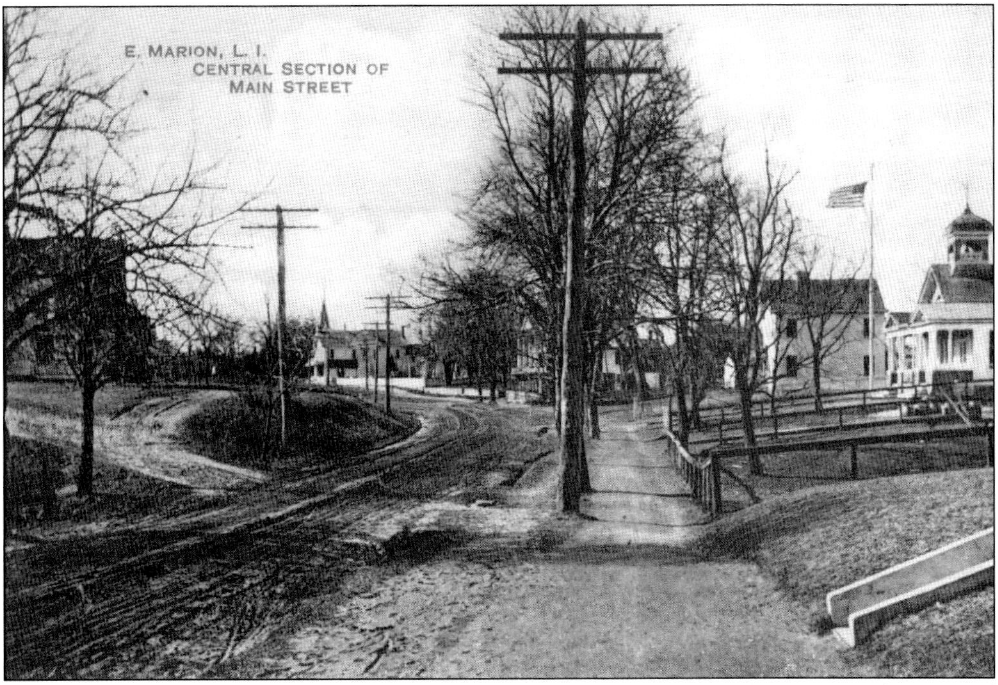

MAIN ROAD IN EAST MARION LOOKING WEST, C. 1900. Loren Rowley, the photographer, moved down the street a little bit and turned his camera 180 degrees to the west. Here, the new school sits proudly on the north side of the road, and in the distant background the distinctive tower of the Anker Store can be seen next to firehouse.

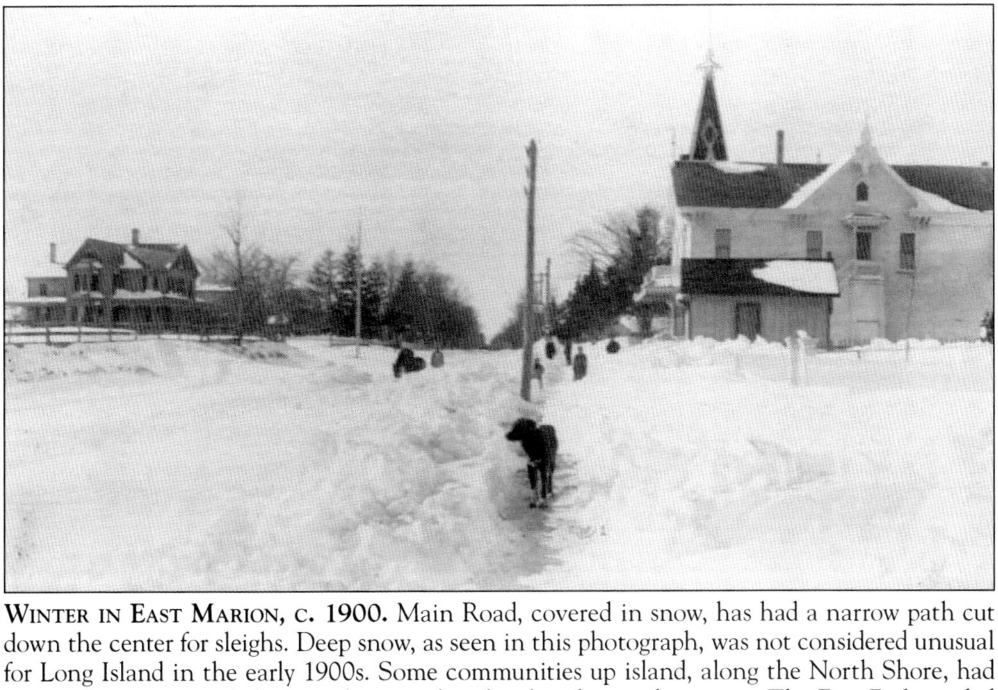

WINTER IN EAST MARION, C. 1900. Main Road, covered in snow, has had a narrow path cut down the center for sleighs. Deep snow, as seen in this photograph, was not considered unusual for Long Island in the early 1900s. Some communities up island, along the North Shore, had competitive 20-man sled teams that raced each other during the winter. The East End avoided such frivolous pursuits and left sledding to the youngsters.

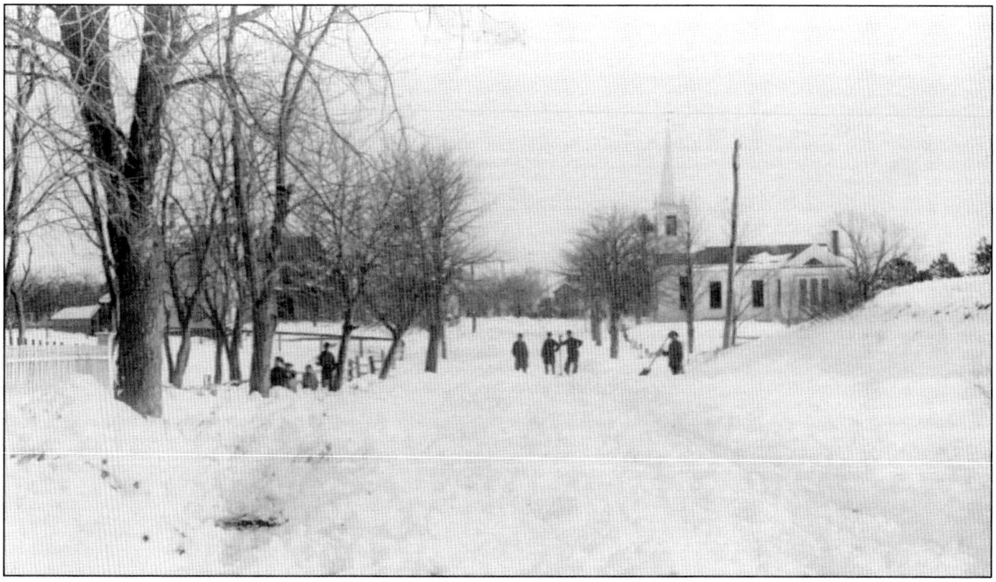

MAIN ROAD IN THE SNOW LOOKING EAST TOWARDS THE BAPTIST CHURCH, C. 1900. Note the large group of men working by hand to clear a path down the center of the road for travelers. While East Marion also had a road crew, a man and horse with a snow plow to move most of the accumulation, it was the responsibility of the residents along the road to make sure enough snow was cleared for free passage.

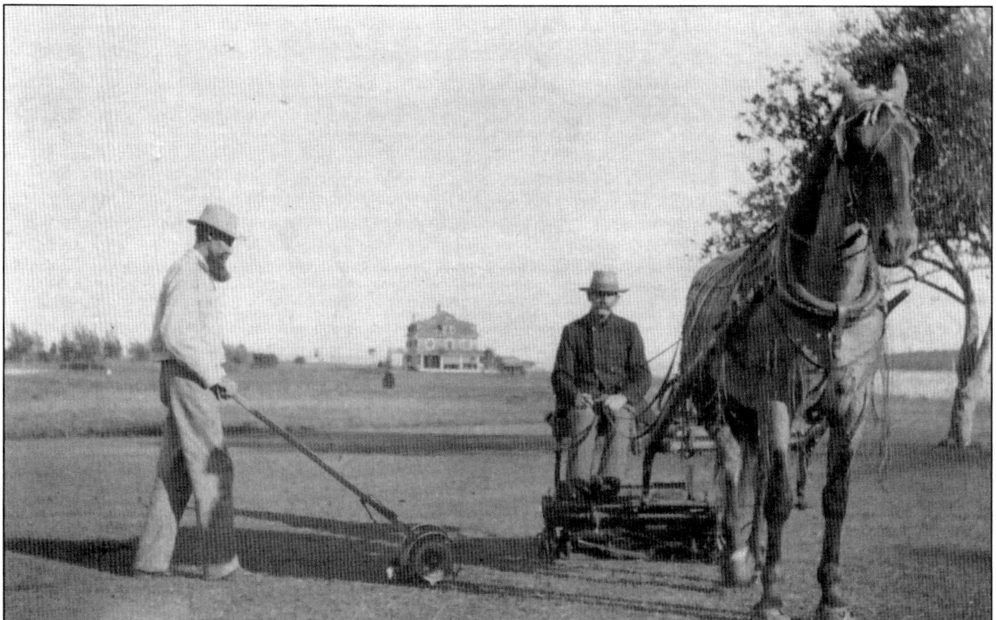

FISH ESTATE, EAST MARION, C. 1900. Egbert Griffing is driving a horse-drawn mower, and Oliver Cauklins is posed with a new hand-reel mower. The men are on the 73-acre estate owned by Latham Avery Fish on Peconic Bay between Gillette Drive and Shipyard Lane, one of the new summer estates that appeared across East Marion after 1900. The family summered in East Marion until 1937. The property was eventually added to the neighboring Merkle estate.

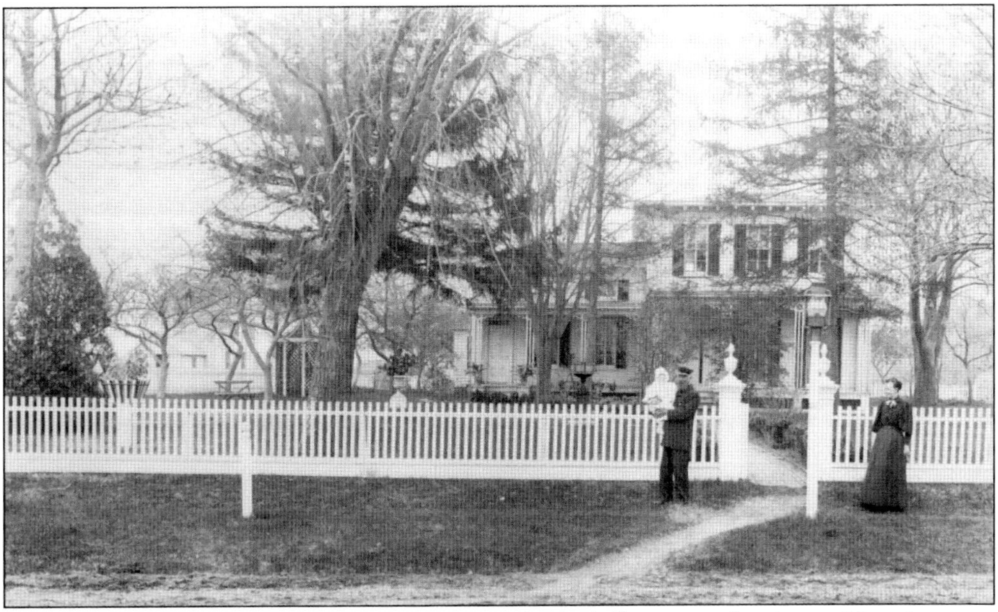

Benjamin Clark Tuthill and Family, c. 1870. The Tuthills are posed in front of their home on Main Road in East Marion. Tuthill, who brought the post office to his general store in East Marion, is posed outside his house holding his daughter Ella. His wife, Rebecca, stands near the front gate. Tuthill, who was a very successful businessman, eventually sold his store to Clarence Ankers.

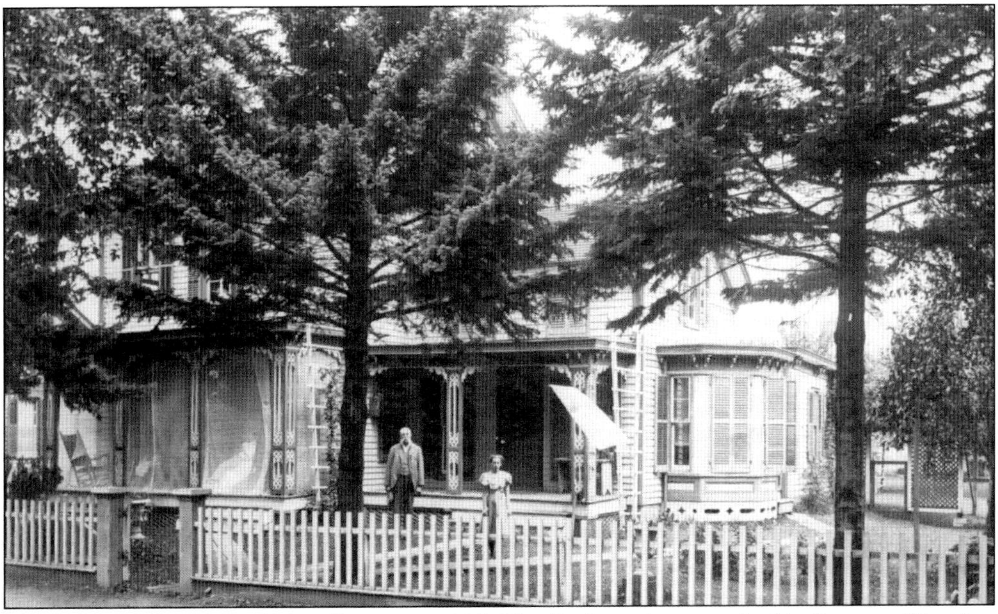

Captain Leander and Bertie Beebe, c. 1905. The Beebes, photographed by Reverend Rowley, pose outside their home in East Marion. Leander Beebe grew up and lived for many years on Skippers Lane in Orient. He was the owner and the captain of the schooner *George L. Fessenden* for a time. Around 1900, Beebe decided to change careers, and he moved to this home on Main Road in East Marion and became a lumber dealer.

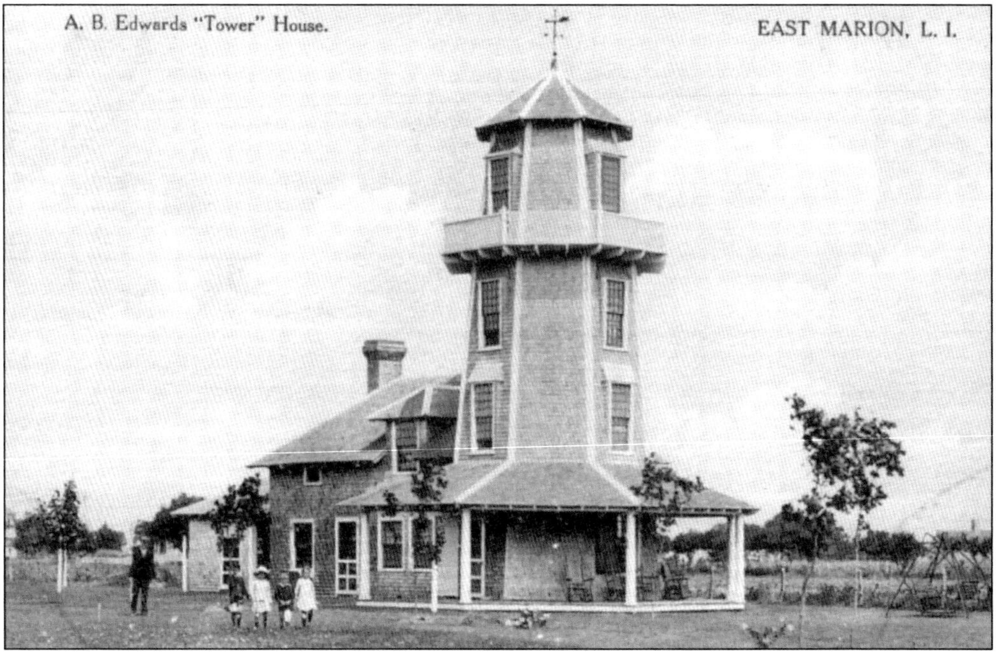

Tower House, c. 1930. This unusual home was built with a viewing tower for the owner's pleasure. The Tower was simply a summer house for Alfred B. Edwards of Manhasset, New York. The structure was built prior to 1931, and it stood in the Rabbit Lane Summer Colony at the end of Rabbit Lane in East Marion, offering spectacular views. Sometime before 1950, the tower was taken down, but the house still stands.

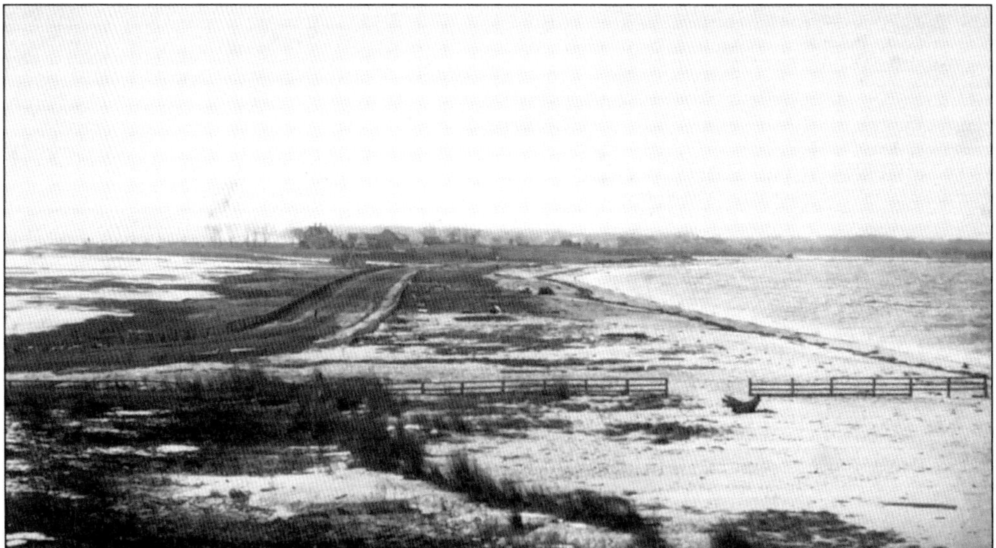

The Causeway Looking West, c. 1870. Before the roadway was paved, the area was known for years as either the beaches or hard beach, seemingly depending on which side of the causeway one lived. This early photograph illustrates how narrow the physical connection is between Orient and East Marion. Over the centuries, storms regularly have swept over this narrow stretch of beach, cutting the connection between Orient and the rest of Long Island.

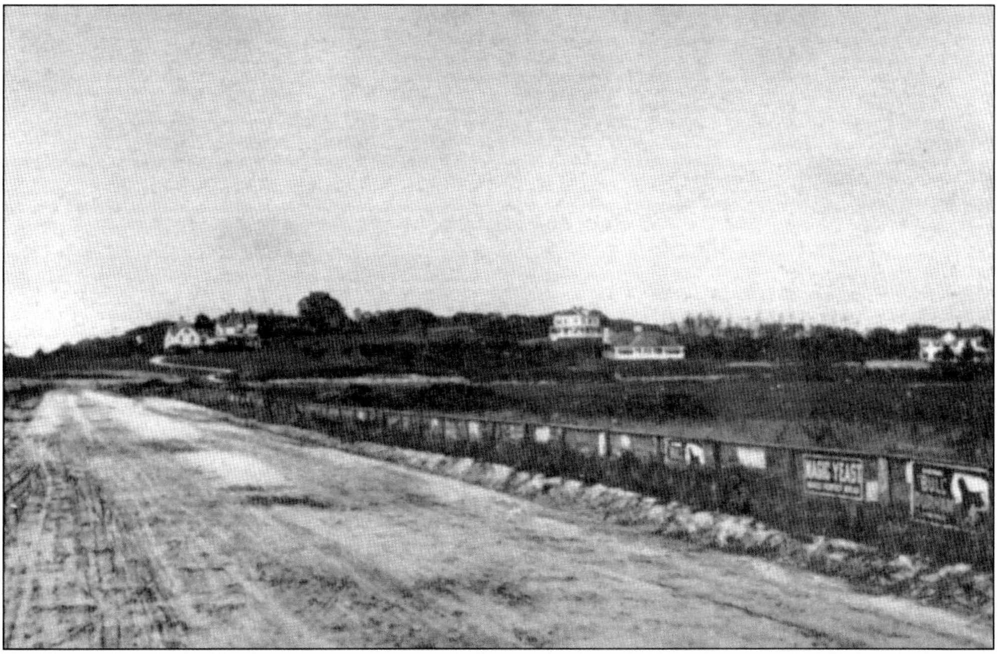

The Causeway Looking East, c. 1910. To preserve the road, residents installed a wooden fence along the causeway to trap the storm debris that always accumulated. The long fences also provided ideal advertising space for local businesses. The road shown here is the old Main Road, which circled around the north end of the pond. Today, the causeway cuts across the middle of the pond, which is to the right of this image and south.

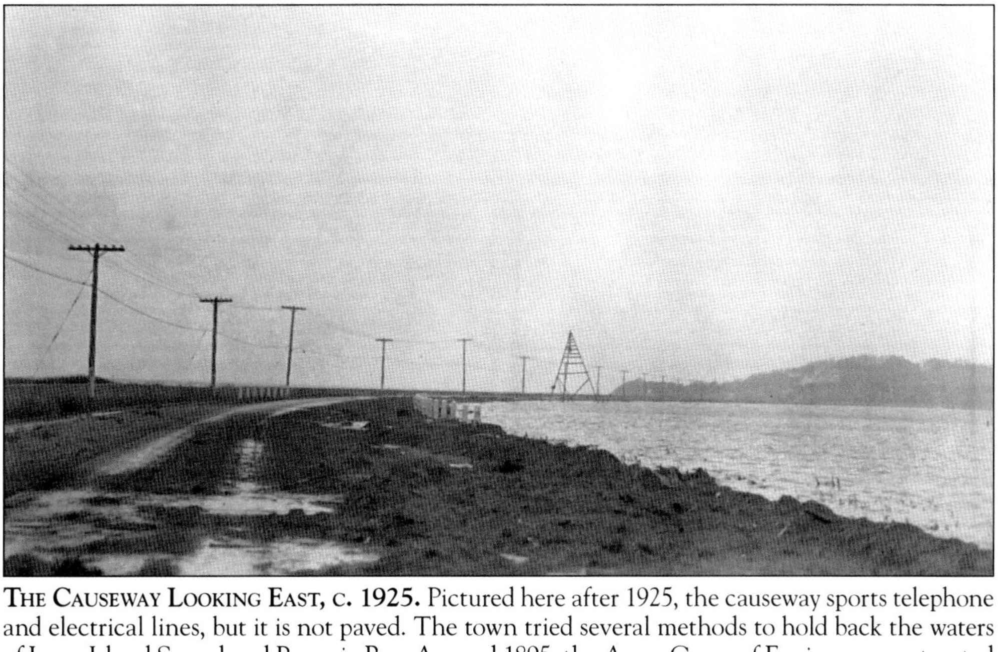

The Causeway Looking East, c. 1925. Pictured here after 1925, the causeway sports telephone and electrical lines, but it is not paved. The town tried several methods to hold back the waters of Long Island Sound and Peconic Bay. Around 1895, the Army Corps of Engineers constructed a seawall on the north side of the pond, along the road. In 1902, Clarence Birdseye, who owned the property, sued the government, claiming they never asked permission to build.

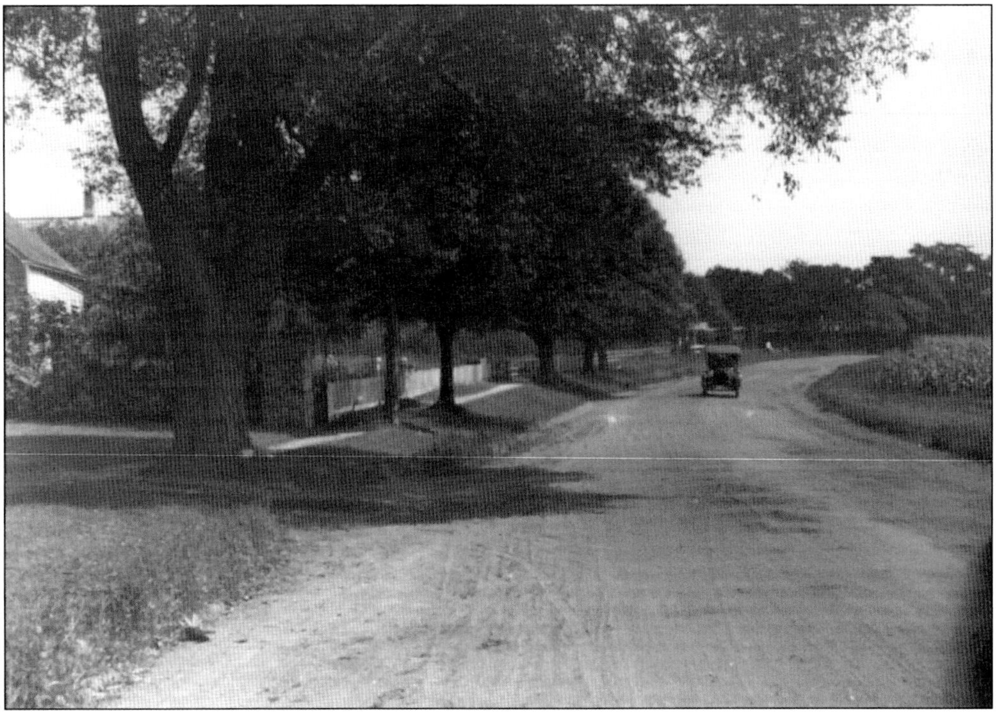

MAIN ROAD, ORIENT, C. 1910. Main Road climbs up a slight rise into Orient. The Dyer farm, now the Latham farm, appears on the right. Prior to 1938, cherry trees lined Main Road into Orient. Rev. Henry Clark, who was at the Congregational church from 1849 to 1856, led a campaign to plant trees around Orient. Visitors commented that traveling down the street when the cherry trees bloomed was like going through a snowstorm.

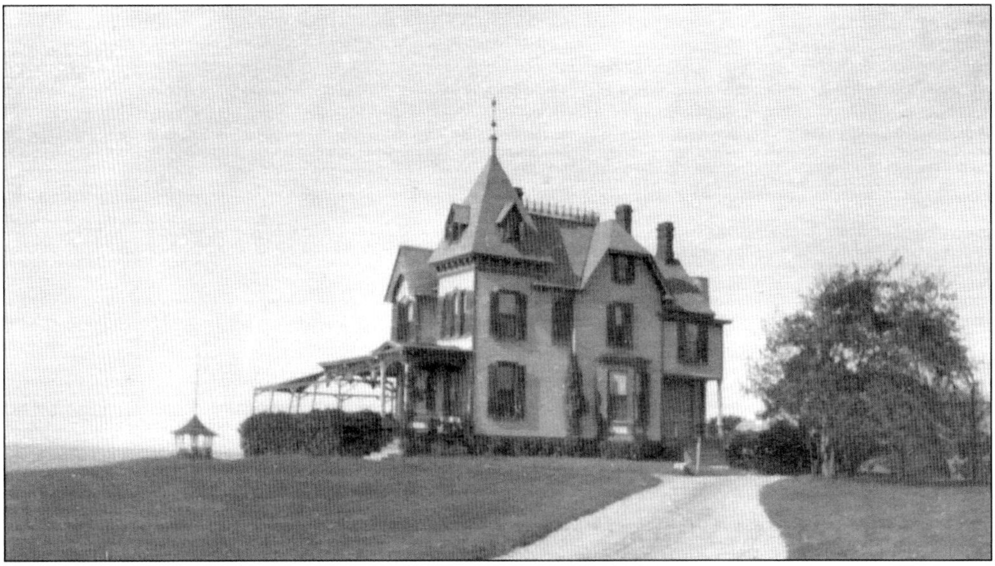

THE CEDARS, C. 1915. In 1883, after William Wilson Stephenson had returned from the Civil War, he built the Cedars. Stephenson, who was a lawyer with a practice in Brooklyn, originally used the house as his summer home. Until recently, the house has remained in the Stephenson family, and it overlooks both Long Island Sound and Peconic Bay.

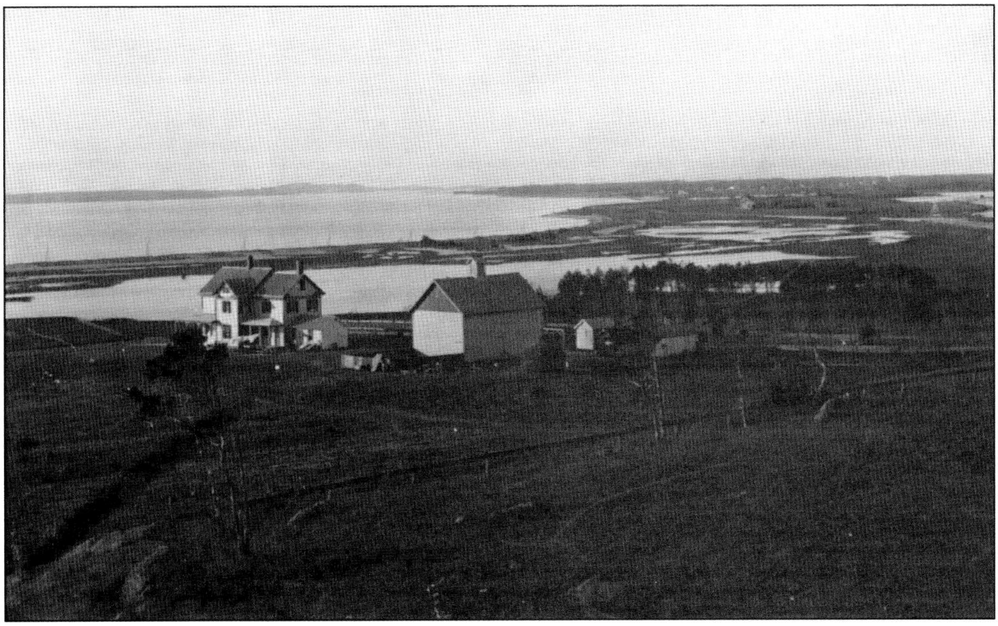

The Hill, Orient, c. 1890. This image looks downhill towards the causeway and East Marion. The hill from which this photograph was taken has had a number of names over the years—Pete's Hill, Brown's Hill, and Stephenson Hill. Nowadays, most refer to it as just the Hill. In this image, one can see the Morris family house on the left and John Miller's house on the right.

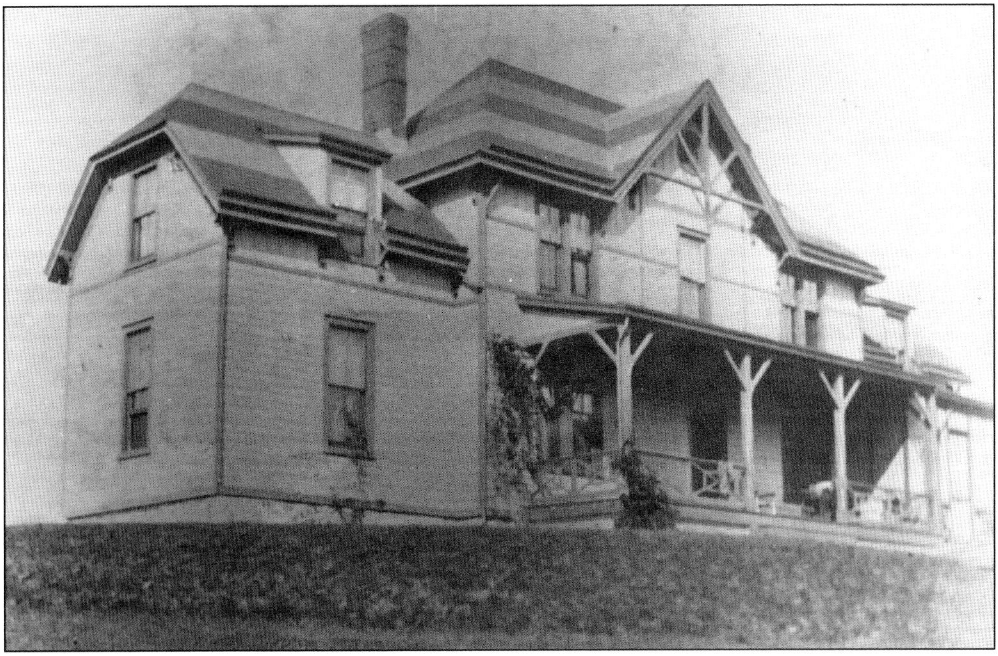

Birdseye House, c. 1895. The summer home of Clarence Birdseye is at the top of the Hill. He spent summers in Orient as a child, beginning in 1894. The house, called Interwellen, which means between the waters, was built in 1885. The original owners were reputed to have installed a large chain connected to a boulder in the basement to prevent the house from being blown away in the event of a hurricane.

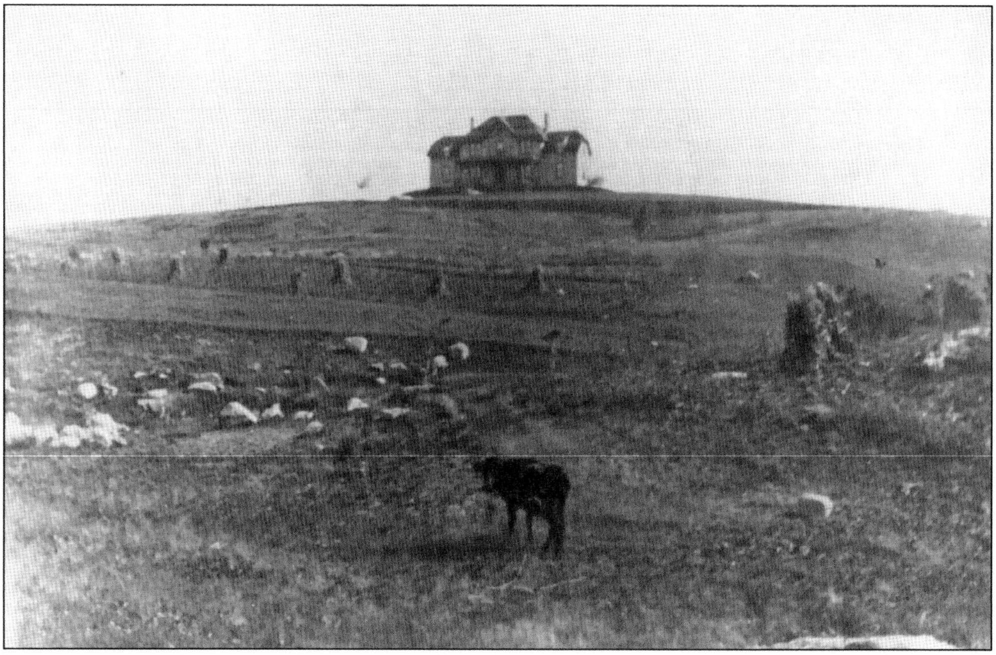

BIRDSEYE HOUSE FROM A DISTANCE, C. 1885. Unlike today, the Hill was all fields, with few houses and no trees. The lack of foliage and the crest's vantage point provided the owners with enviable, sweeping views of both Long Island Sound and Peconic Bay. Clarence Birdseye recalled that as a young boy he enjoyed exploring nature with the other boys of the area.

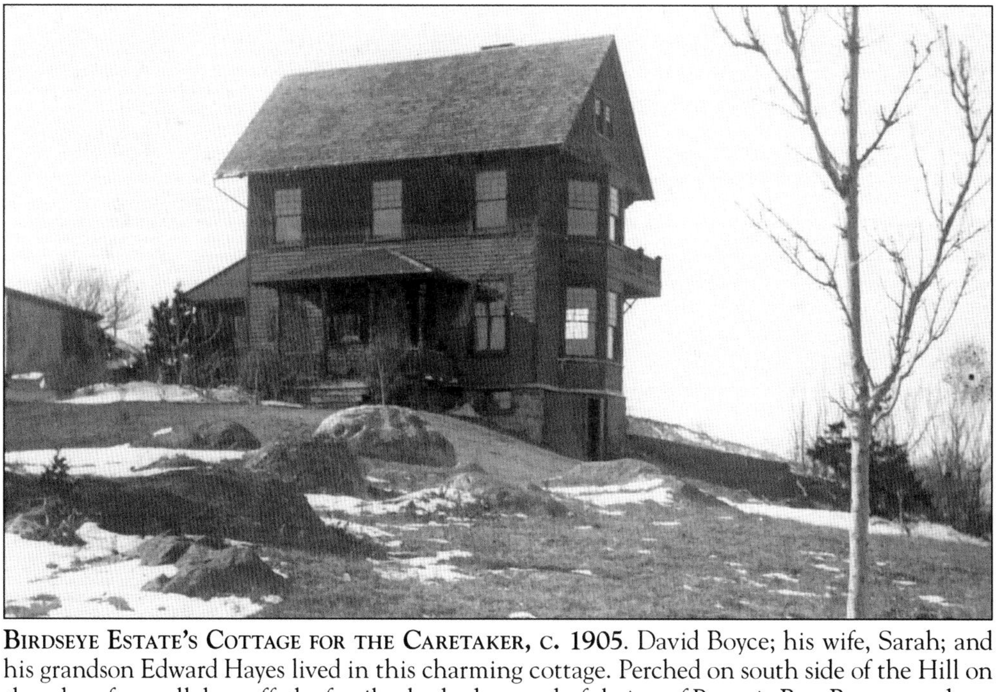

BIRDSEYE ESTATE'S COTTAGE FOR THE CARETAKER, C. 1905. David Boyce; his wife, Sarah; and his grandson Edward Hayes lived in this charming cottage. Perched on south side of the Hill on the edge of a small drop off, the family also had a wonderful view of Peconic Bay. Boyce acted not only as the gardener and general laborer on the property, he also served as the chauffeur when the family was in residence.

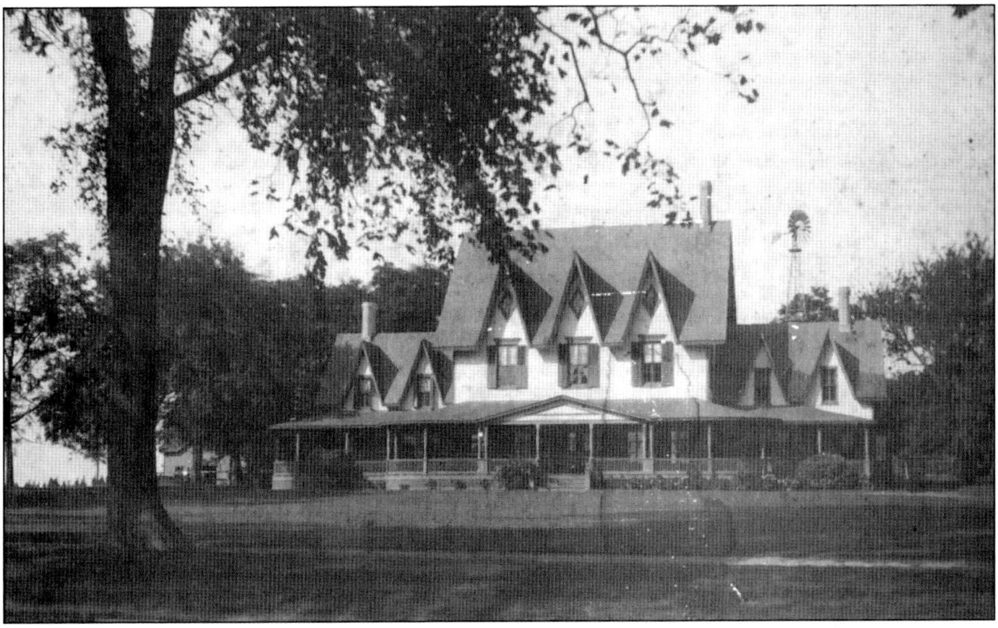

SEVEN GABLES, C. 1920. Orient's House of the Seven Gables was owned by Caleb Dyer. The house was located on Main Road between Back Lane and Pete's Hill Road, directly across from Dyer's farm fields. The house was one of the more spectacular and well-photographed losses during the 1938 hurricane. The wind sweeping across Dyers farm field hit the house and ripped the front half of the roof from the building.

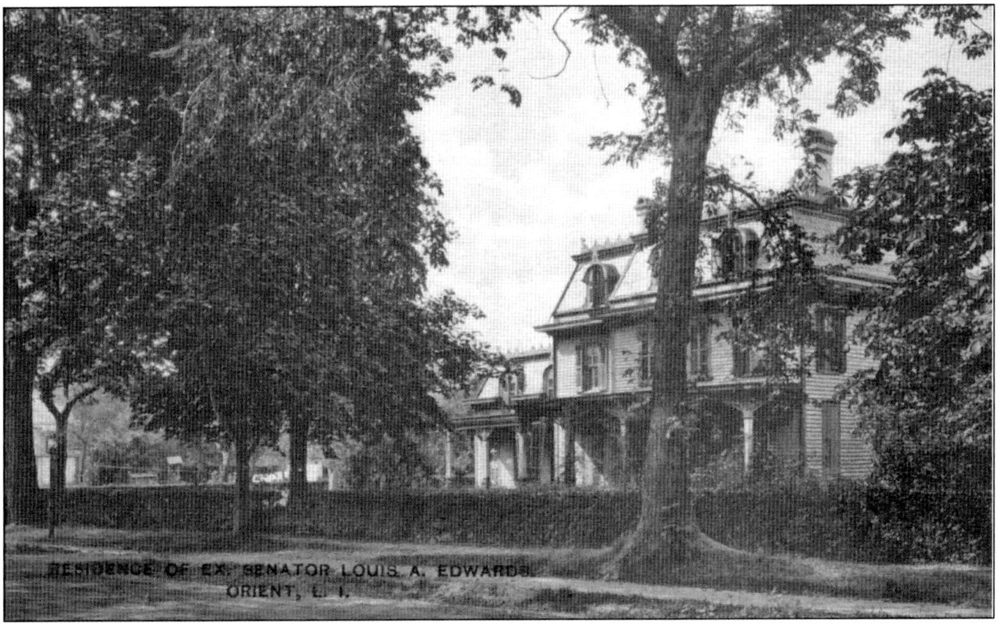

LEWIS EDWARD'S HOUSE, C. 1905. The Edwards' Second Empire home is located on Main Road across from Village Lane. In 1870, Edward built the Second Empire–style house for his third wife, Emma Beers. After Emma Edward's death, the house was inherited by her niece Adeline Beers House. The House family used the residence as their summer home, and Ruth and Grace House retired to Orient after long careers in the education field.

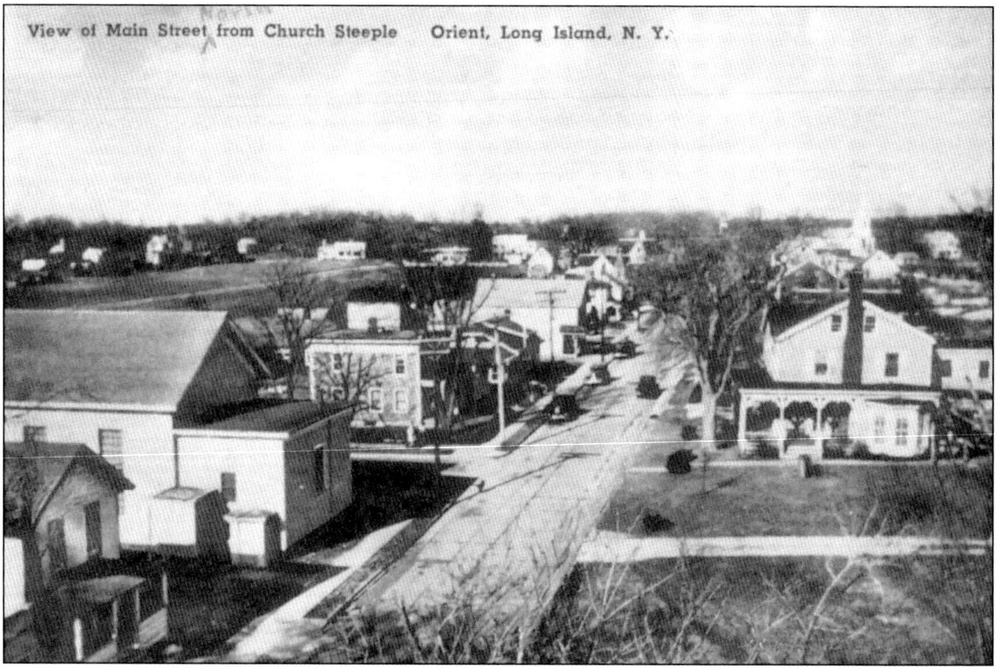

VILLAGE LANE LOOKING NORTH FROM THE STEEPLE OF THE METHODIST CHURCH, C. 1935. This view is not much different from the one that can be enjoyed today. One of the major differences is the absence of the homes along Oysterponds Lane.

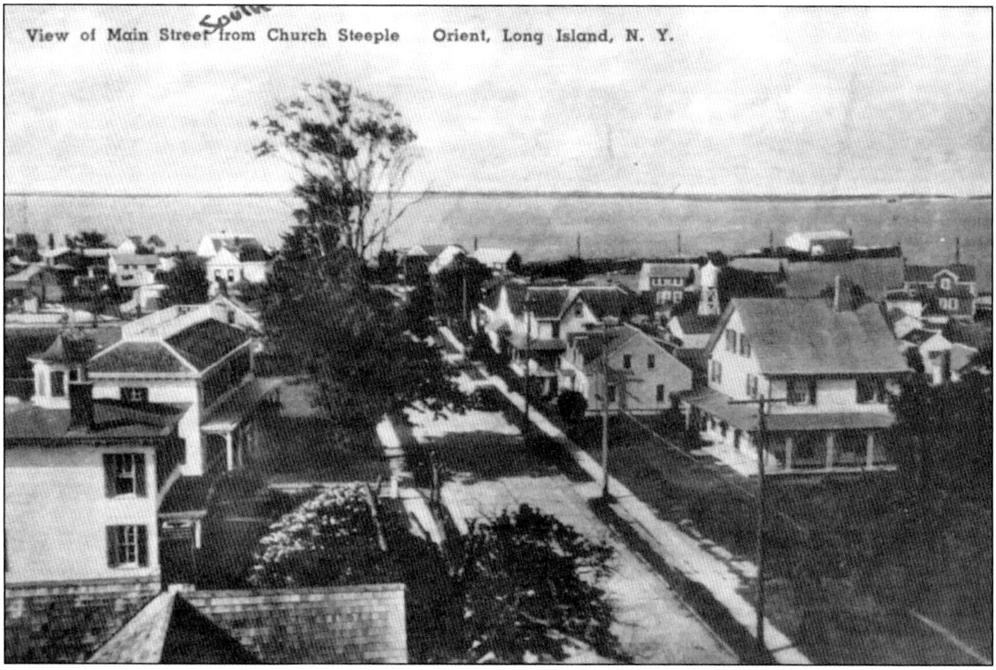

VILLAGE LANE LOOKING SOUTH FROM THE STEEPLE OF THE METHODIST CHURCH, C. 1935. This view shows the south side of the hamlet towards the Orient Wharf. This image and the one above were probably taken just before the 1938 hurricane. Several structures, such as the small water tower to the right, and the large trees pictured here were destroyed in the storm.

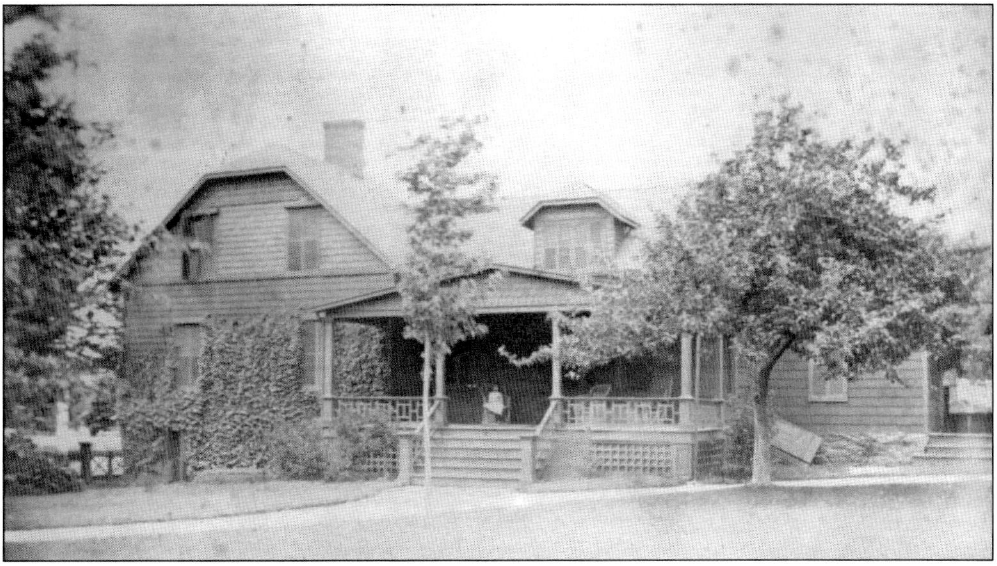

HALLELUJAH PARK HOUSE, C. 1900. The building originally stood north of the Methodist church, but it was moved around 1905. It took a week and a half to move the house less than a mile to Main Road, next to Dyer's farm. The man hired to move it drank a quart of whiskey daily, then napped. The horse pulling the house would halt when it heard "oh-oh-oh" in a sympathetic voice, so the neighborhood children said it over and over again.

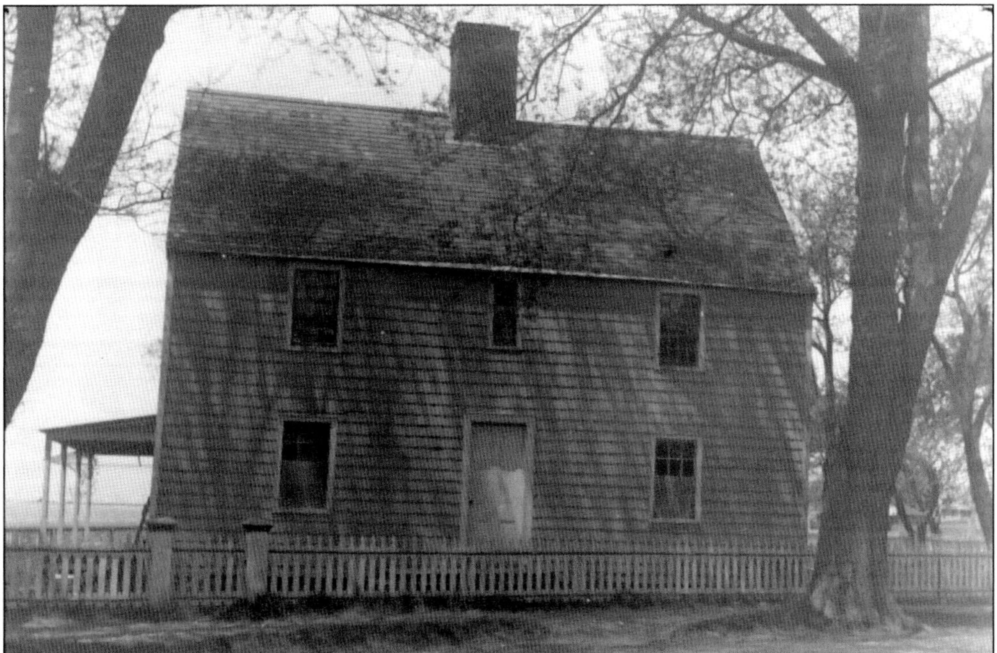

REVOLUTIONARY WAR COTTAGE, C. 1935. The house pictured here was built around 1730 by Richard Shaw. This is the house from which Augustus Griffin's father, Jasper, made his daring escape by jumping out of a second-floor window to elude British soldiers who were ransacking the house. Griffin was one of the Revolutionary War soldiers conducting guerrilla warfare on the occupying forces in the area.

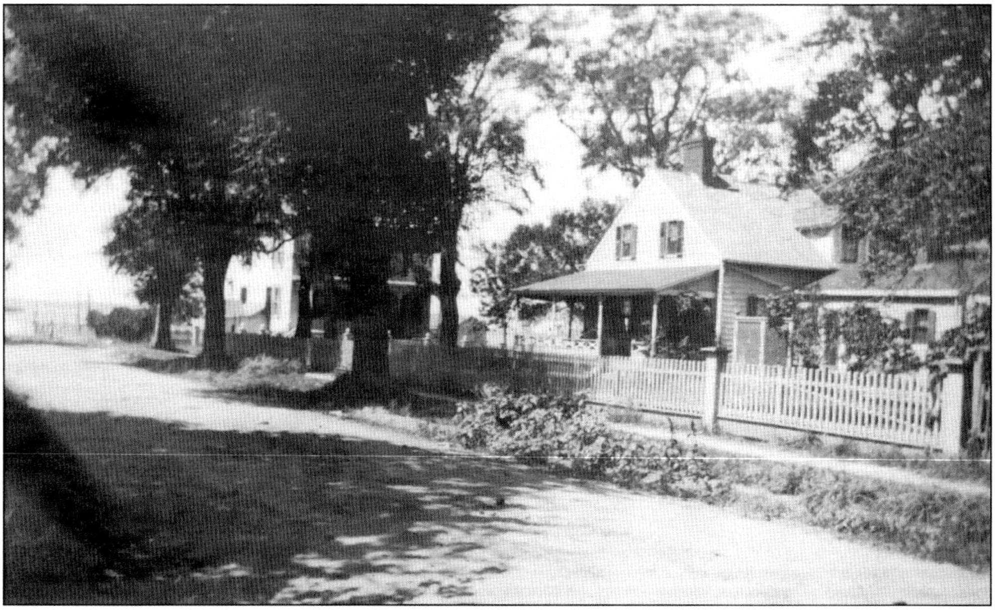

George Bristow's House, c. 1880s. Bristow, a musical genius, began performing at age 11 in a New York City theater orchestra; at 16, he was first chair in the New York Philharmonic. Just after this photograph was taken, Bristow refused to move his summer home's sidewalk to line up with that of his neighbor James Douglass. Douglass purchased the property across from Bristow's and built a large home, known as the Spite House, to block Bristow's view of the harbor.

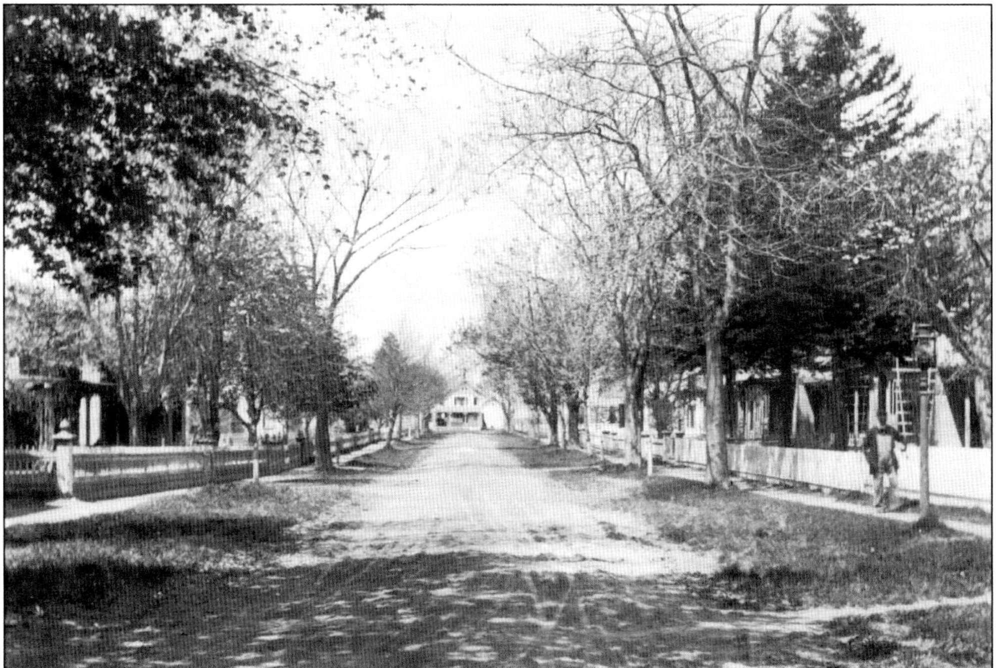

State Street, c. 1870. Originally known as State Street, the street was renamed Skippers Lane around 1946, the same time that Village Lane changed its name. The renaming was in honor of nine ship captains that had made their homes along the roadway.

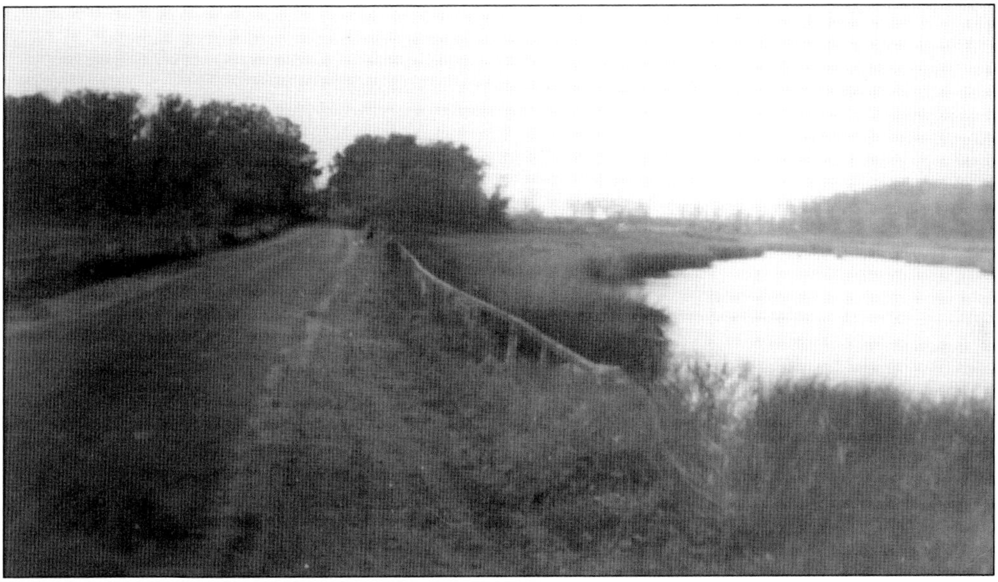

Narrow River Road, c. 1935. Narrow River Road winds along the river, looking north toward Main Road. The eastern side of the river was a large marsh, which was drained and partially turned into farmland. The western side of the river was mostly owned by the Hallock family, as part of their large farming enterprise. Lucius Hallock noted in his diaries that some of the fields along the river were ruined due to saltwater flooding.

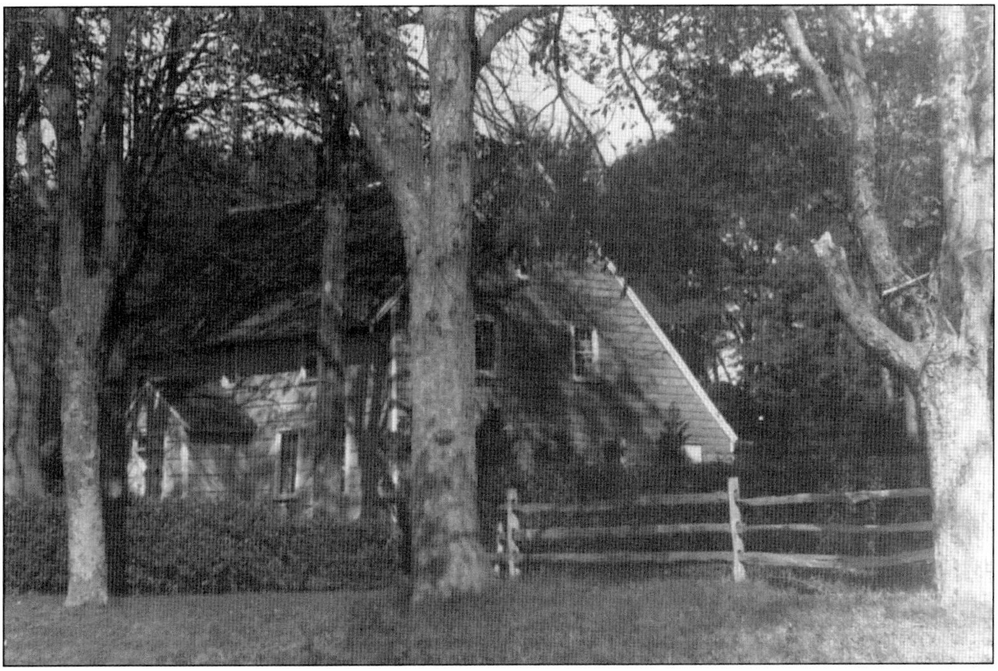

Terry-Mulford House, c. 1930. Located on Main Road, this is one of the oldest houses on the East End, built for Thomas Terry shortly after the founding of Southold and passed down in the family until after the Revolutionary War. Purchased by William Helms, it was sold to Elisha Mulford in 1805. The Mulford family remained in the house until 1900, when it was purchased by Dr. Henry Heath of Brooklyn. In 1979, the Mulford family reacquired the house.

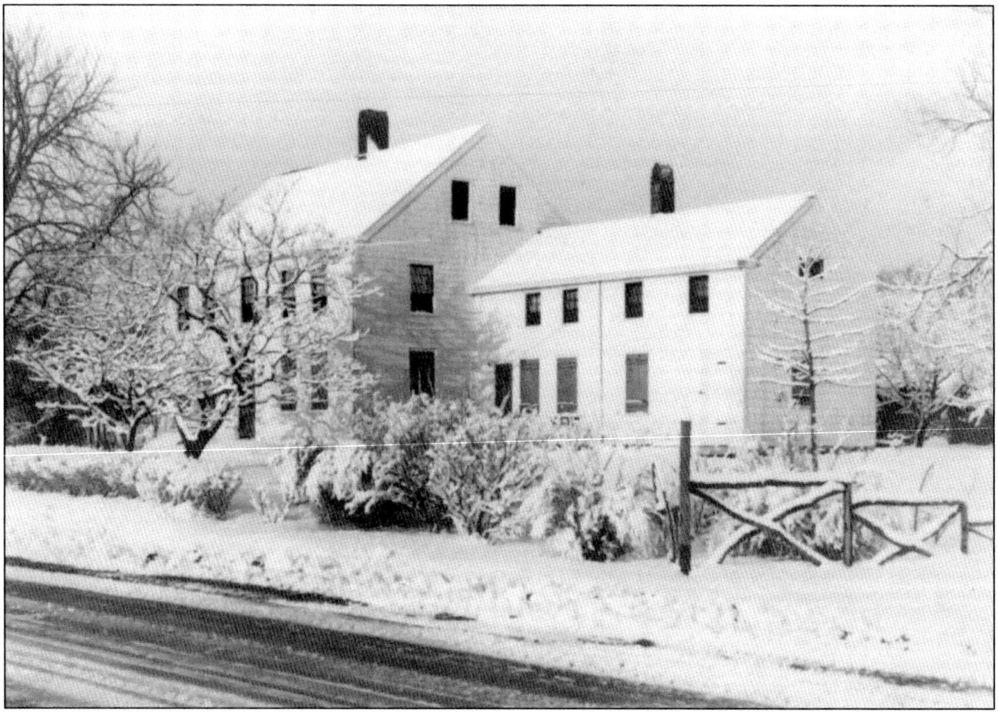

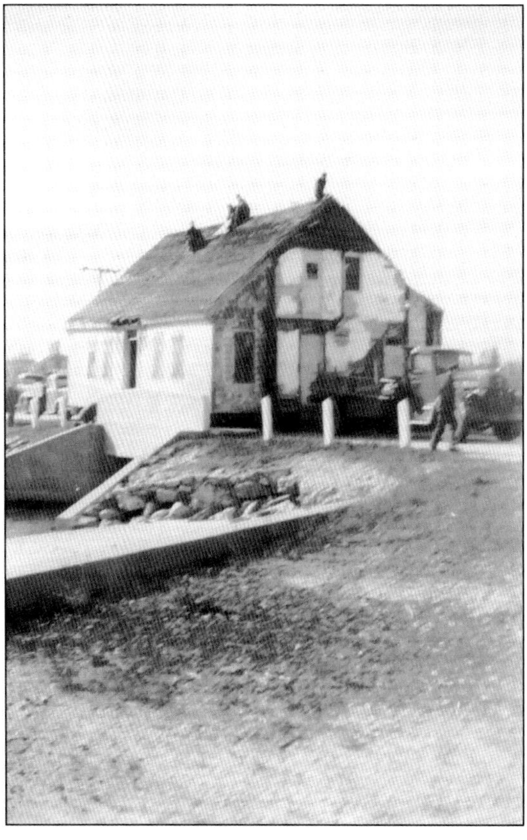

TERRYWOLD, C. 1900. Terrywold is the second-oldest house in Orient and the oldest house still in the same family. This house has been continuously lived in by the Terry family since its original construction between 1674 and 1684. The main section of the house was added to the original structure around 1700. Today the 11th generation of the family continues to live in Terrywold. (Courtesy of Diana Whitsit.)

MOVING A HOUSE, C. 1940. This house crossing the bridge at Dam Pond once stood at the head of Shipyard Lane in East Marion. It was moved by Nelson and Mary Chapman from East Marion to Orient Point. Relocating houses and other buildings has been a time-honored tradition for thrifty North Fork residents. The men sitting on the roof of the building were stationed there to move any wires or tree branches that might hit the house.

Seven

LEISURE

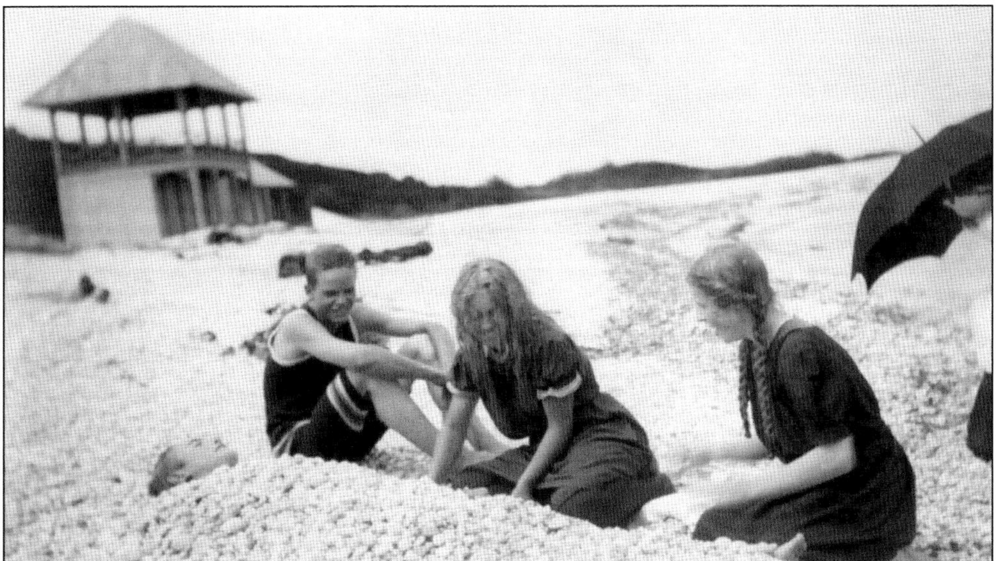

BEACHGOERS, C. 1900. After the menhaden fish-rendering factories left the North Fork, the tourist trade abounded in the East End from the 1870s to the advent of the automobile. Here, visitors amuse themselves on the sound beach in between swimming. The small buildings in the background are changing rooms, which dotted the beaches on the north and south sides of the Oysterponds area.

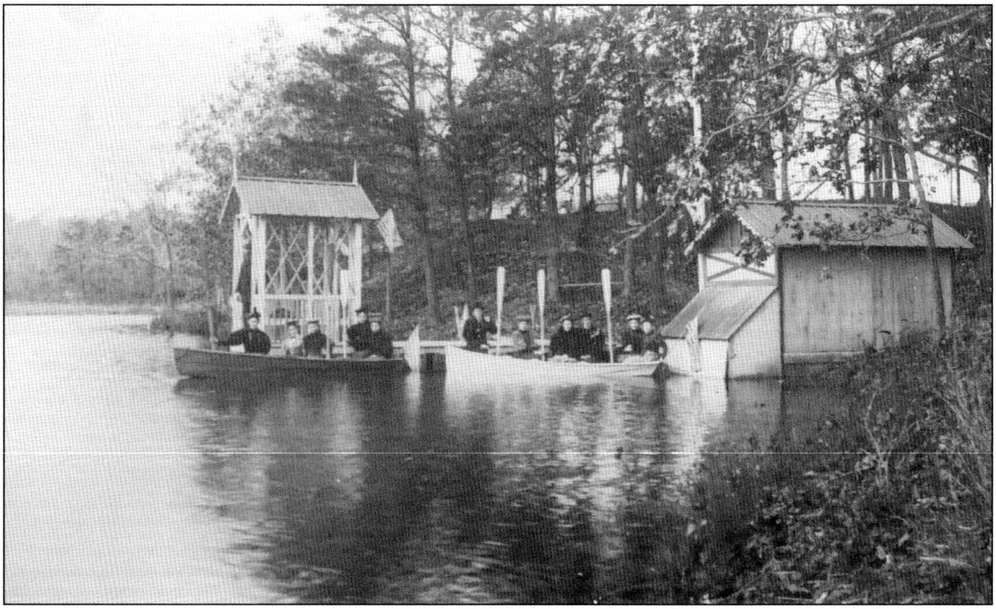

Rowers on Lake Marion, c. 1900. Lake Marion also provided visitors with the pleasure of rowing on the placid waters of a lake, rather than the more challenging waters of the bay or sound. The small boathouse was located on the north side of the lake, and East Marion residents used it on a regular basis.

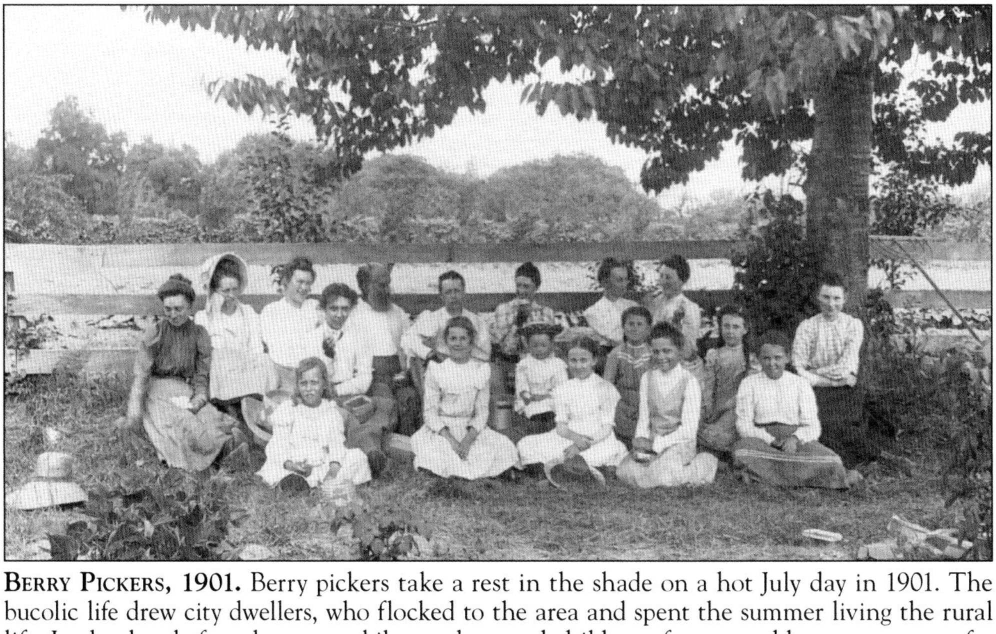

Berry Pickers, 1901. Berry pickers take a rest in the shade on a hot July day in 1901. The bucolic life drew city dwellers, who flocked to the area and spent the summer living the rural life. In the days before the automobile, mothers and children often rented houses or rooms for the entire summer, while fathers who had to work commuted out to the East End on weekends to visit the family.

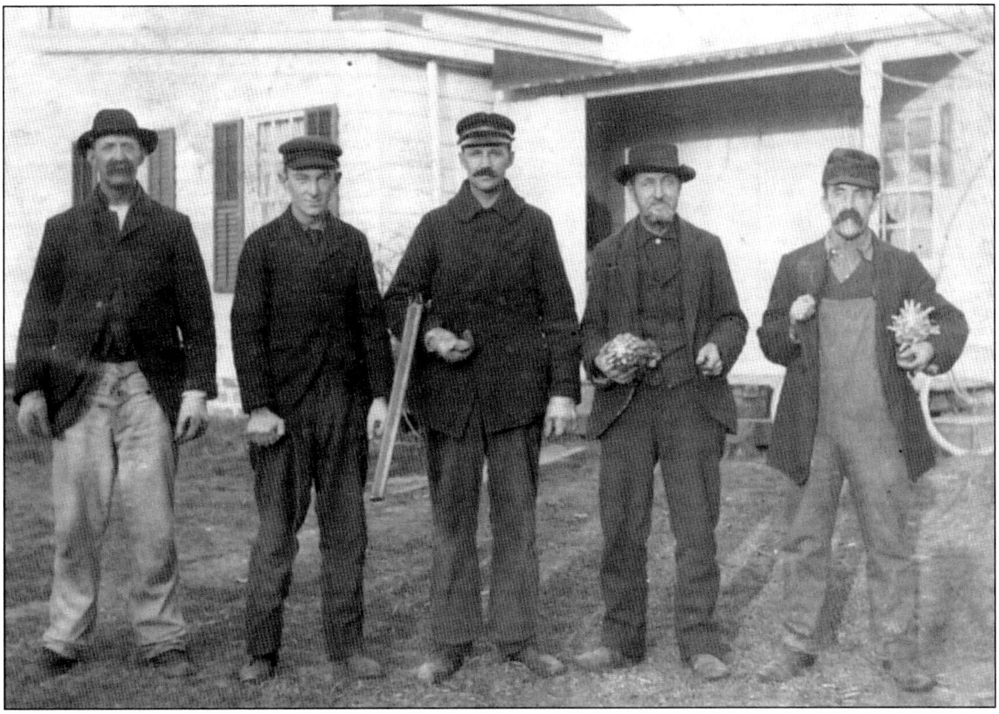

HUNTERS, C. 1910. In the fall, hunting, particularly for waterfowl, was very popular. Hunting enthusiasts flocked to the area to join locals in search of flocks of old squaw, canvasback, merganser, and black ducks. Here, hunters pose before the hunt. The man on the far right is holding a large conch shell, which could have a hole drilled into it to make a horn.

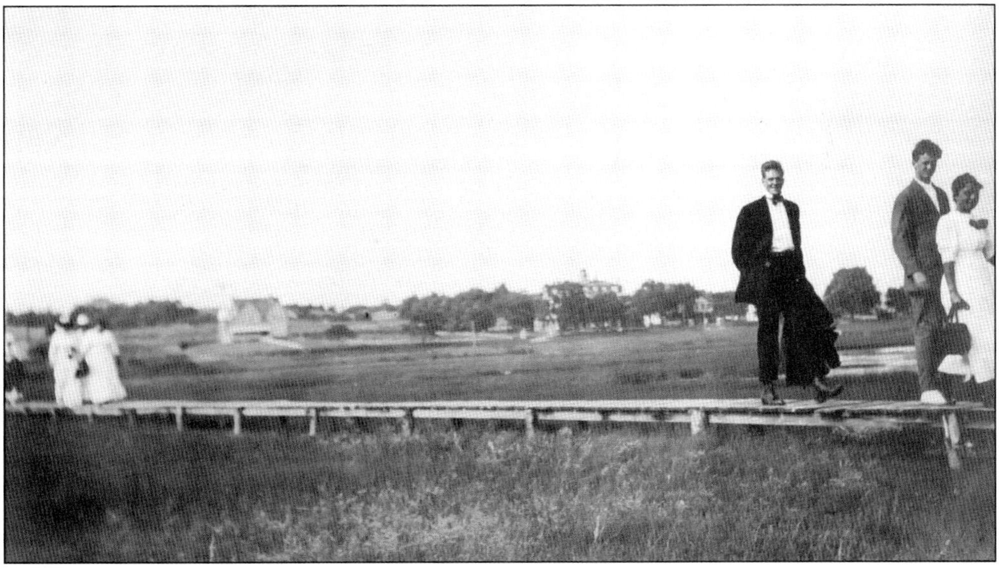

VISITORS FROM MOUNT PLEASANT HOUSE CROSSING ORIENT CREEK, C. 1900. A wooden walkway extended from the Old Crab's Shack to the north of the oyster ponds to the beach on the far side. The walkway extended over the marshy grasslands bordering the ponds, and a narrow bridge spanned the water of the pond. Guests at the Mount Pleasant House often used the walkway over to small beach on the south side of the oyster ponds to relax along Peconic Bay.

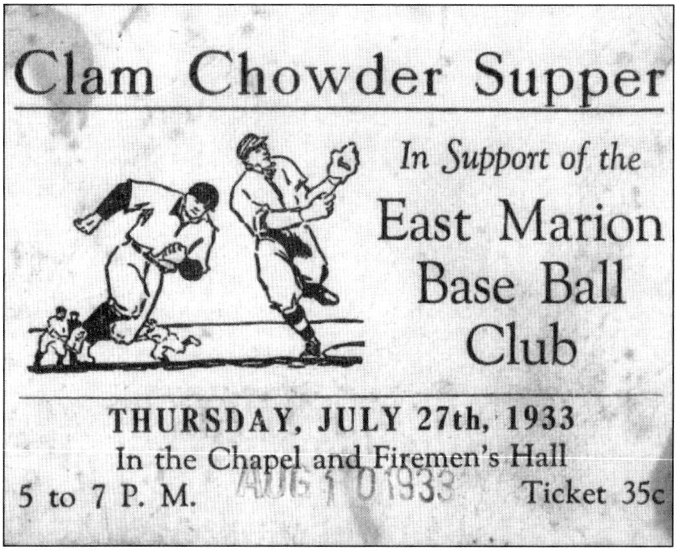

EAST MARION BASE BALL CLUB, 1933. This ticket and some scorebooks are what remain of the East Marion Base Ball Club. The club had a field south of Main Road between Bay Avenue and Old Orchard Lane. The team started in 1869 and called themselves Wenonda after a Native American character in an 1857 book by Franz Hoffman. The team eventually split into several teams, which included the East Marion Nines and the Enterprise of East Marion.

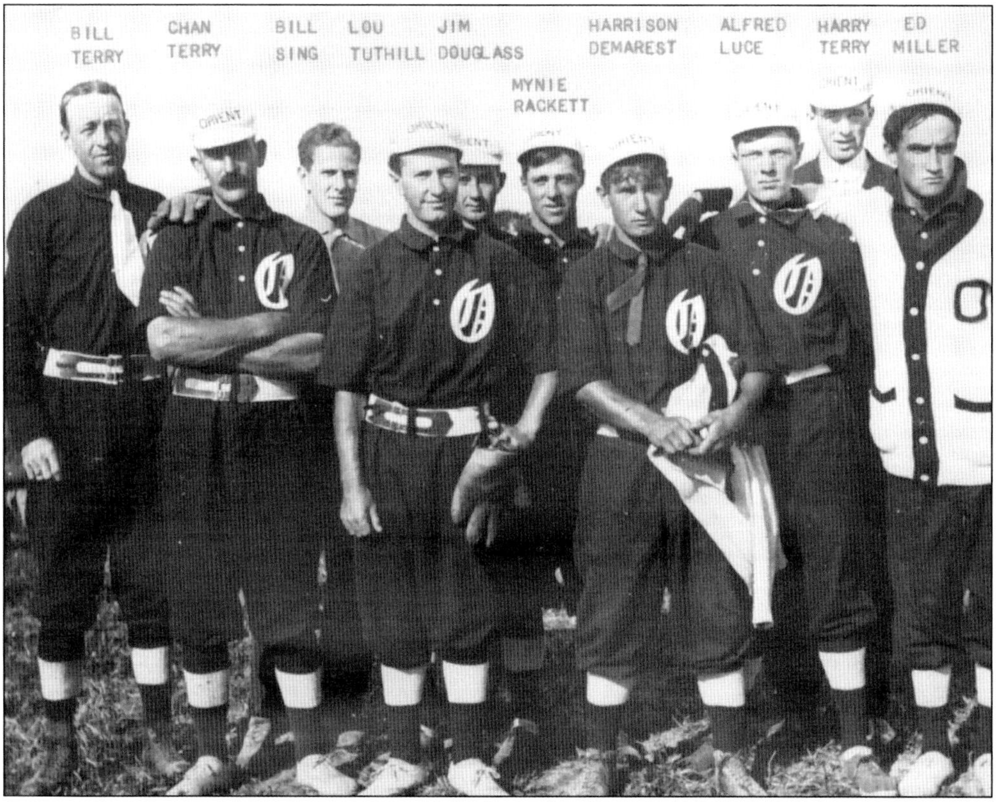

ORIENT BASE BALL CLUB, C. 1908. Orient also had a local baseball team, which played on a farm field that belonged to Bill Terry. The 1908 Orient baseball team pictured above in uniform are, from left to right, Bill Terry, Chan Terry, Bill Sing, Lou Tuthill, Jim Douglass, Mynie Rackett, Harrison Demarest, Alfred Luce, Harry Terry, and Ed Miller.

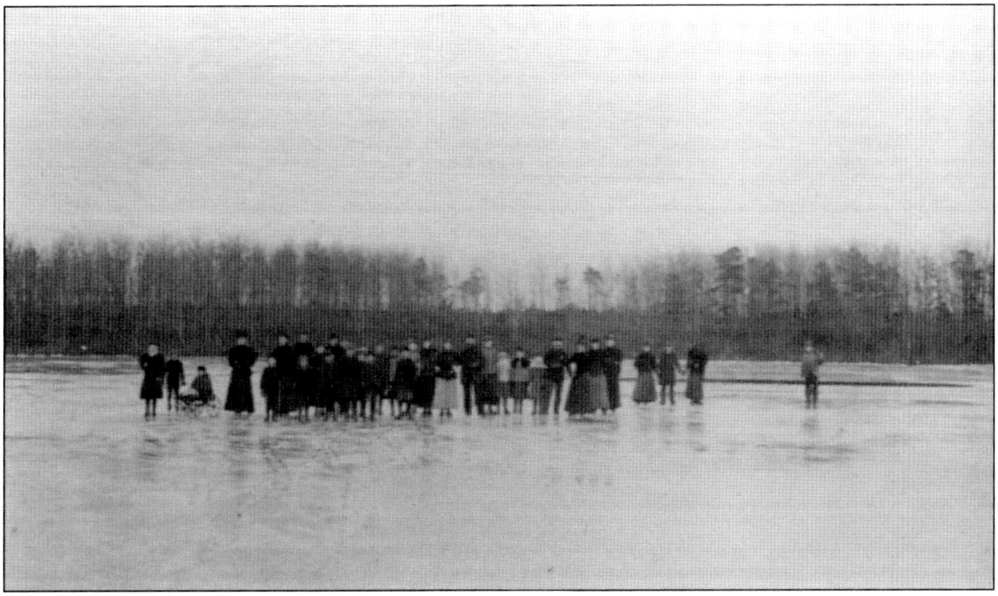

Ice Skating on Marion Lake, 1897. The winter was often a time for socializing. Whenever the smaller bodies of water froze, residents turned out to enjoy the freedom of skimming over the ice and viewing the familiar surroundings from a new perspective. On Christmas Day 1897, this photograph was taken by Rev. Loren Rowley of the ice skaters on Marion Lake.

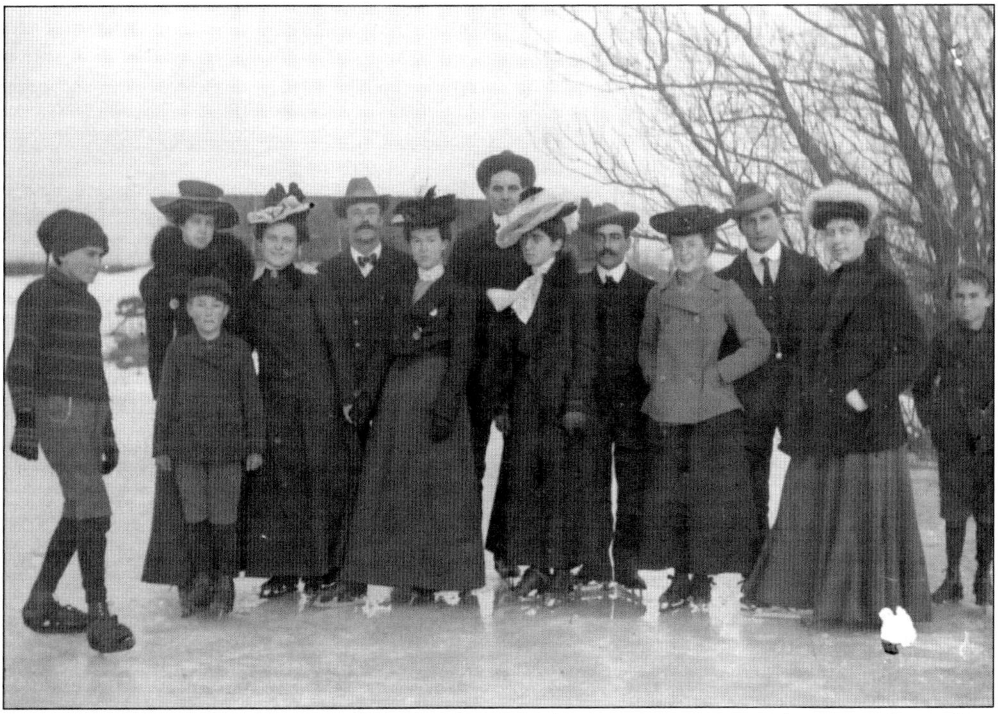

Ice Skating on Majors Pond, c. 1900. Here, ice skaters on Majors Pond pause to have their photograph taken. From left to right are Vinton Richard, Seward B. King, Nan Latham, Jess Vail, Eldridge P. Latham, Carrie W. Latham, Florence Douglass, Fred Terry, Samuel Vail, Lillian Vail, Fred Hommel, Flora Wilcox, and Milton Miller.

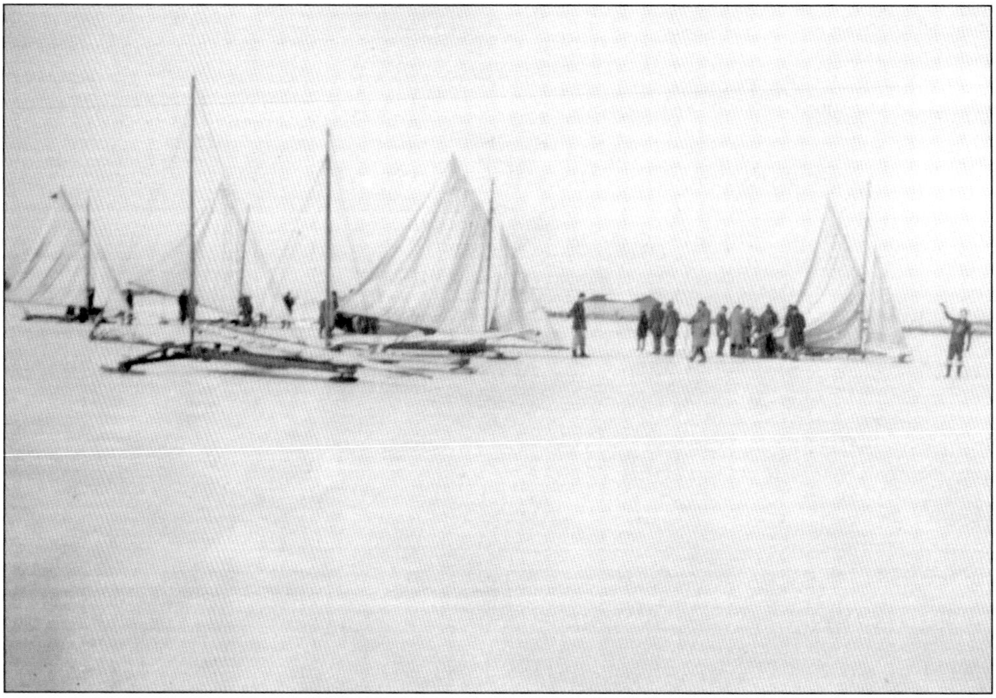

Iceboating in Orient, 1934. Whenever the weather gets cold enough to freeze the small bays, the iceboats, or scooters as they are sometimes called, are taken out of storage and brought down to the water. Here, iceboats are gathered for an exciting sail across Hallocks Bay. Iceboats have been clocked moving as fast as 55 miles per hour.

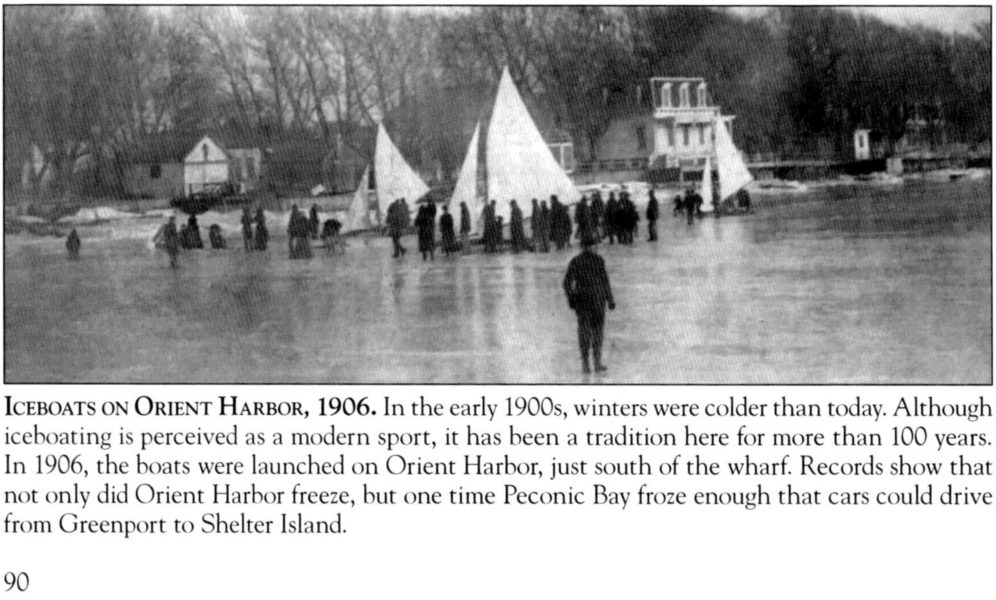

Iceboats on Orient Harbor, 1906. In the early 1900s, winters were colder than today. Although iceboating is perceived as a modern sport, it has been a tradition here for more than 100 years. In 1906, the boats were launched on Orient Harbor, just south of the wharf. Records show that not only did Orient Harbor freeze, but one time Peconic Bay froze enough that cars could drive from Greenport to Shelter Island.

Orient Wharf in the Snow, c. 1960. Before 1800, there were few roads on Long Island, so transportation by water was a necessity. The Orient Wharf was built in 1740 by Richard Shaw, who soon abandoned the structure. In 1828, Caleb Dyer rebuilt and expanded the dock, and it was incorporated in 1837 as the Oyster Ponds Wharf Company. Within 10 years, the dock was again falling apart. In 1848, a group of residents bought the wharf and rebuilt it with rock.

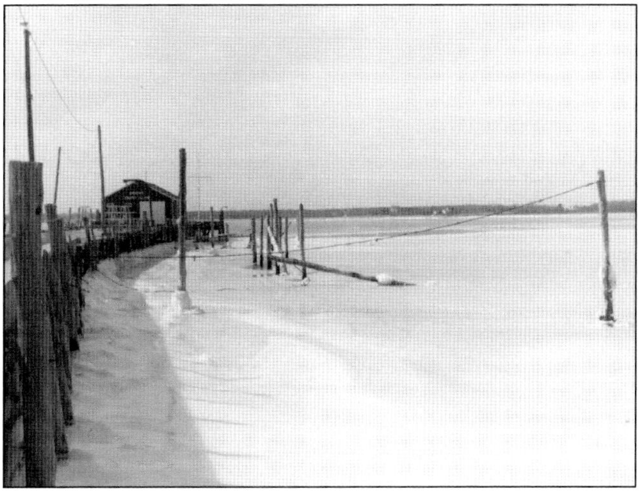

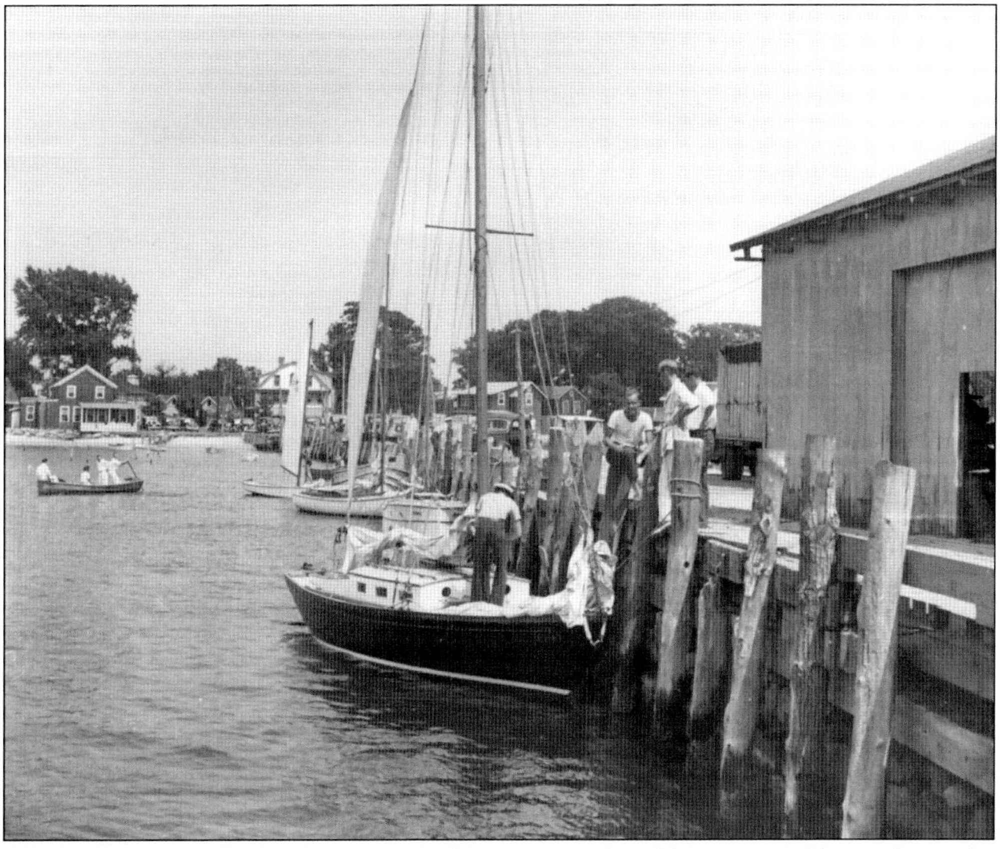

Orient Yacht Club, c. 1940. In 1933, the Orient Yacht Club was started by residents who wanted to race their boats. By 1940, the club was formalized and incorporated. It was not until 1994, when the Wharf Company sold the wharf to the yacht club, that the club finally found a permanent home. Here, Nelson Chapman prepares his sailboat for a day. Howard Sharman is sitting with crossed legs on the piling.

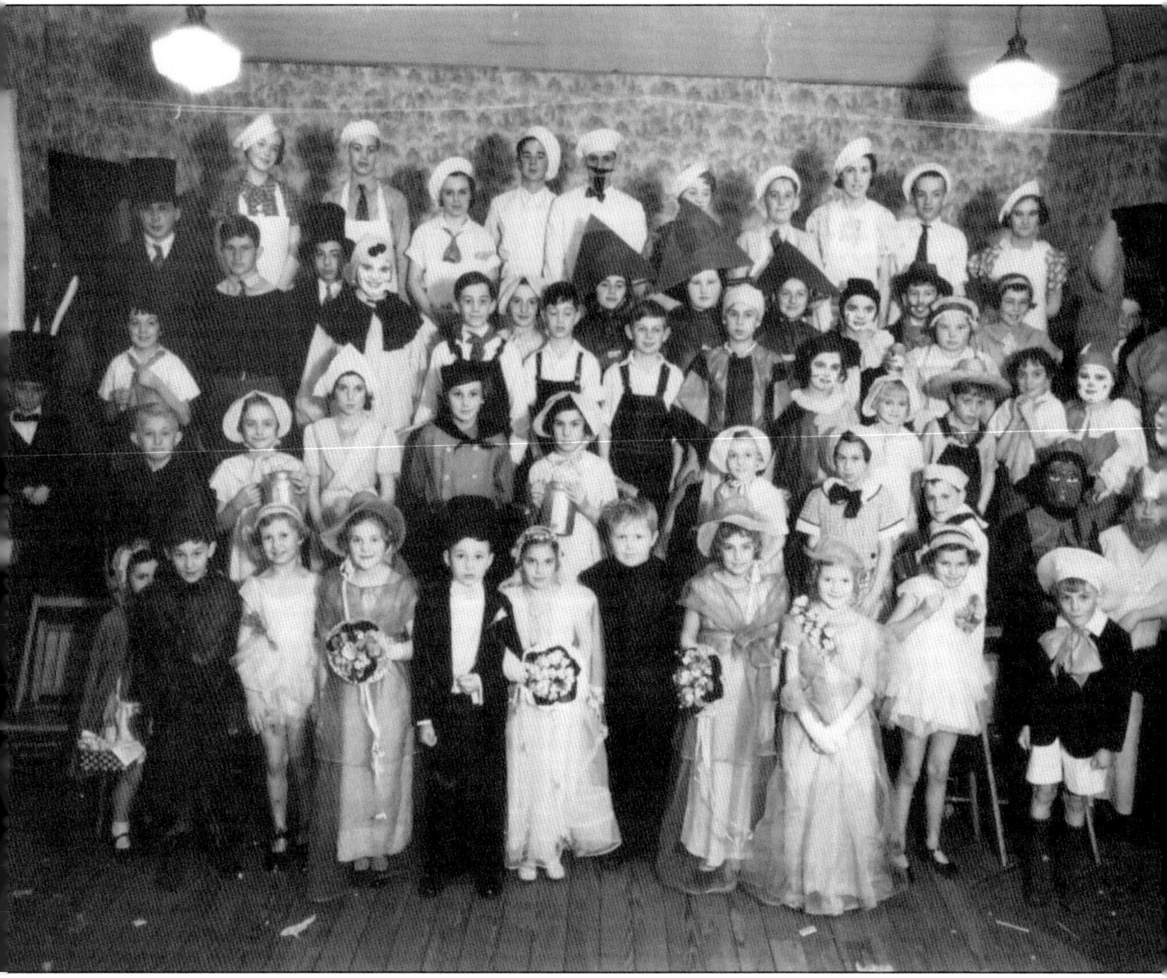

Children of East Marion, 1935. Rural communities were always looking for something to do in the days before the invention of television. In February 1935, all of the children of East Marion were gathered together by the East Marion Craft Club to put on a play. The production was called either the *Wedding of the Painted Doll* or *Dolly of the Follies*. Pictured are, from left to right, (first row) Marjorie Traffica, George Arnold, Janis Brown, Janet Gagen, Gordon Rackett, Ann Vail, Ronald Edeen, Shirley Traffica, Irene Beck, Betsey Brown, and Donald Terry; (second row) Dan Dzenkowski, Alice Denkowski, Lillian Brown, Sarah Brown, Catharine Arnold, Viola Skidmore, Virginia Rackett, Sam Skidmore, Jimmy Rogers, and Jennie Boken; (third row) Ken Ketcham, Betty Ketcham, Jean Ellen Dzenkowki, Bud Ketcham, and Muriel Ketcham; (fourth row) Madeline Gagen, Douglas Rogers, Bob Ketcham, Stanley Rutkoski, Robert Arnold, Helen Brown, Betty Bryant, and Hope Vail Jetter; (fifth row) Peter Dykowitz, Lawrence Tuthill, Albert Abersmith, Jean Ellen Brown, Helen Arnold, Hattie Rogers, Marcella Dzenkowski, Catharine Getches, Stanley Dykowitz, Barbara Ketcham, and Jackie Bryant; (sixth row) Marie Beck, Milton Rogers, Dotey Leicht, Donald Jetter, John Arnold, Gertrude Shaffer, Russell Terry, Mardie Brown, Jimmie Getches, and Ida Arnold.

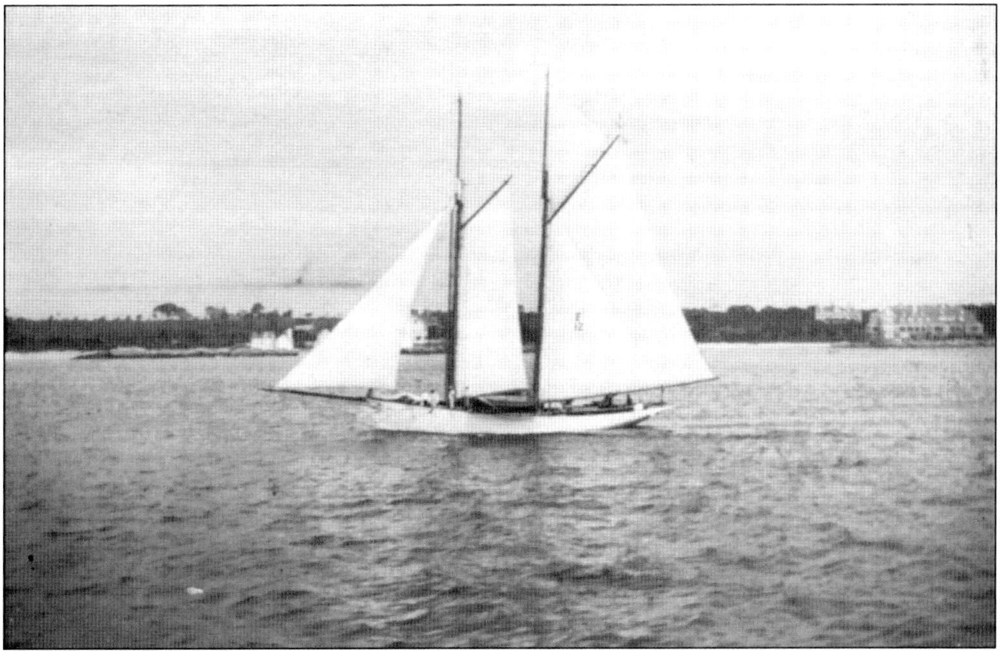

EAST MARION SHORELINE, C. 1930. An anonymous sailboat cruises past the East Marion shoreline. Boating was and is immensely popular, and many clubs sponsored sailing races to and around the east end of Long Island. Visitors to the area also frequently chartered rides on local sailboats to tour the small islands surrounding the North Fork, such as Gardiner's Island and Plum Island.

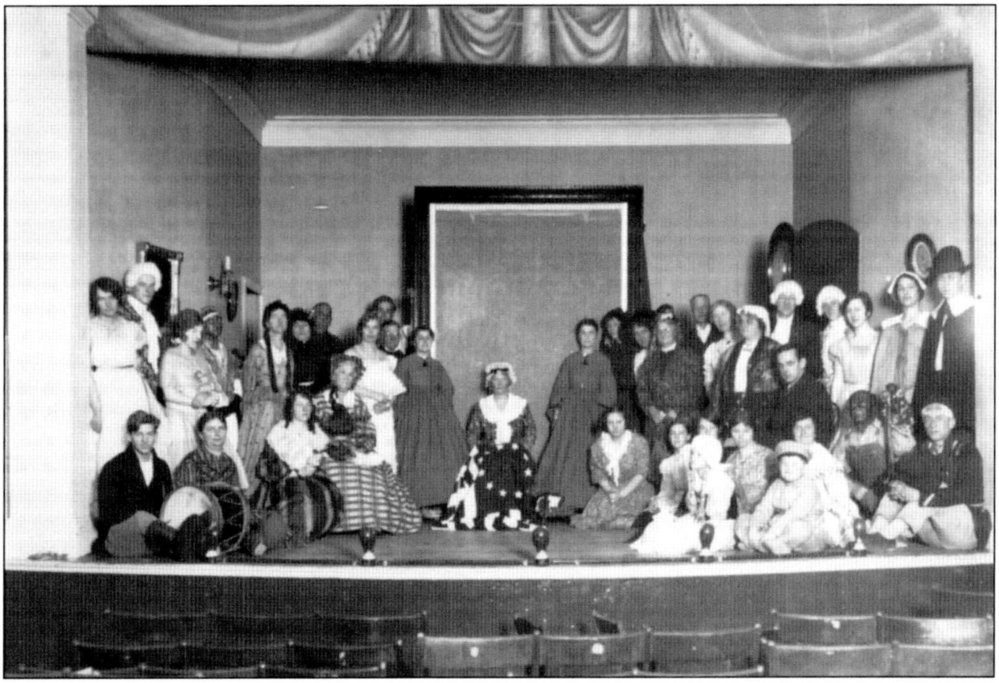

DAUGHTERS OF THE AMERICAN REVOLUTION, 1929. On March 12, 1929, the DAR put on a historical drama in Poquatuck Hall. The production spanned the history of the New World from the Pilgrims to the Civil War.

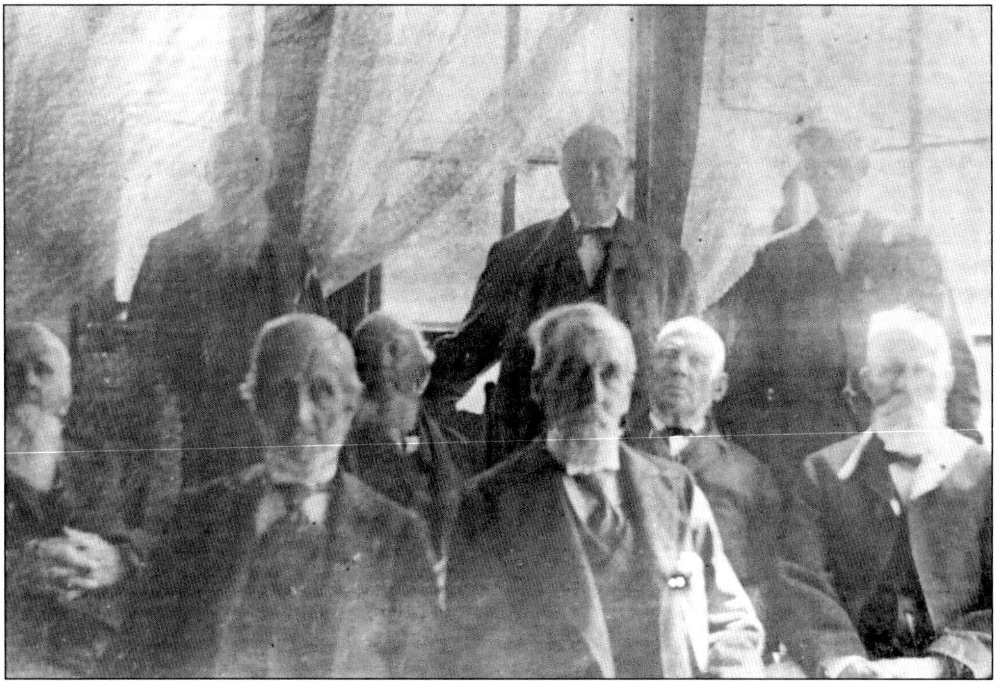

OLD CAPTAINS CLUB, 1898. Once a year, retired captains of oceangoing vessels of Orient met as the Old Captains Club. Pictured are, from left to right, (first row) Capt. Marcus Brown (age 81) and Capt. Henry Rackett (age 82); (second row) Capt. David Edwards (age 80), Capt. Thomas Poole (age 90), Capt. Lester Terry (age 83), and Capt. George K. Rackett (age 81); (third row) Capt. William Corwin (age 79), Capt. William Terry (age 80), and James Henry Young, host.

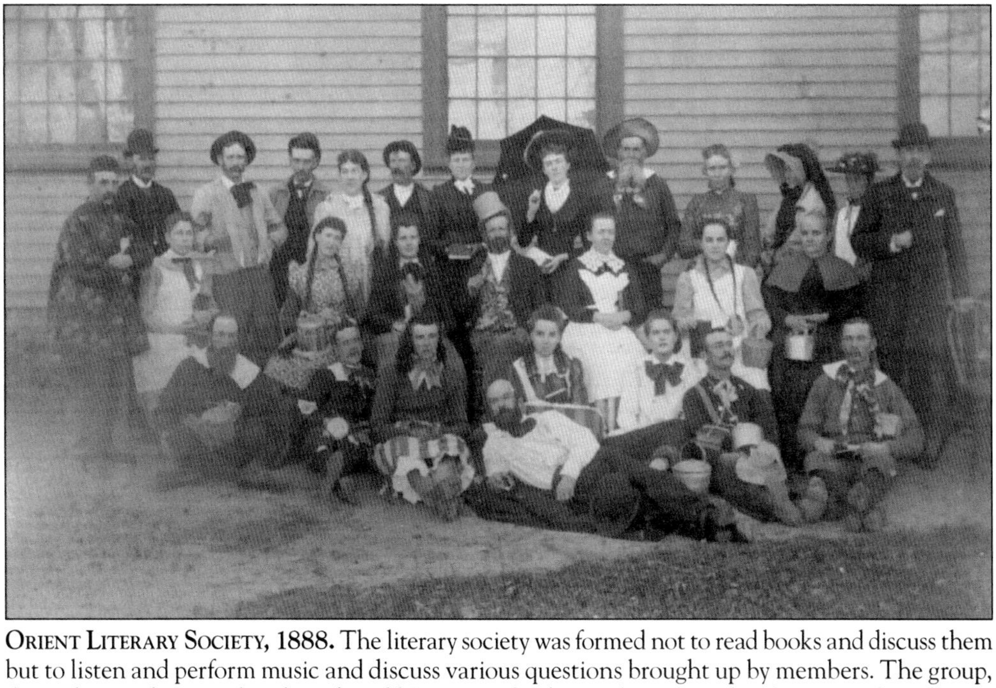

ORIENT LITERARY SOCIETY, 1888. The literary society was formed not to read books and discuss them but to listen and perform music and discuss various questions brought up by members. The group, dressed to perform in the play *The Old District School*, posed on the side of Poquatuck Hall.

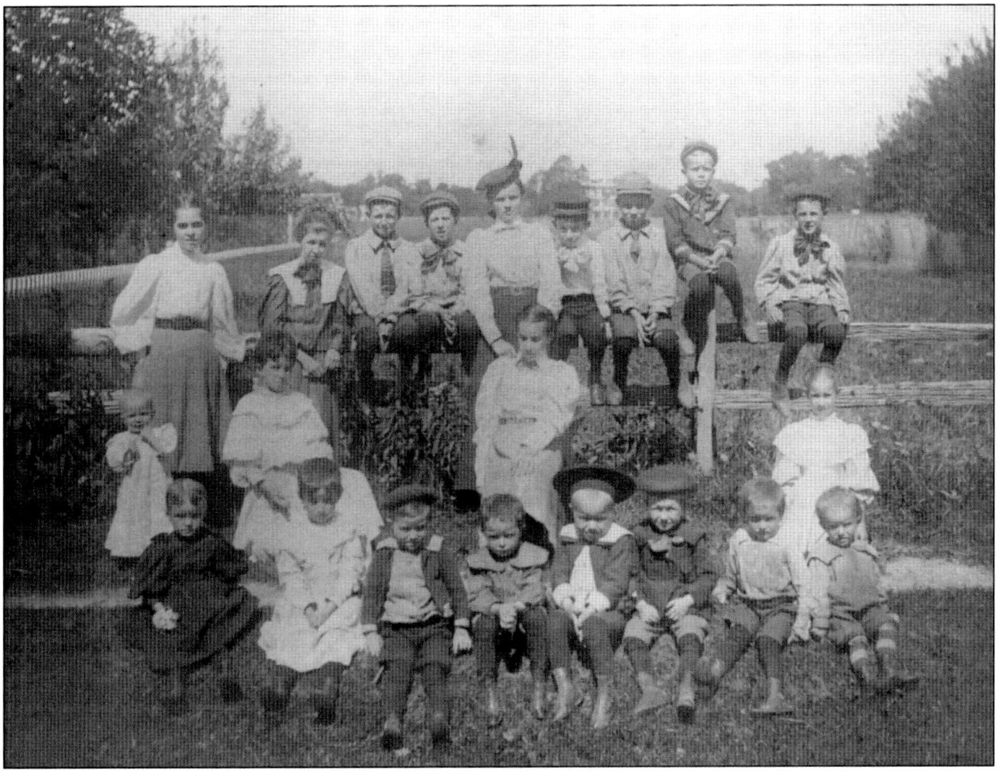

The State Street Gang, c. 1896. One of State Street's (now Skippers Lane) nicknames was "Kid's Alley" because of the large number of children who lived along the street. Pictured here are, from left to right, (first row) Ruth Conklin, Abbie Tuthill, Walter Rackett, Edgar Tuthill, Alfred Luce, Chatfield Tuthill, Lewis Tuthill, and unidentified; (second row) Cora Tuthill, Marion Tuthill, Bertie Beebe, and Leah Luce; (third row) Eva Rackett, Nancy Latham, Ralph Latham, Myron Rackett, Edith Conklin, Ross Kenyon, Bert Luce, Harry Conklin, and George Latham.

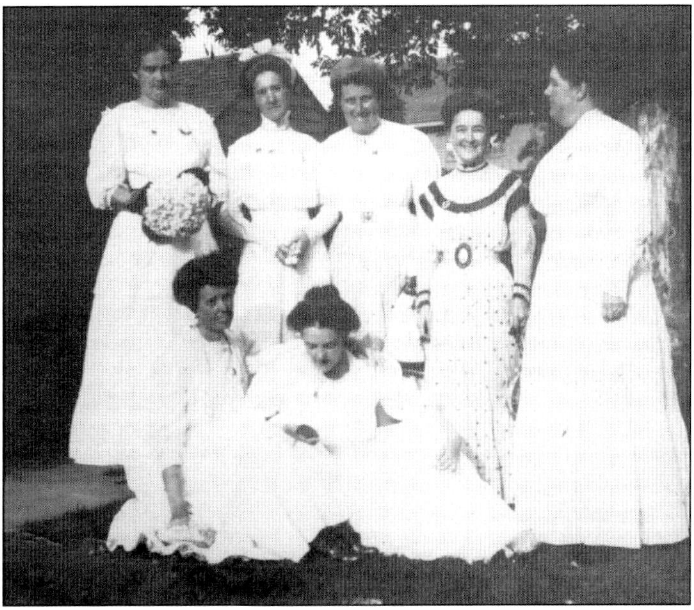

Busy Bees, 1909. The Busy Bees was one of the many clubs of Orient. Members are, from left to right (first row) Leila Young and Mabel Young; (second row) Stella Young, Mary Young, Sadie Stephenson, Florence Rush, and Josie Heath.

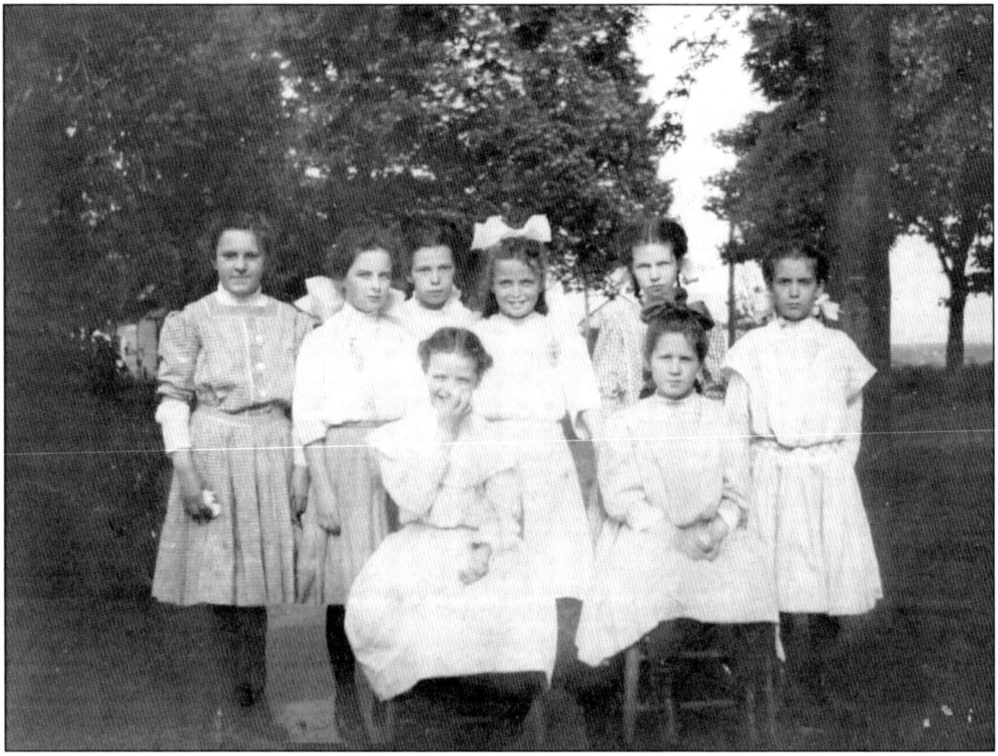

Busy Bees Junior, 1910. The adult Busy Bees also formed a similar club for the younger members of Orient. Pictured in the image are May Tuthill (first row, seated right), Leila Tuthill (second row, far left), and Hilda Rackett Wilcox (second row, second frome left).

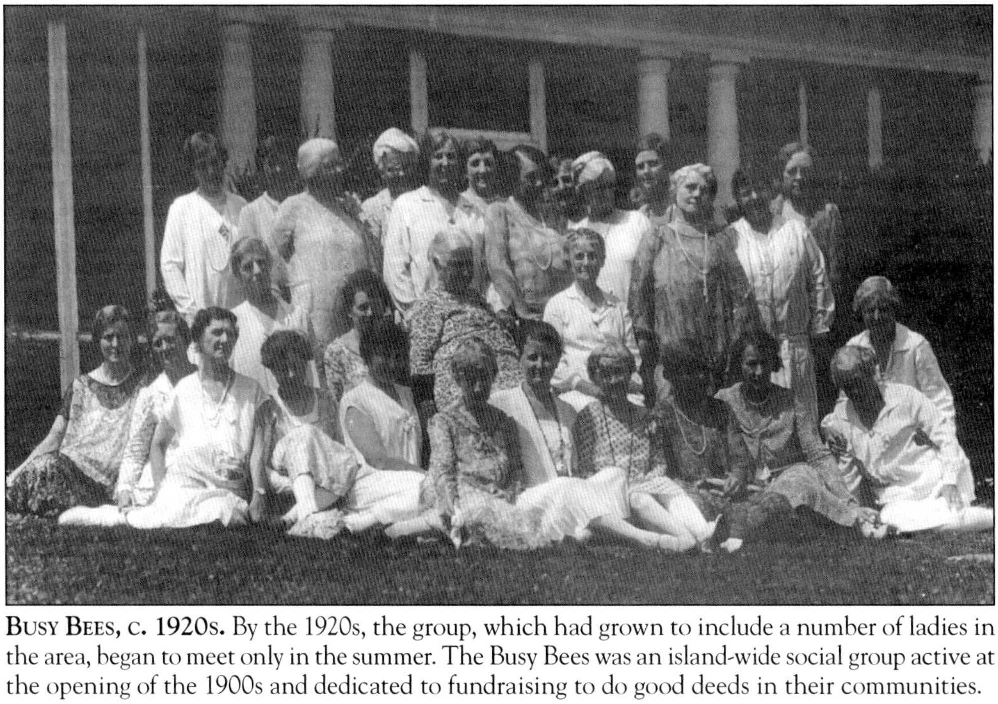

Busy Bees, c. 1920s. By the 1920s, the group, which had grown to include a number of ladies in the area, began to meet only in the summer. The Busy Bees was an island-wide social group active at the opening of the 1900s and dedicated to fundraising to do good deeds in their communities.

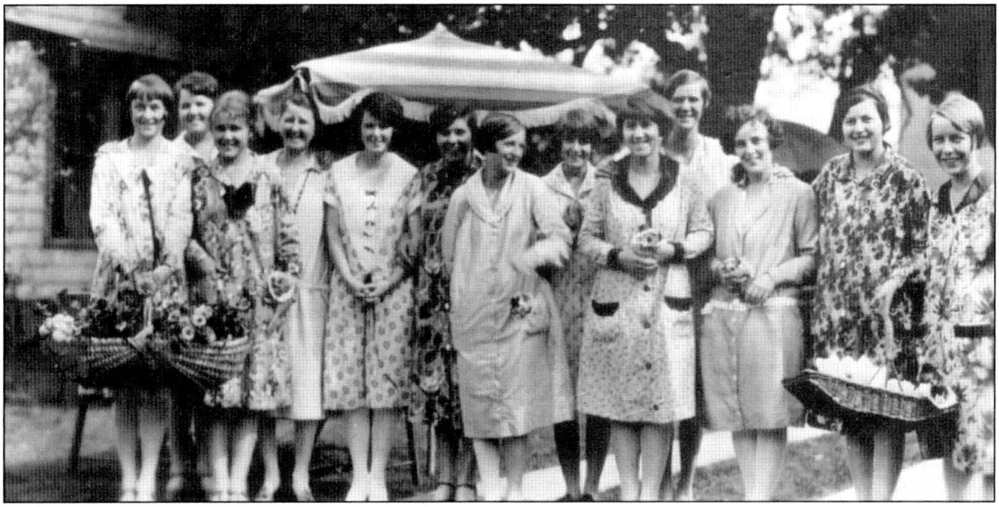

Picksies, c. 1929. The Picksies was an Orient group for older teenage girls, organized by Isabelle Knobloch around 1928. Pictured are, from left to right, Martha Terry, Florence Adams Berry, Mary Anna Vail, Isabelle Knobloch, Lillian Vail Hallock, Mae Ryder Conklin, Cathryn Young Gaul, Blanche Latham Clingen, Elizabeth Beebe Vail, Sarah Adams Wiggs, Ruth Vail Luce, Cele Hester, and Helen McClymont Robertson.

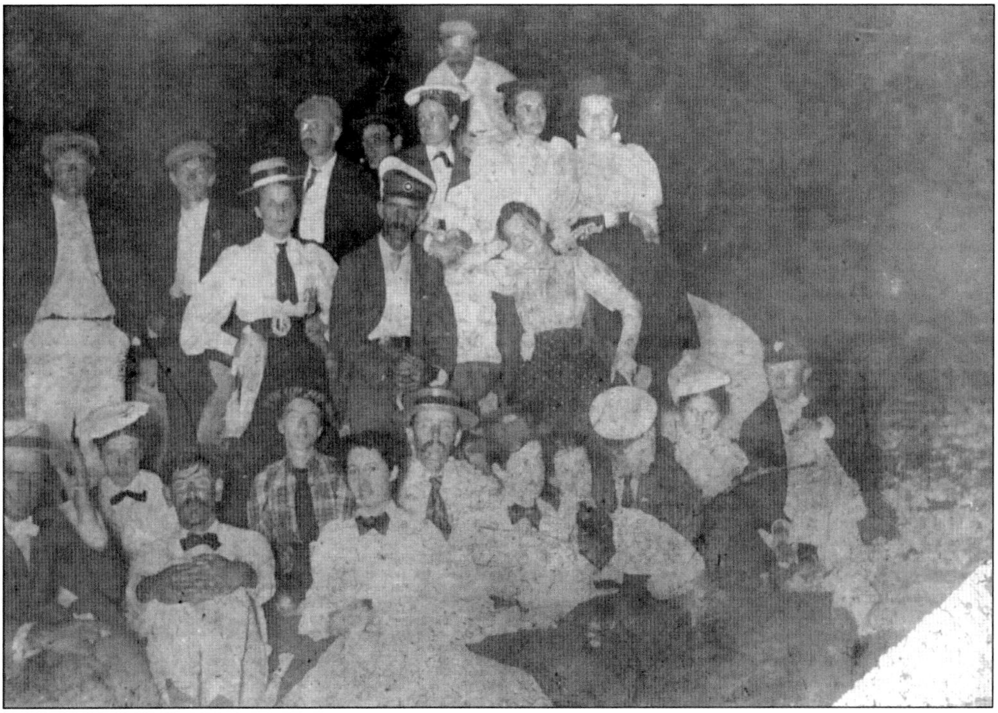

Grasshoppers, c. 1900. This photograph of the Grasshoppers was taken during a nighttime beach picnic, with only a flashlight for light. People in the club included Harry Raynor, Grace Stephenson, Mabel Young, Florence Bush, William Westerfield, Jason Westerfield, Ed Franklin, Stuart Young, Lulu Potter, Edward Edwards, Gus Edwards, Alfred Merritt, Minnie Andrews, Mary Young, Louis Young, Sadie Stephenson, Edna Potter, Frank Stephenson, Hiram Franklyn, Gertie Heath, May Heath, ad Leila Young.

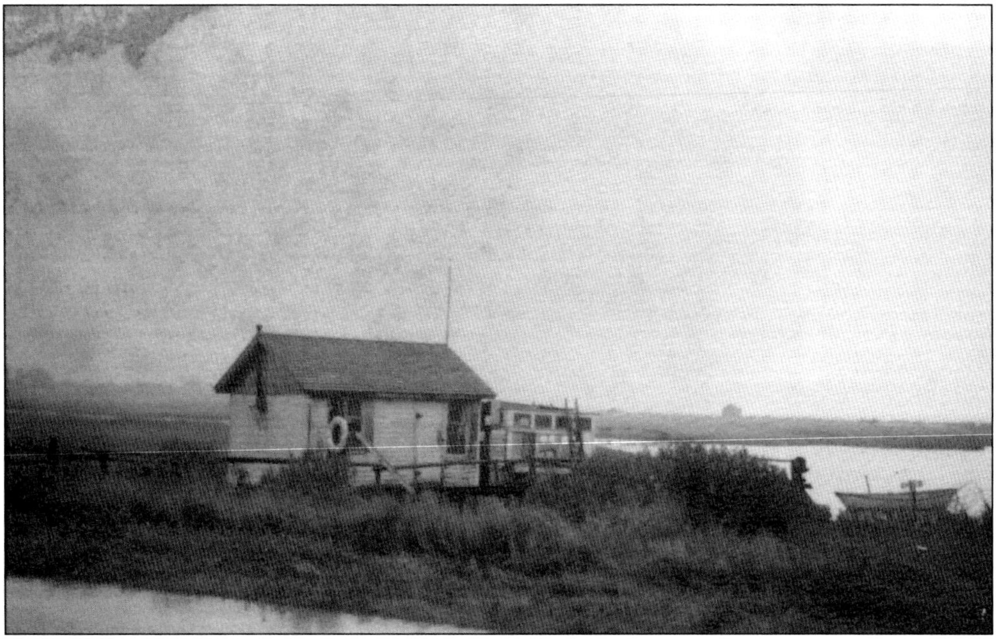

OLD CRAB'S SHACK, C. 1935. One of the most recognizable landmarks in Orient is the small shack on the east side of the causeway. Known as the Old Crab's Shack, the structure was the former laundry building from the Mount Pleasant House and was turned into a clubhouse for the men-only club the Old Crabs. An informal club, members met to relax, converse, and share a drink away from the hustle and bustle of home.

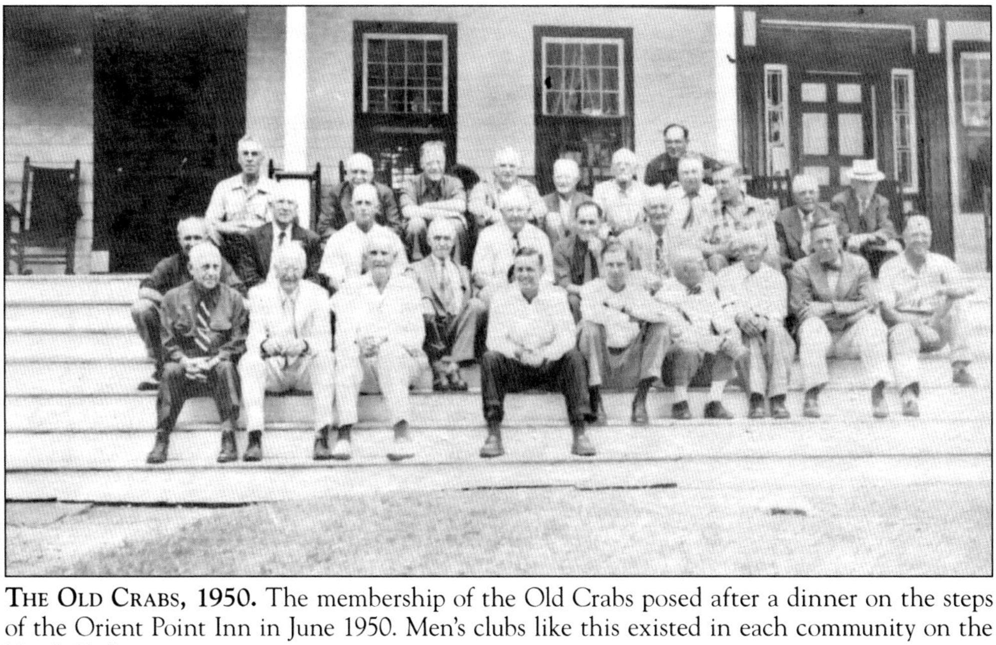

THE OLD CRABS, 1950. The membership of the Old Crabs posed after a dinner on the steps of the Orient Point Inn in June 1950. Men's clubs like this existed in each community on the North Fork.

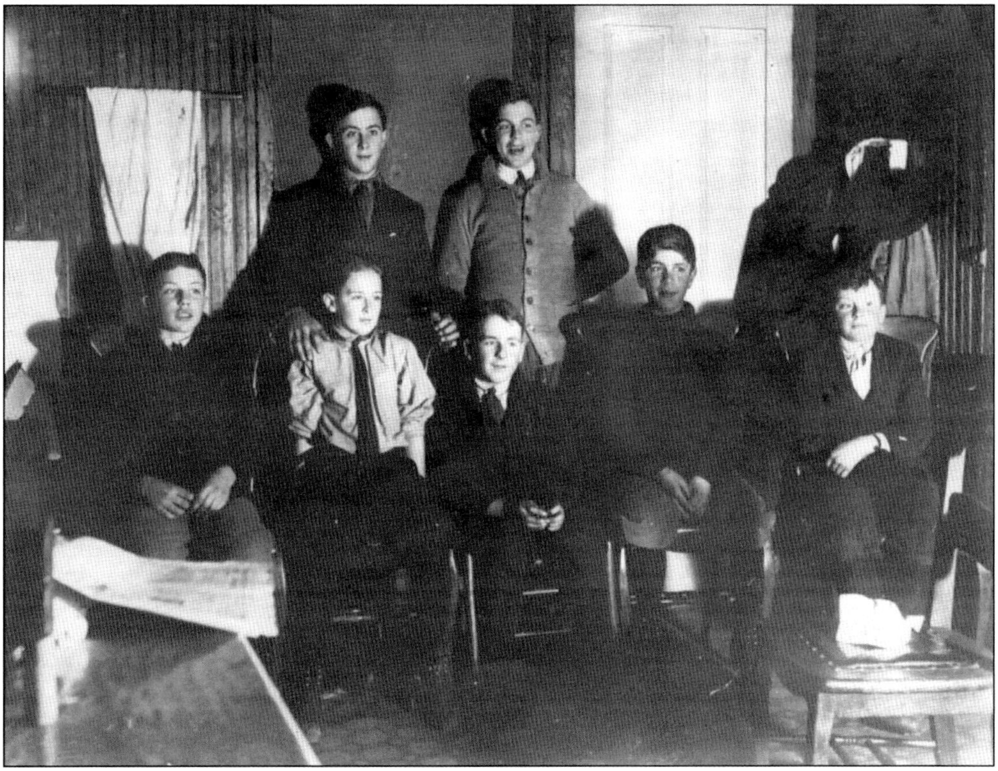

ORIENT BOY SCOUT PACK NO. 306, 1914. The pack gathers in Joseph Potter's kitchen for their meeting; the Orient Boy Scouts were organized the year before, in 1913. Pictured here are, from left to right, (first row) Archer Karcher, Lawrence Potter, Leonard Vail, Gerald Latham, and Kenneth Tabor; (second row) Donald Rackett and Donald Vail. Their Scoutmasters were Frank Douglass and L. Vinton Richard.

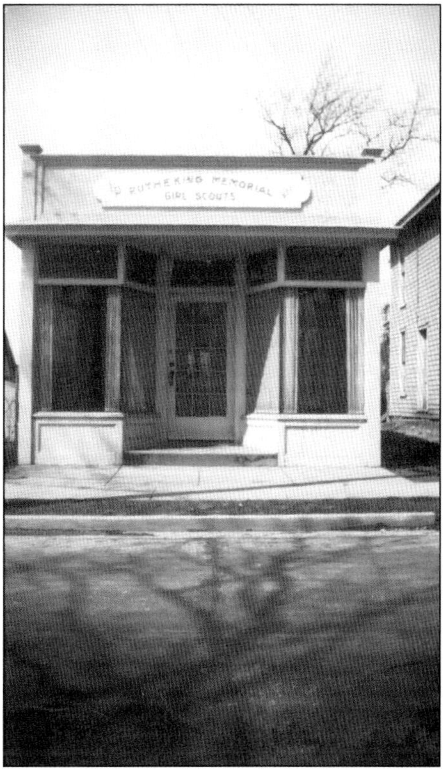

RUTH KING MEMORIAL GIRL SCOUT HALL, 1931. In 1928, this building, formerly the Orient A&P, was given to the local Girl Scouts in memory of Ruth King. The Ruth King Memorial Association was established to promote the local Girl Scout movement. The building was a meeting place for the Poquatuck troop of Girl Scouts, separate from the Girl Scouts of America. The association was dissolved in 1983 and taken over by the Orient Community Activities.

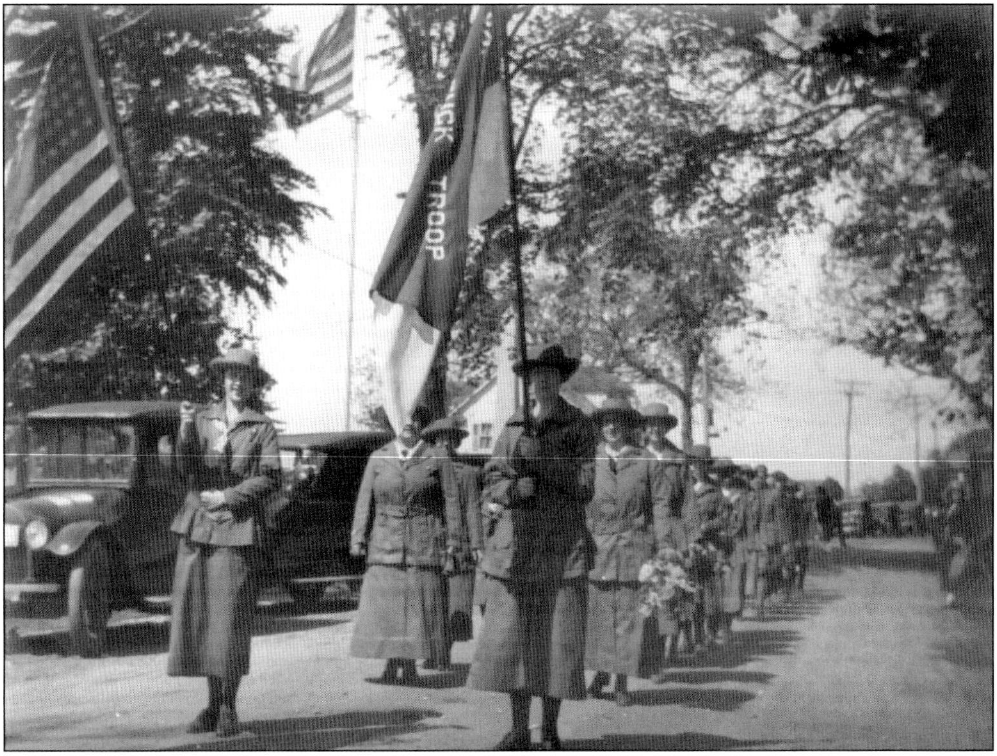

GIRL SCOUTS ON PARADE DURING A DECORATION DAY CELEBRATION, C. 1900. Pictured here in formation from left to right are (first row) Edna Mae Tabor Beebe and Grace Tuthill; (second row) Gladys Frank and Jessie Terry; (third row) Evelyn Terry Kluge. The remaining marchers in the parade moving down Village Lane are unidentified.

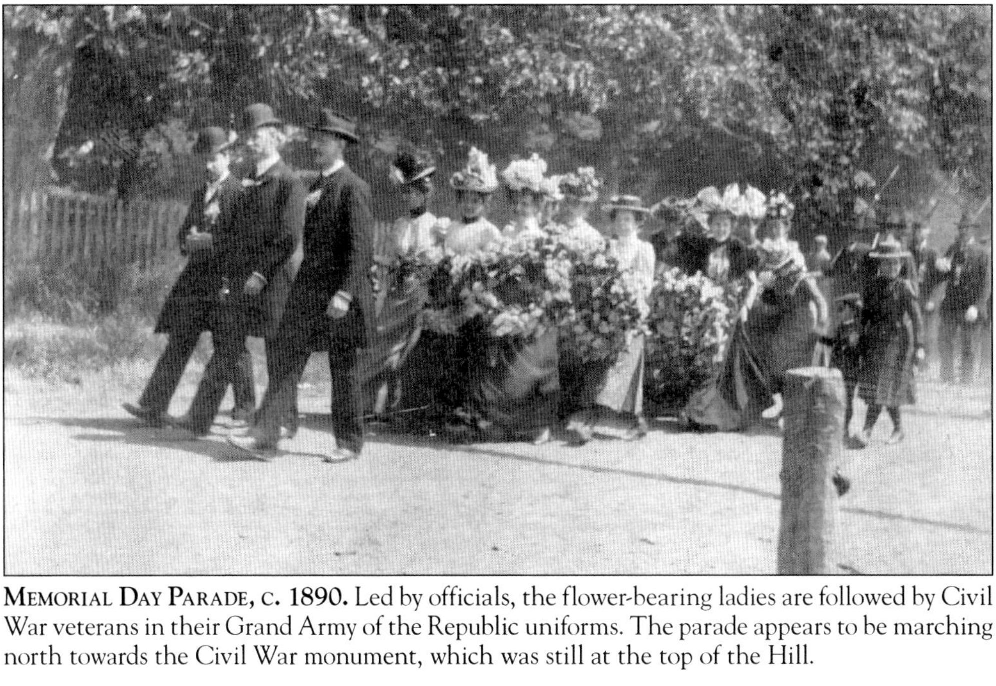

MEMORIAL DAY PARADE, C. 1890. Led by officials, the flower-bearing ladies are followed by Civil War veterans in their Grand Army of the Republic uniforms. The parade appears to be marching north towards the Civil War monument, which was still at the top of the Hill.

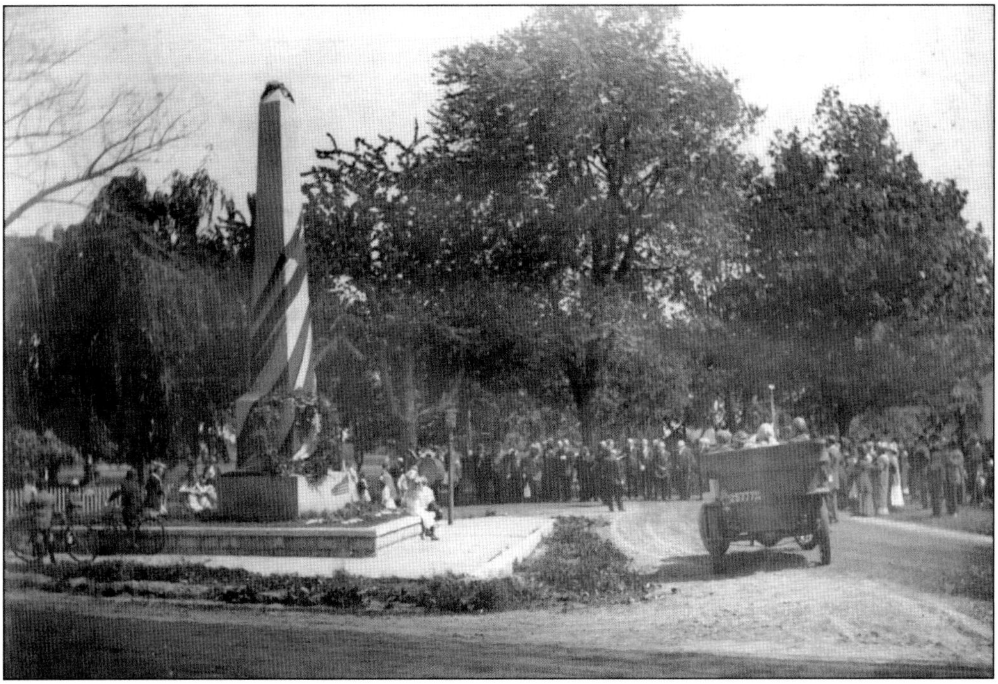

Honoring the Civil War Soldiers, 1913. May 30 was Decoration Day, and the beautifully decorated Civil War obelisk is situated at its new home at the top of Village Lane. Youngsters, the Orient Band, and the now much older Civil War veterans pay their respects to their deceased comrades in arms while parade watchers mill about the lawn and the side of the road.

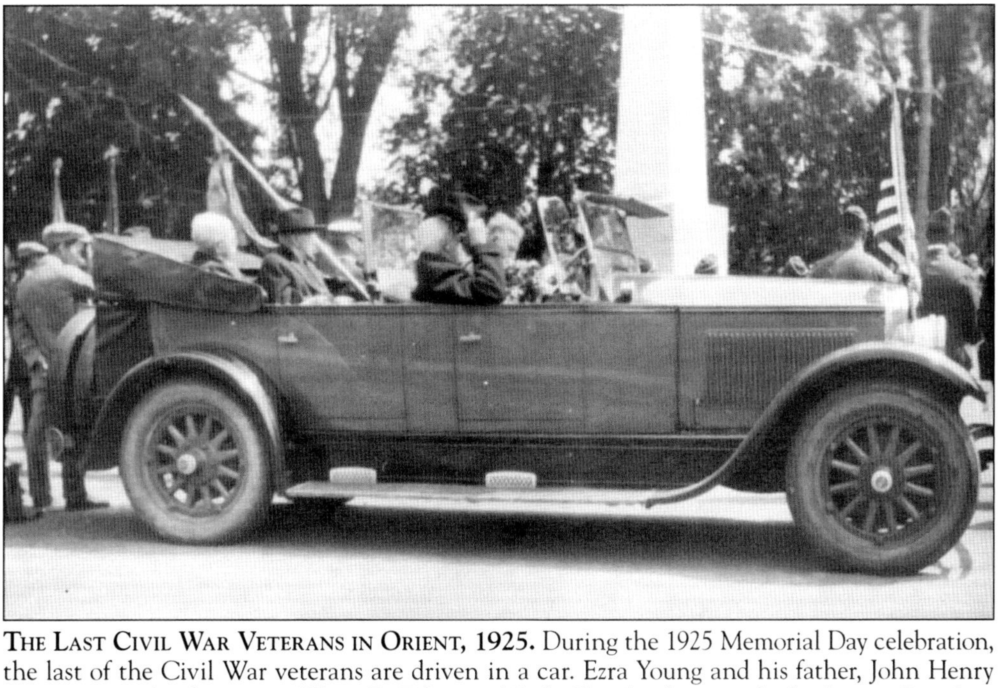

The Last Civil War Veterans in Orient, 1925. During the 1925 Memorial Day celebration, the last of the Civil War veterans are driven in a car. Ezra Young and his father, John Henry Young, sit in the front seat. Elbert E. Tabor and Jack Cleveland are in the back seat. Standing among the marchers are members of the Greenport American Legion.

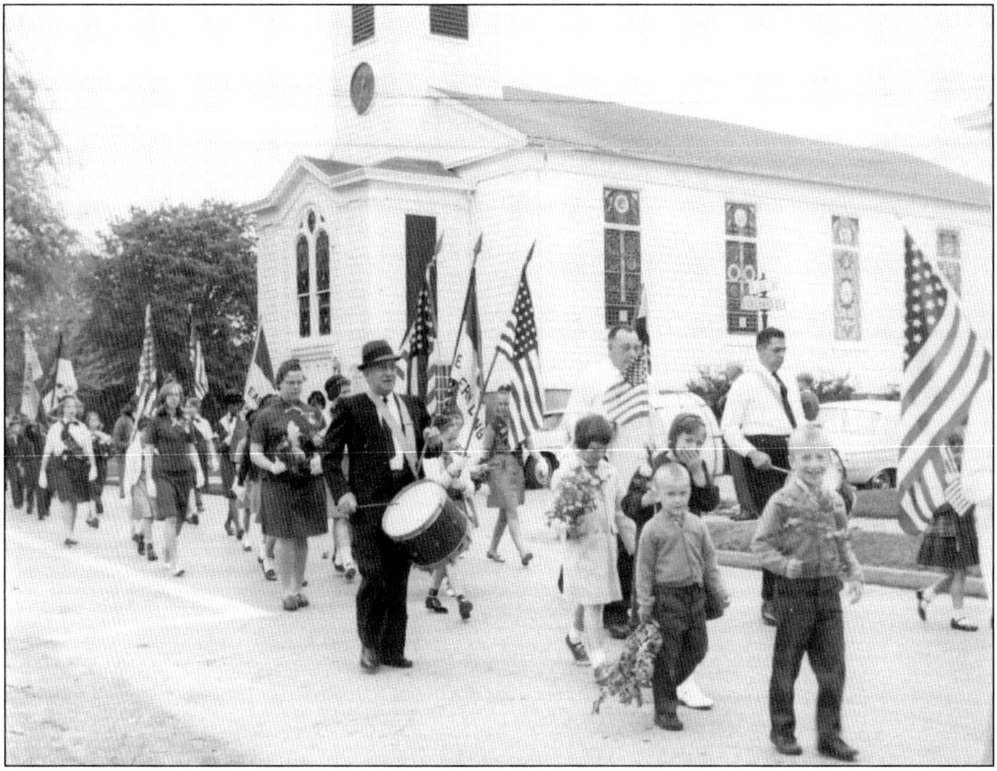

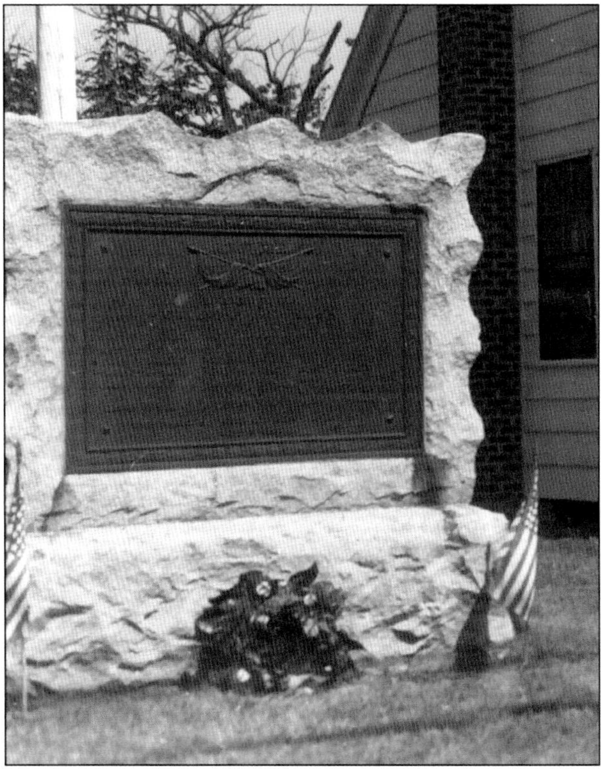

Memorial Day, 1966. The Boy Scouts and Girl Scouts march on Village Lane, past the Orient Methodist Church south towards the World War I memorial at the foot of the Orient Wharf.

East Marion World War I Soldiers' Memorial, 1949. According to the memorial, East Marion sent 15 young men into the battlefields of Europe. Only two, Stacy T. Brooks and Bryant E. Clark, did not make it back home alive. Brooks was killed on the battlefield in France, and Clark died in Dover, England, of pneumonia in 1918.

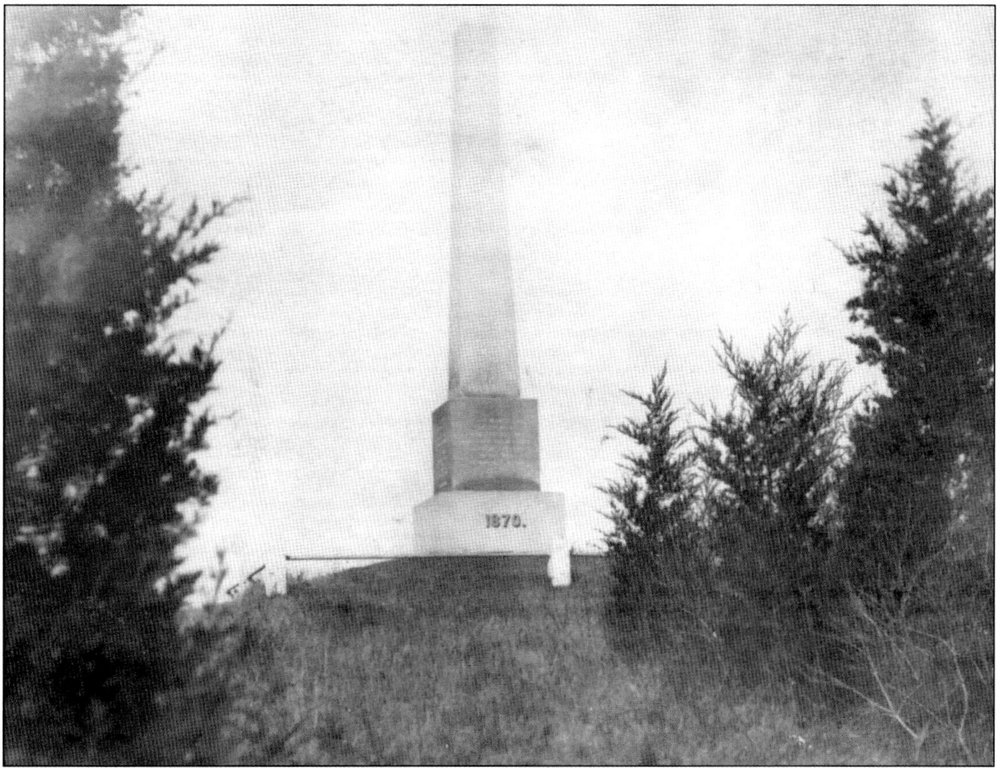

PETE'S HILL SOLDIERS' MONUMENT, 1904. In 1866, a committee from the Orient Congregational Church designed and raised the funds for a granite obelisk to honor Civil War veterans. The monument was originally situated at the crest of Pete's Hill (the Hill). The committee known as the Ladies Monumental Aide Society was ironically headed up by two men, William H. Wilcox and Marcus B. Brown.

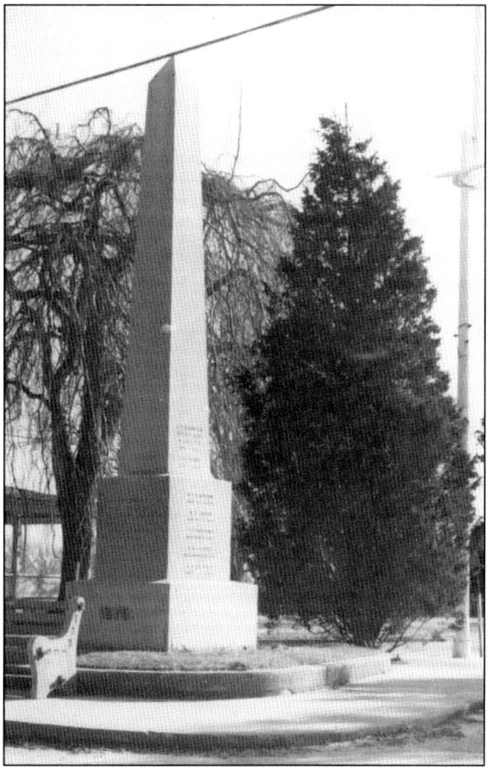

SOLDIERS' MONUMENT, c. 1940. The community soon decided that the obelisk was too far away. By 1906, the monument was slid down the hill to its current location at the top of Village Lane and Main Road. The corner of the Thomas Poole House property (also known as the Cabbage Patch House) was cut off to create the new site, and Village Lane was divided to either side of the monument.

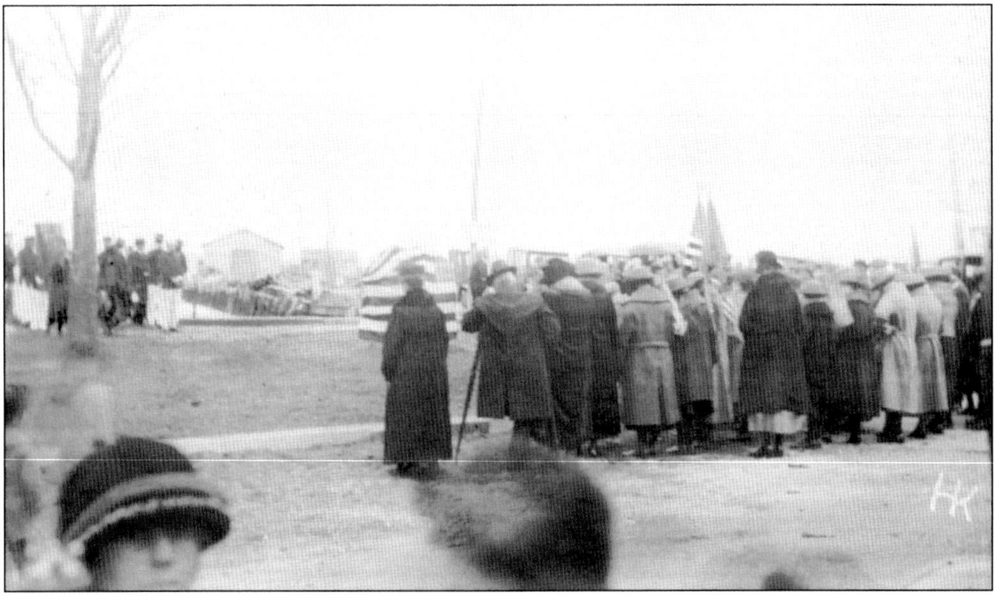

Dedication of the Orient World War I Soldiers' Memorial, c. 1920. The memorial is located on a small triangle of land on the south side at the base of the Orient Wharf. The site is the former location of Cleveland Blacksmith shop. Residents of Orient deeply felt the loss of the three young men who died during the war.

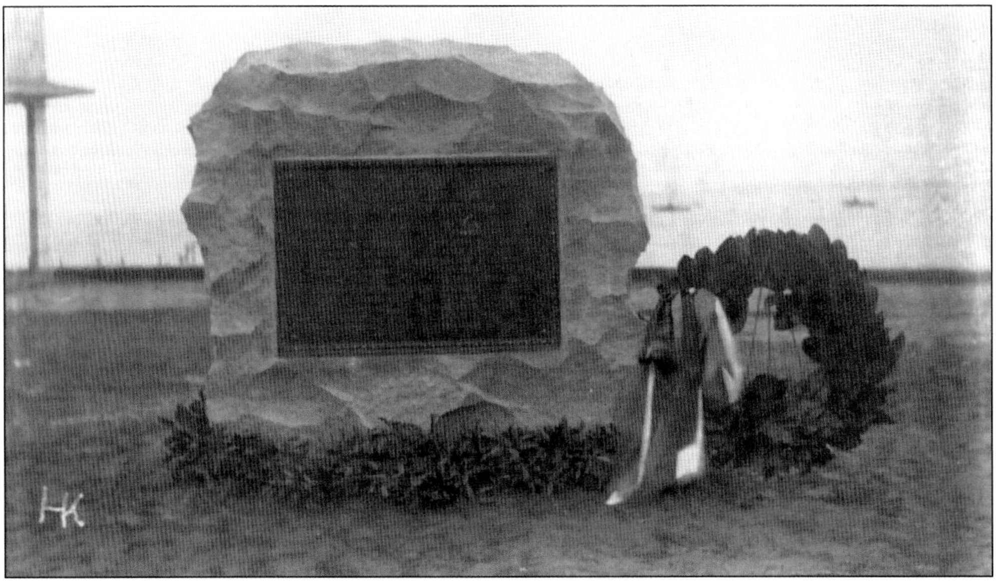

Orient World War I Soldiers' Memorial, c. 1920. In 1917, twenty-four young Orient men answered the call to go across the pond. Burton F.S. Potter, William H. Beebe Jr., and John W. Jones died in service. Potter was the first man of Southold town to die, thus giving him the honor of having the local VFW post named after him. This memorial sits at the foot of the Orient Wharf.

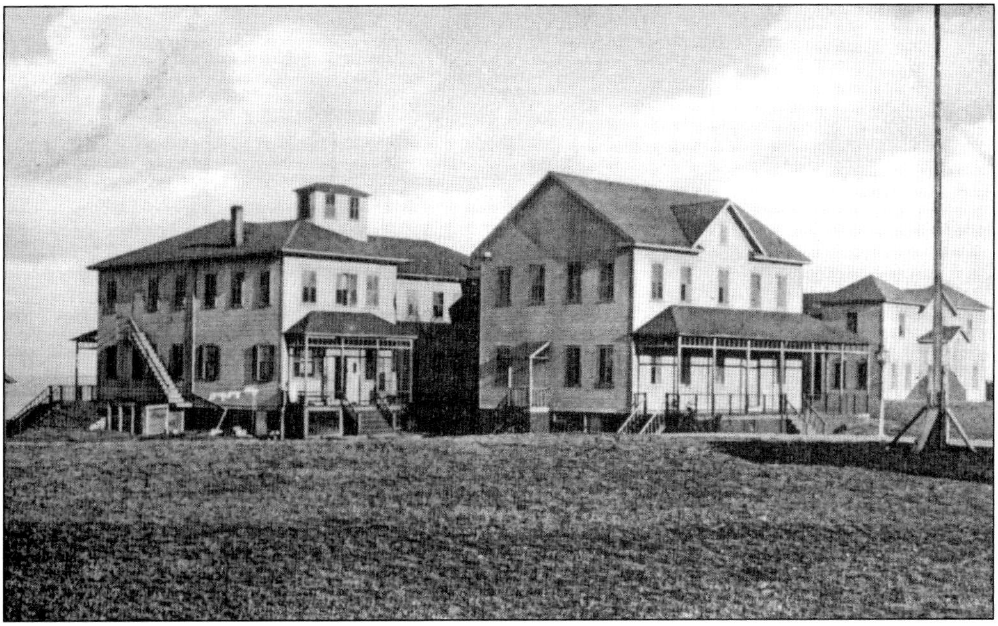

St. Thomas Summer Home in East Marion, c. 1907. In 1893, St. Thomas Episcopal Church in New York City started a neighborhood outreach program. The church created a summer camp for children living on Manhattan's east side to get out of the city for a couple of weeks each summer. Children were brought to the camp by train or ferry, then met by wagons and brought to East Marion.

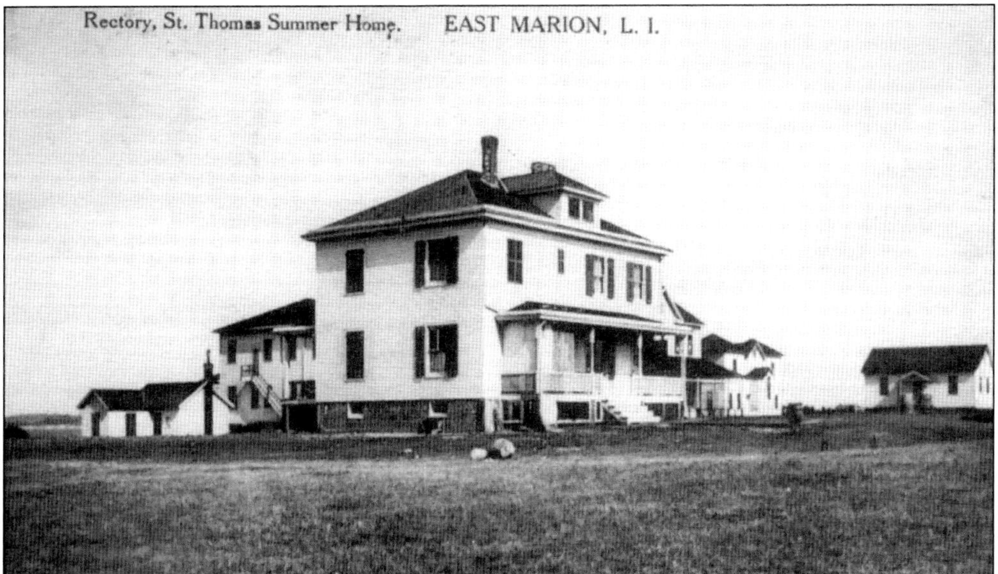

Rectory at St. Thomas, c. 1910. The camp was located on 60 acres in northern East Marion. Boys and girls attended separate sessions, and parents paid on a sliding scale based on income. Religious instruction was of course provided. By the second summer of operation, children were arriving in groups of 100 to 125 in a single session, and the camp served approximately 600 campers each summer.

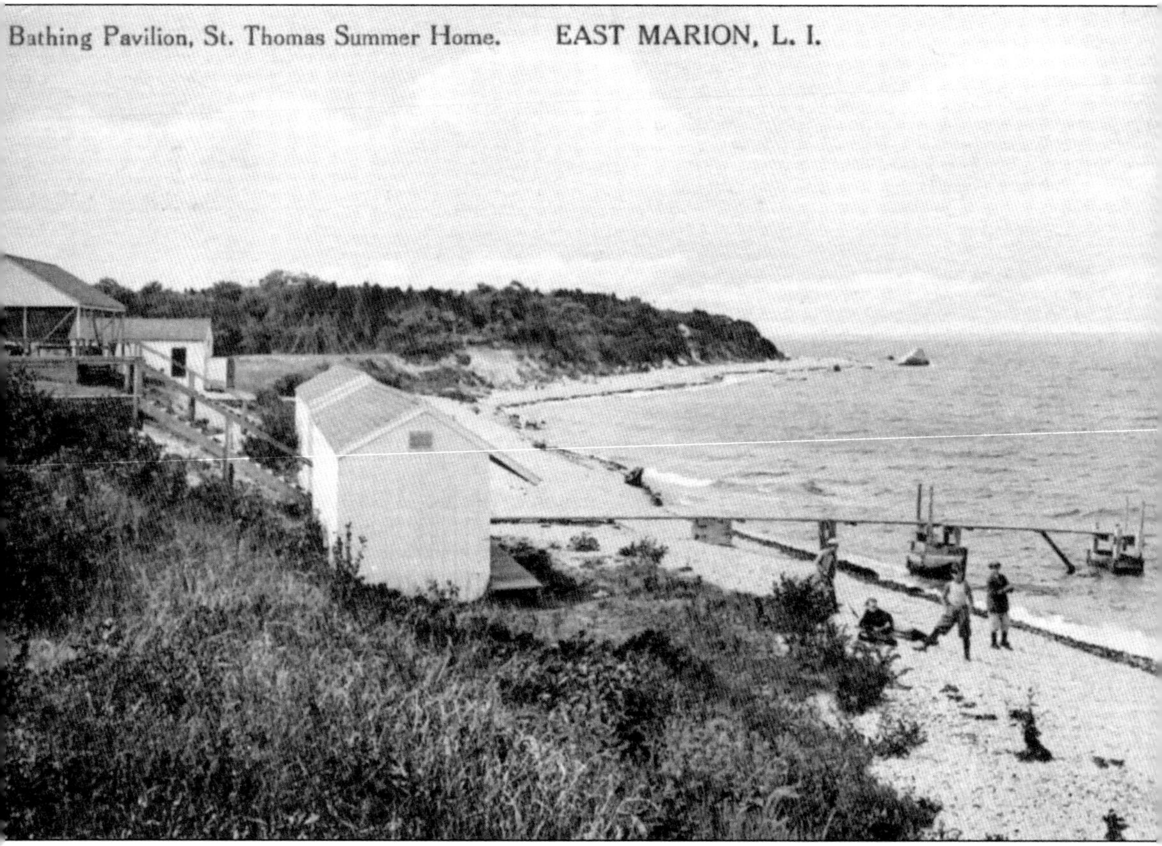

Bathing Pavilions on Long Island Sound for St. Thomas, c. 1910. The property featured 6,000 feet of shoreline along the sound, perfect for swimming. The summer camp closed in 1925, faced with expensive new state regulations. The property was sold in 1937 to George M. Tisdale of New York City for a gravel-mining operation. The large dormitory building burned down around 1939, and witnesses said the fire in the early morning lit up most of East Marion like it was daylight.

Eight

1938 Hurricane

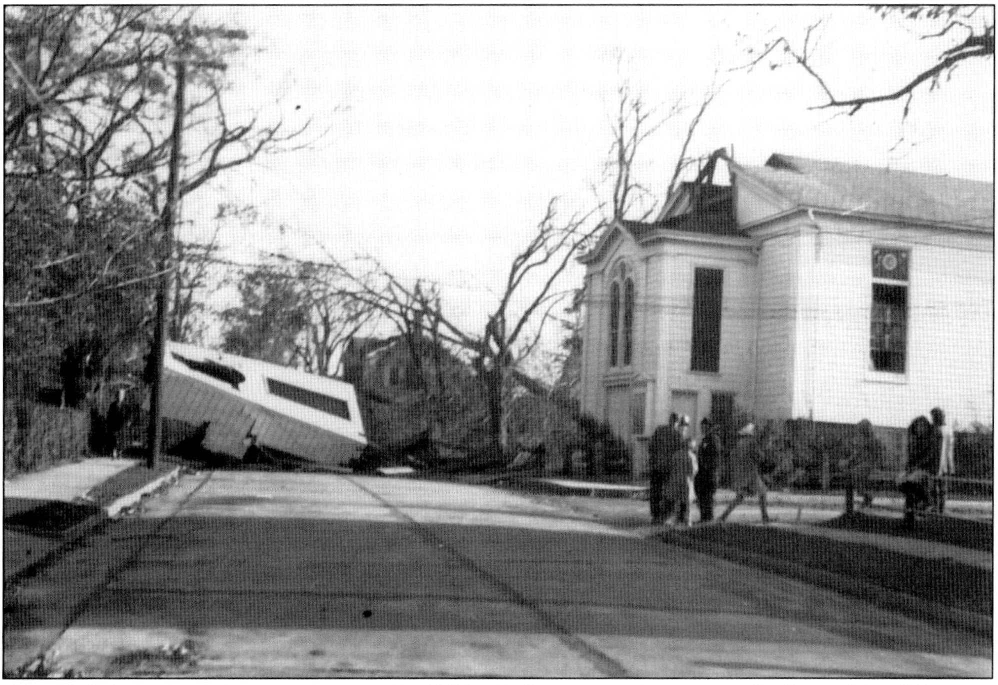

Orient Methodist Church, 1938. In 1938, the hurricane known as the Long Island Express roared through the East End of Long Island. While the South Fork of Long Island bore the brunt of the devastation, the storm also wreaked havoc on the North Fork. The Methodist and Congregational churches had their steeples torn off and thrown into the street. The original steeple clock, created by William Conklin, was lost to the storm.

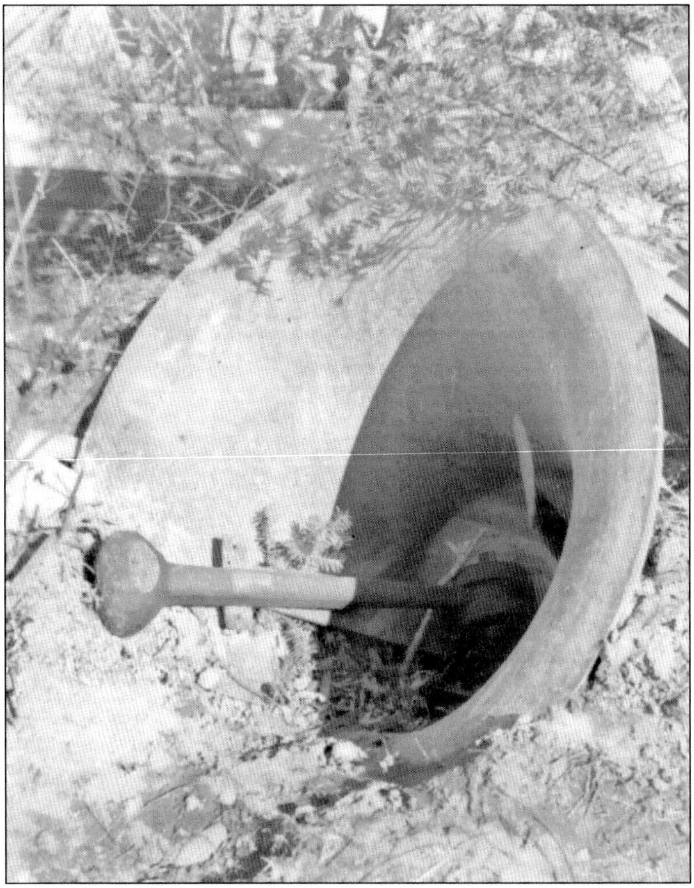

ORIENT CONGREGATIONAL CHURCH BELL, 1938. The bell from the church tower fell with such force into the ground that, at first, the teams clearing the debris assumed it was lost to the winds. After moving several trees and the remains of the steeple, it was found that the bell had hit the soft ground so hard that it had buried itself all the way up to the rim.

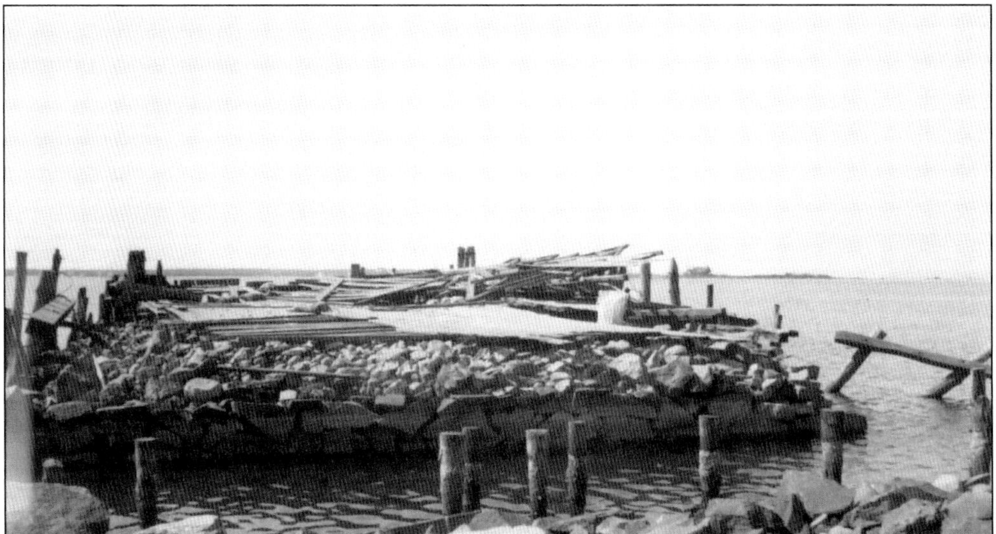

ORIENT WHARF, 1938. The wharf also suffered considerable damage; the buildings that had once stood on it were swept away, and the water ripped up a considerable amount of rock and timber.

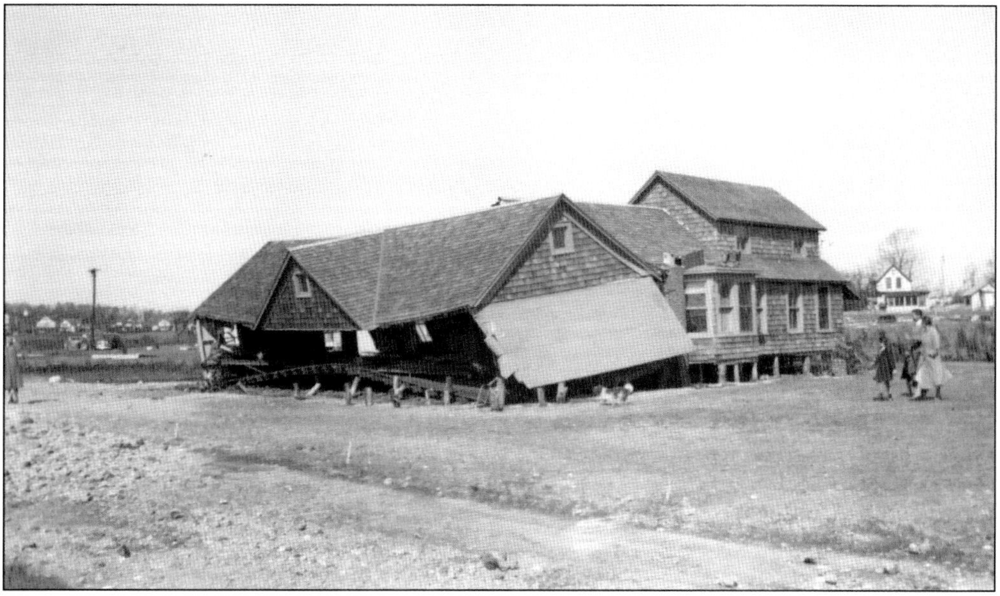

George Younie's Bungalow, 1938. The Younie bungalow was the last house on Water Street, now known as West Bay Avenue, in the aftermath of the 1938 hurricane. The force of the water sweeping over the house and into the farmland now know as Poquatuck Park collapsed the front of the building during the storm.

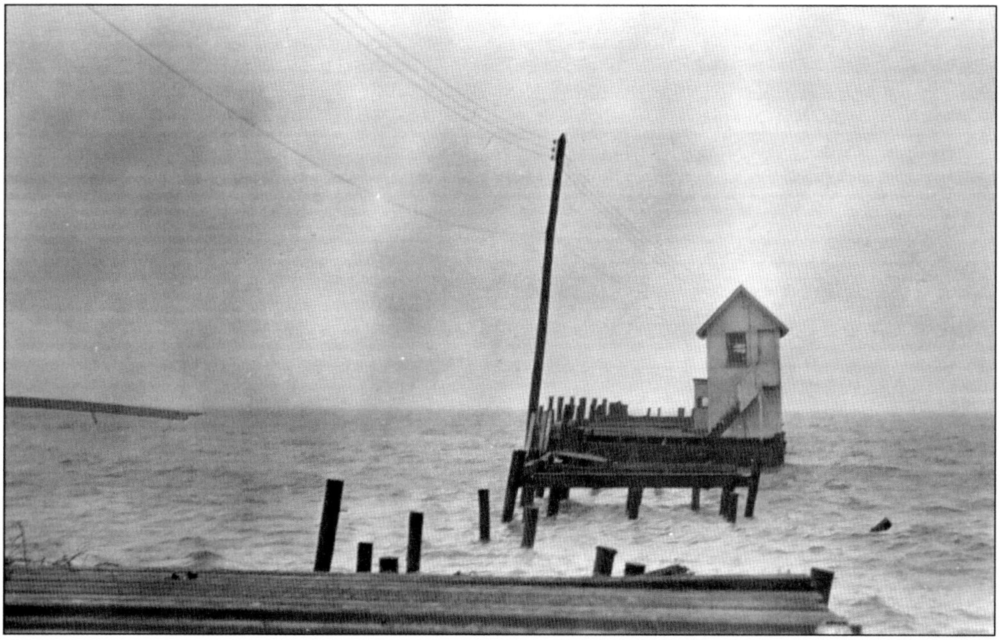

Orient Point Dock, 1938. The storm swept away the center section of the Orient Point ferry dock, but oddly enough, the ticket booth at the far end of the dock remained. The two-story freight house that also stood on the dock was not as lucky.

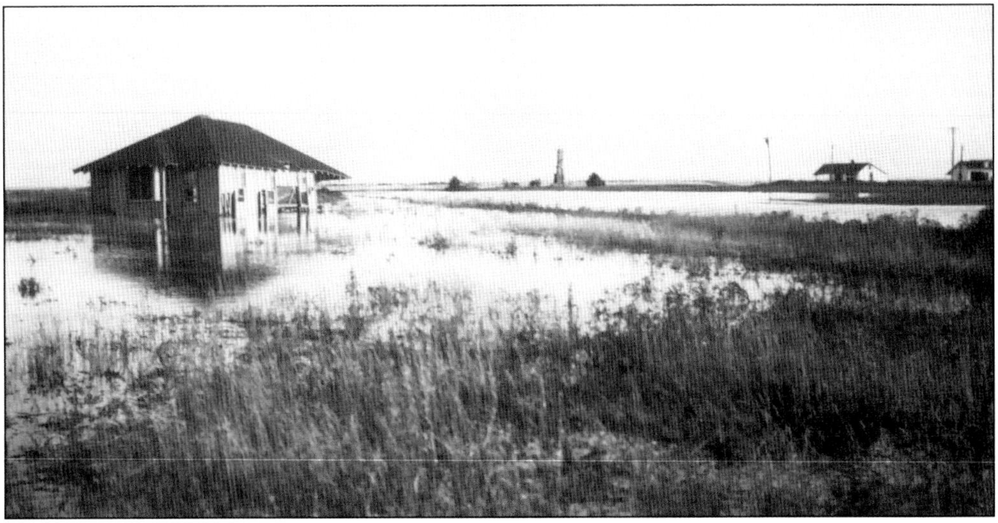

Ray Youngs's Bungalow, 1938. At Orient Point, Ray Youngs's bungalow was floated off its foundation and cleaned out as it was pushed into the center of a field by the point. A lone chimney and fireplace remain standing in the distance.

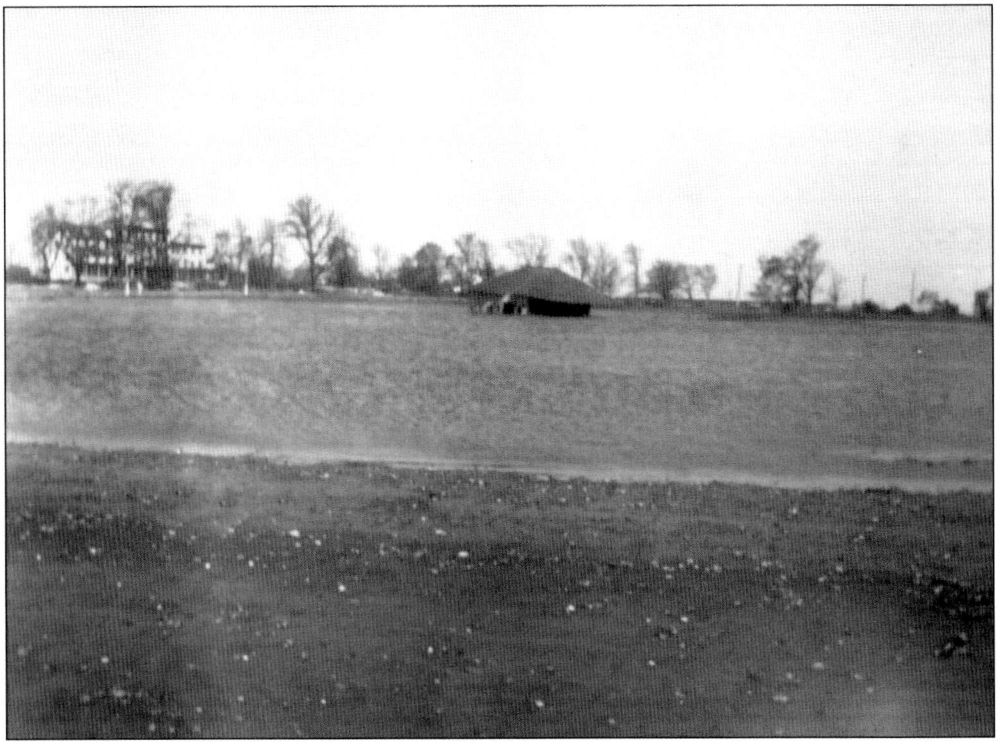

Jiffy Bite, 1938. The snack shack known as the Jiffy Bite, which once stood diagonally across from the Orient Point Inn at the beginning of the road leading along Long Beach Bar, was floated down the street into a temporary pond created in what is today the parking lot of the Cross Sound Ferry. The snack stand sold hot dogs, hamburgers, soda, and ice cream.

Nine

ALONG THE SHORE

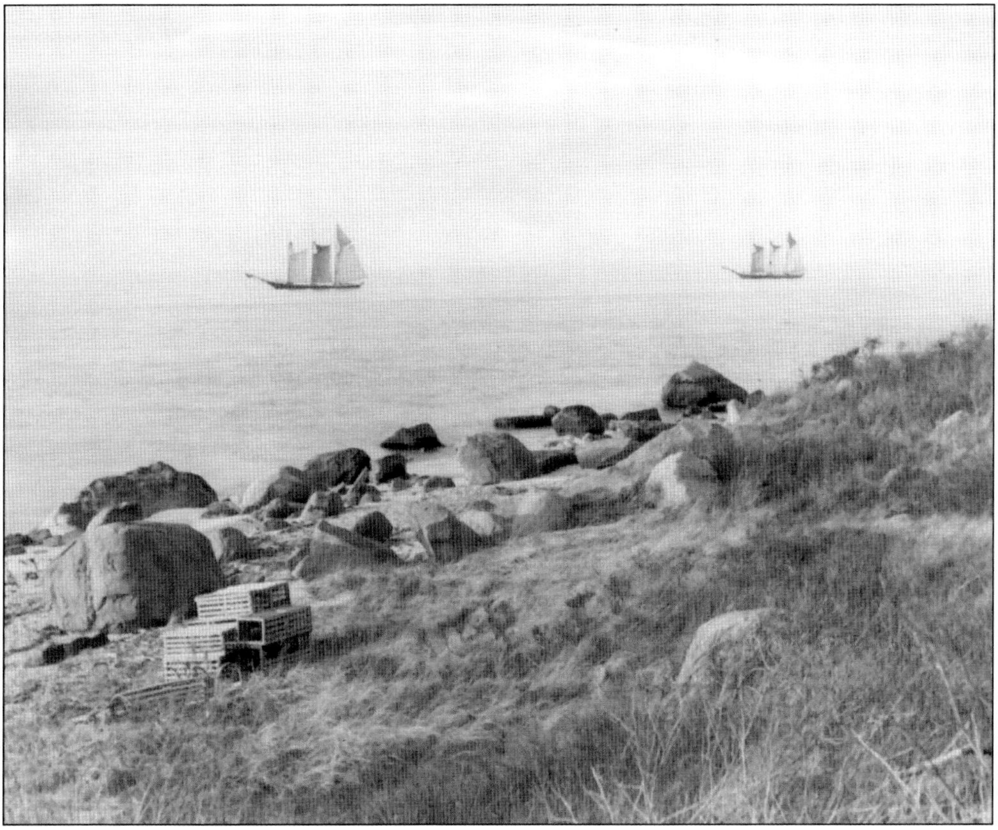

LONG ISLAND SOUND, C. 1870. Bounding the northern edge of the Oysterponds area, Long Island Sound has served for centuries as a highway to communities west of the North Fork to New York City. In this image, two coastermen ships, the most popular method of transportation, are sailing west filled with cargo bound for city markets. Lobster traps are stacked on the beach, waiting to be loaded onto a boat for use.

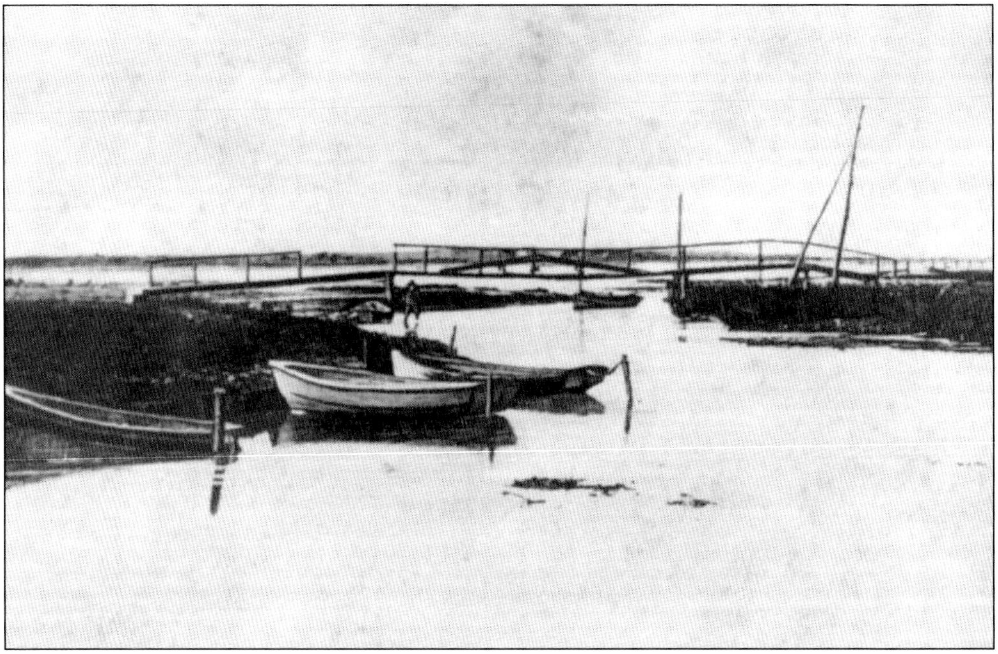

ORIENT CREEK BRIDGE, C. 1900. The bridge was part of the walkway pedestrians had to cross to get from the Old Crab's Shack to the spit of land that separates the Oysterponds from Orient Harbor. It allowed both pedestrians as well as small boats access to their destinations on the beach and the ponds.

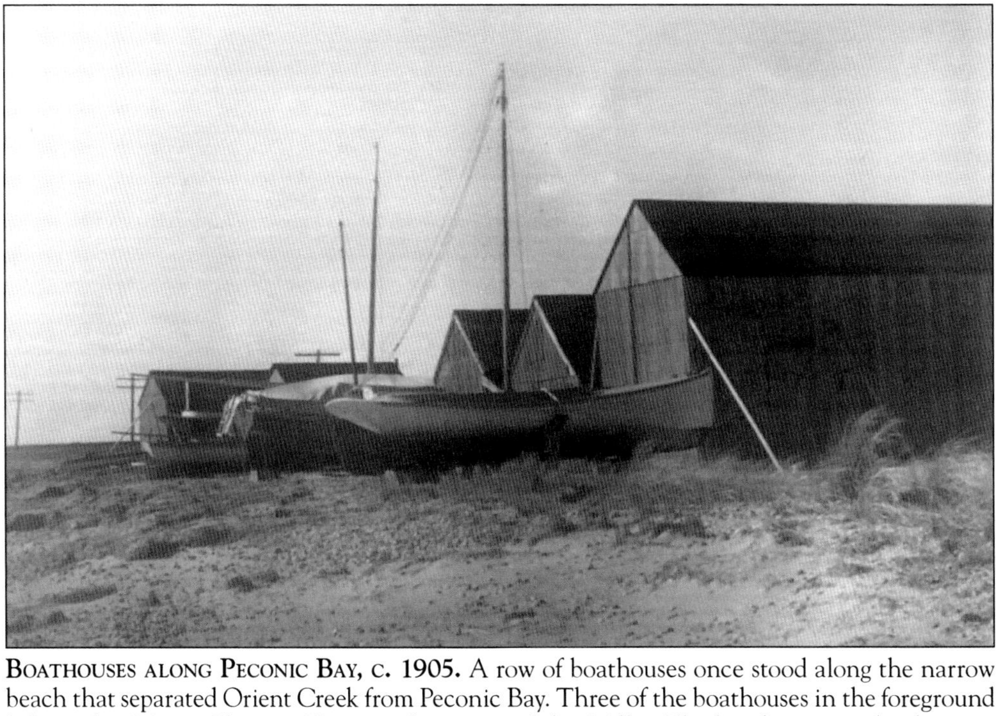

BOATHOUSES ALONG PECONIC BAY, C. 1905. A row of boathouses once stood along the narrow beach that separated Orient Creek from Peconic Bay. Three of the boathouses in the foreground belonged to Mount Pleasant House and its owner, John Miller. The boathouses in the distance were owned by fisherman Robert Adams, who lived close by.

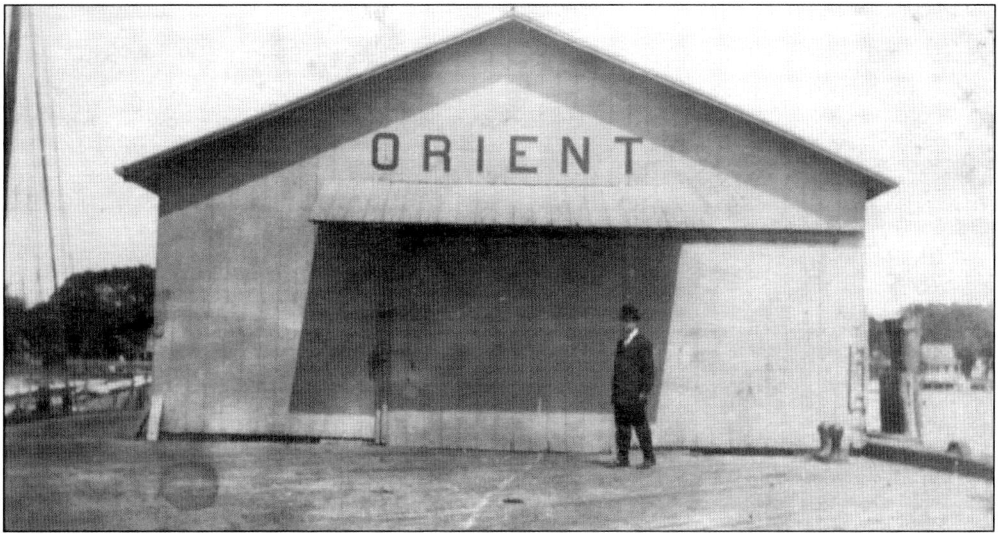

ORIENT WHARF, c. 1900. Cecil Latham stands at the end of the Orient Wharf watching the ferry. This dock was the sight that passengers saw when they arrived and departed Orient. The building over the years served in various functions. The dock, which had been rebuilt in the 1840s, had been expanded in the 1860s and again in 1872, as it became increasingly important to the businesses in the Orient area.

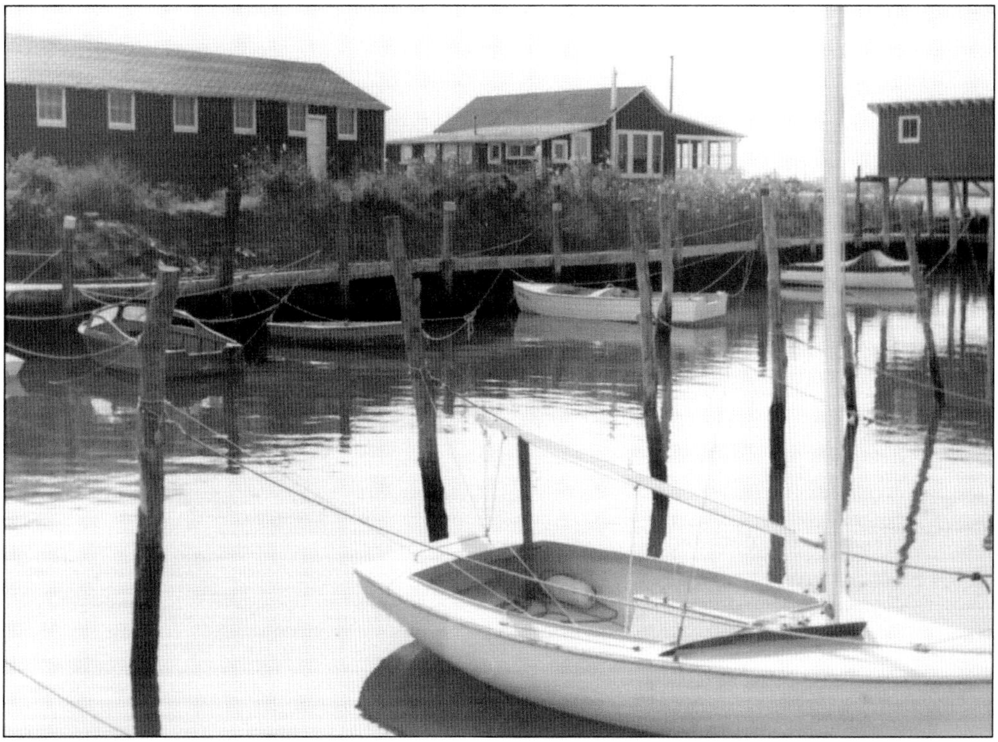

NARROW RIVER, KINGS MARINA, 1966. The marina was created between the late 1940s and early 1950s by Edwin H. King. King dredged out the main boat area, and much of the mud was dumped on either side of the property. He then moved some of his farm sheds to the north and south sides of the property. After King died, the family sold the business in 1972.

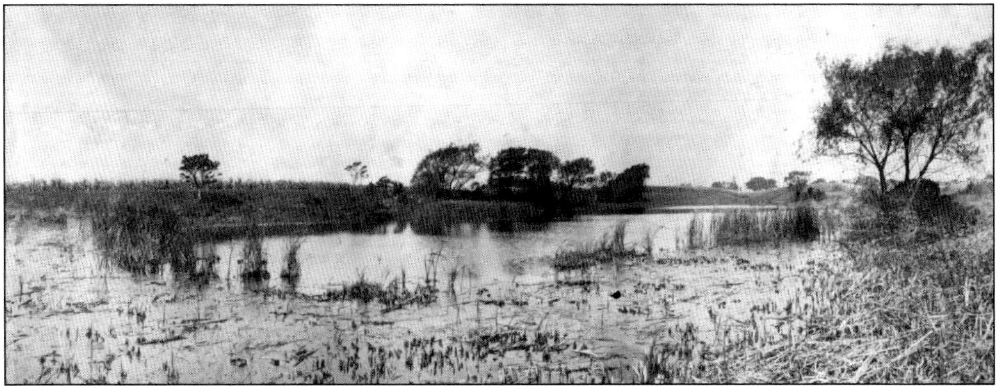

MAJORS POND, C. 1875. The pond is one of three small ponds that are considered local landmarks in Orient Village. These bucolic freshwater ponds were the favorite subjects of local photographers. Majors Pond is located down by Hog Pond Farm. Big Munn and Little Munn Ponds are located along Long Island Sound beside the base of the Hill.

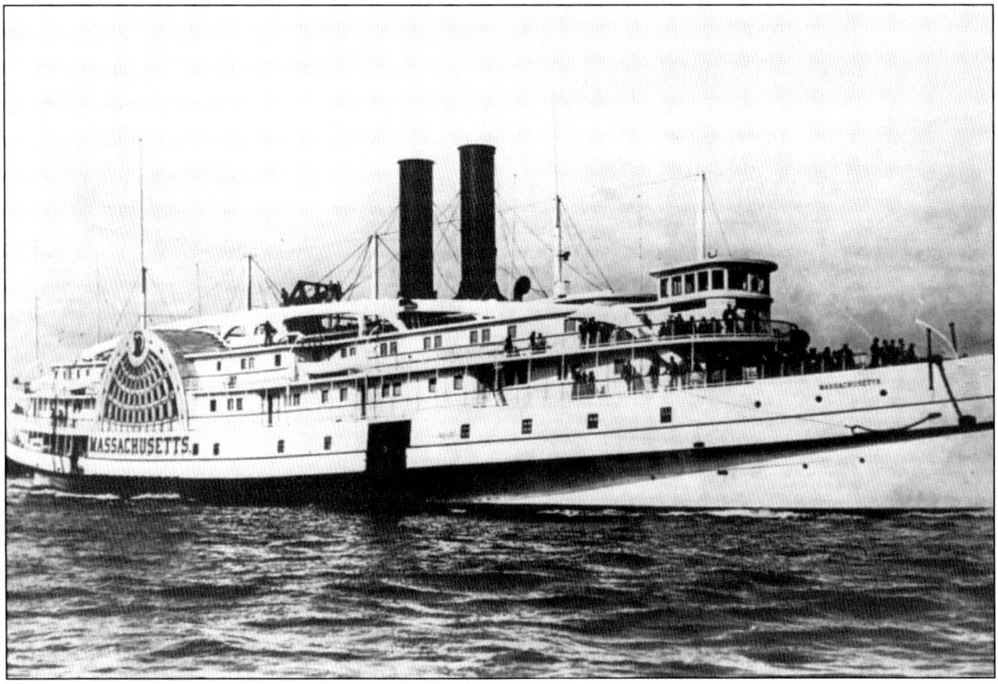

FERRY *MASSACHUSETTS*, 1877. On a regular run to the East End, the *Massachusetts* had the misfortune to run ashore on the western edge of East Marion during a storm, shortly after this photograph was taken in 1877. It was carrying bales of cotton, barrels of oil, and passengers destined for New England and, in an effort to refloat the ship, the crew threw most of the cargo overboard.

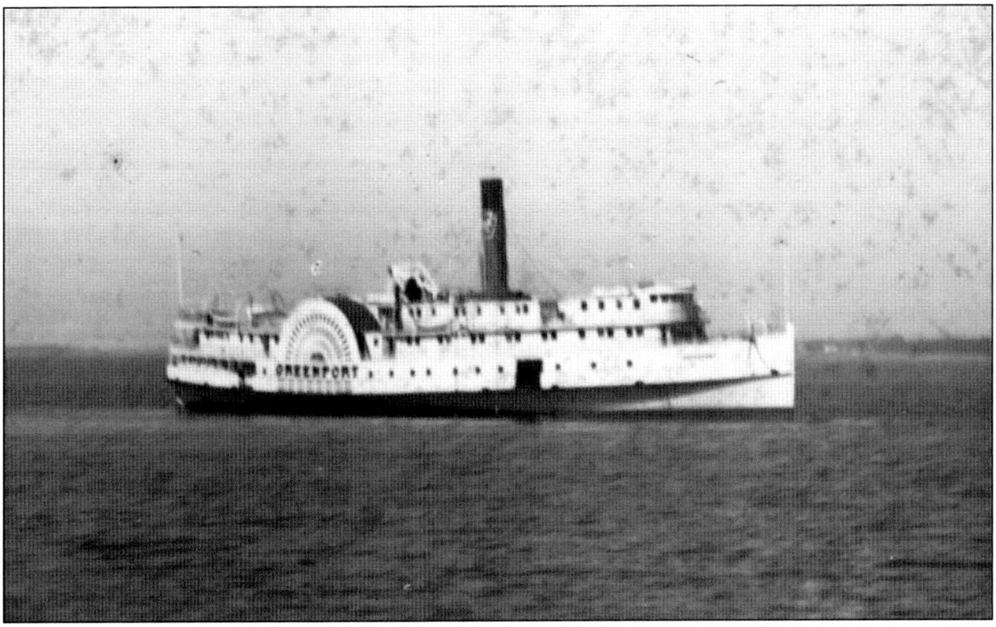

FERRY *GREENPORT*, 1906. On June 25, 1906, the ferry *Greenport* from the Montauk Steamboat line ran aground on a sandbar in Orient Harbor. The ferry was stuck at such a photogenic angle that a number of people ran home and got their cameras to take this image. The next tide lifted the boat off the sand and allowed it to continue on its way.

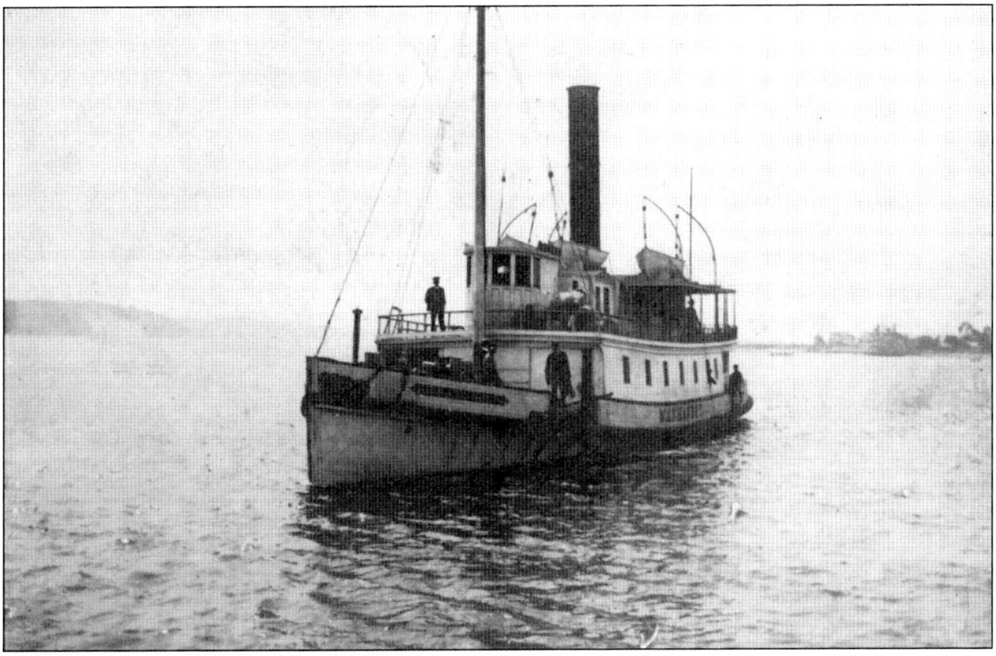

FERRY *MANHANSET*, C. 1907. The ferry *Manhanset* traveled daily from the Peconic Bay area to Connecticut. In 1895, while passing though Plum Gut, Capt. James F. Smith's young son, who was traveling with his father, fell overboard. When Smith heard the commotion, he stopped the ferry and dove overboard searching for his son. Sadly, the boy drowned in the dangerous currents. Smith continued to pass through the gut daily for another nine years.

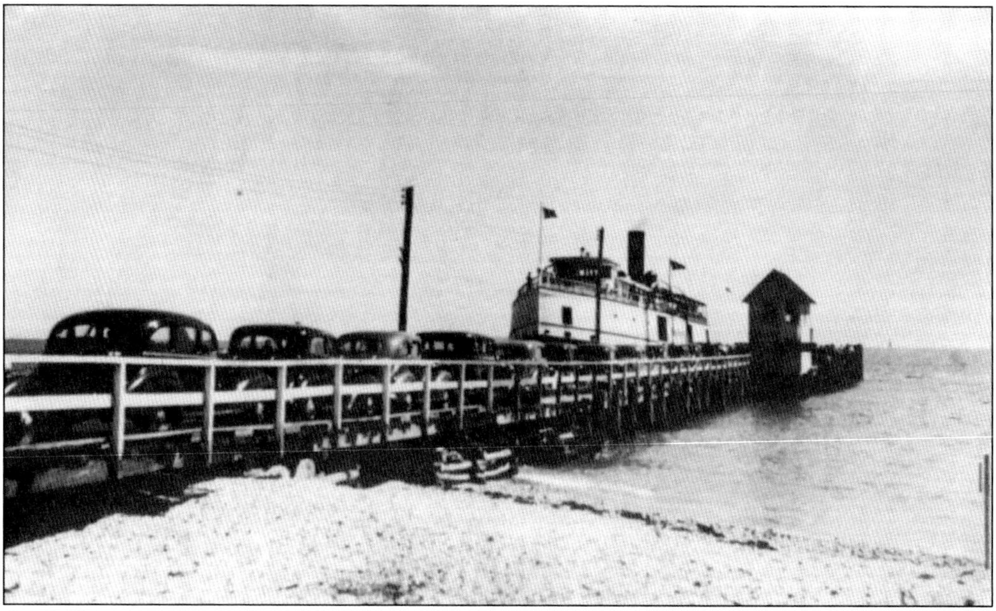

Cross Sound Ferry at Orient Point, 1935. A number of ferry companies have traveled between the North Fork and Connecticut. In this photograph, the steamer *Catskill* is pulling up to the Orient Point Dock in 1935. During the 1940s and 1950s, to get more vehicles onboard, ferry workers would often pack passenger cars into empty trucks also making the trip to Connecticut. They had a dirt ramp built by the shore for this purpose.

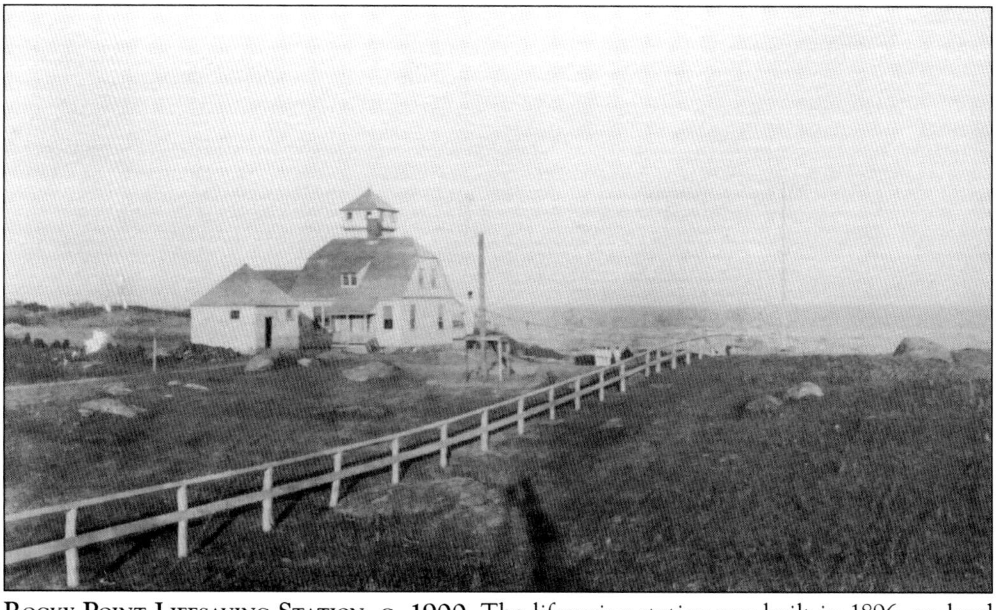

Rocky Point Lifesaving Station, c. 1900. The lifesaving station was built in 1896, on land donated by Anton Furst. The building was sited 50 feet back from the edge of a nearly perpendicular bluff overlooking the sound. The tower commanded a view of miles of sound shore. The masonry work on the station was done by Morris Rogers and Son of East Marion, and a group of six carpenters from East Marion and Greenport constructed the building.

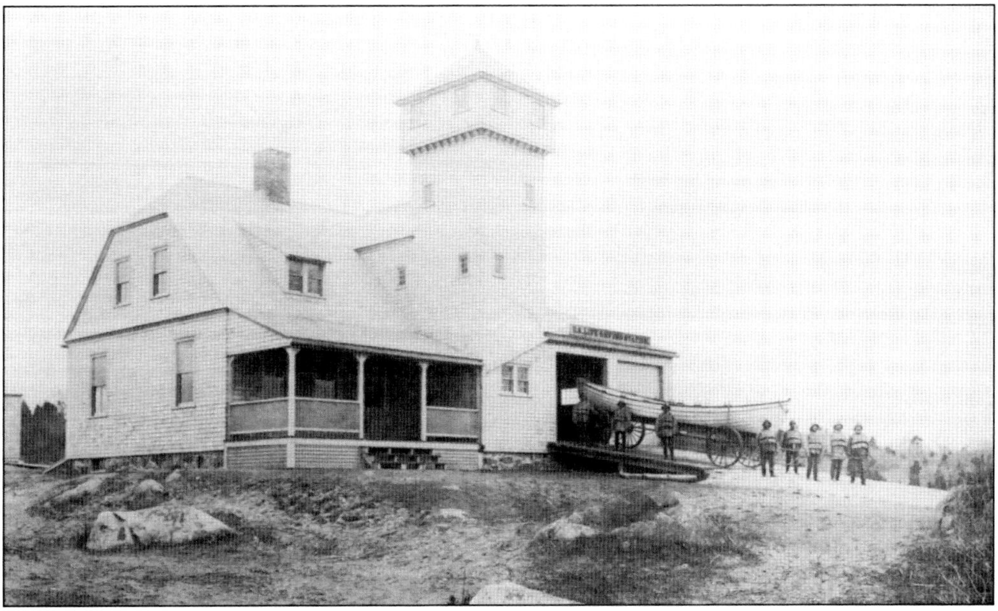

Rocky Point Lifesaving Station, c. 1905. At the front of the station, the crew and their lifesaving boat are posed next to the garage. The US Lifesaving Service was founded in 1848. In 1915, the service was merged with the Revenue Cutter Service to create the Coast Guard. In 1948, the Coast Guard left East Marion, and the buildings became a private home.

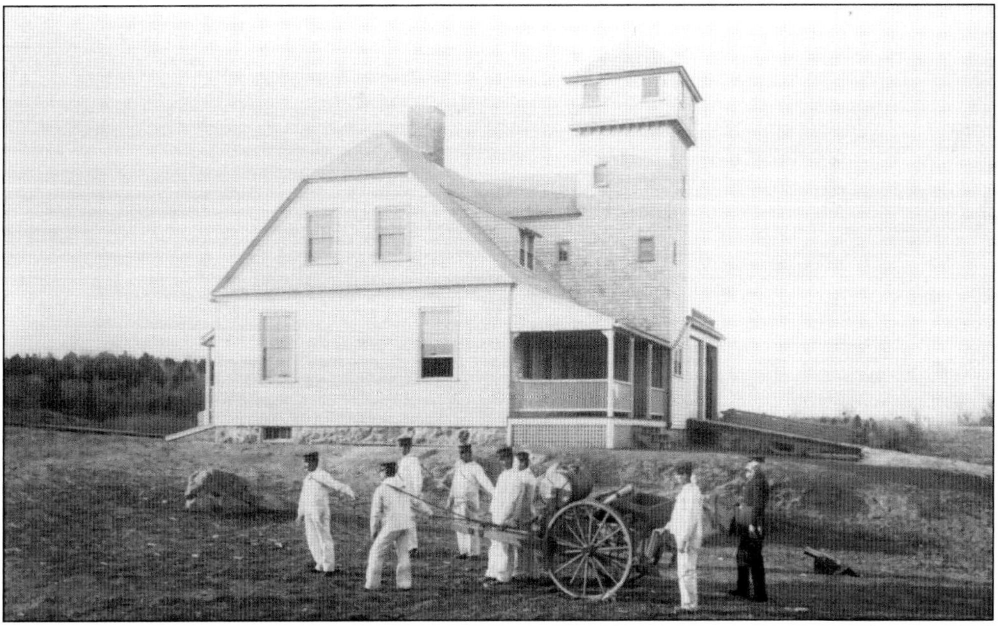

Lifesaving Crew with their Rescue Cart, c. 1905. All of the equipment that the crew had needed to be pulled by the men across the rocky beaches to the site. As part of their duties, members of the lifesaving crew patrolled miles of beach in either direction from the station, keeping watch for floundering ships, distress signals, or victims caught in the currents.

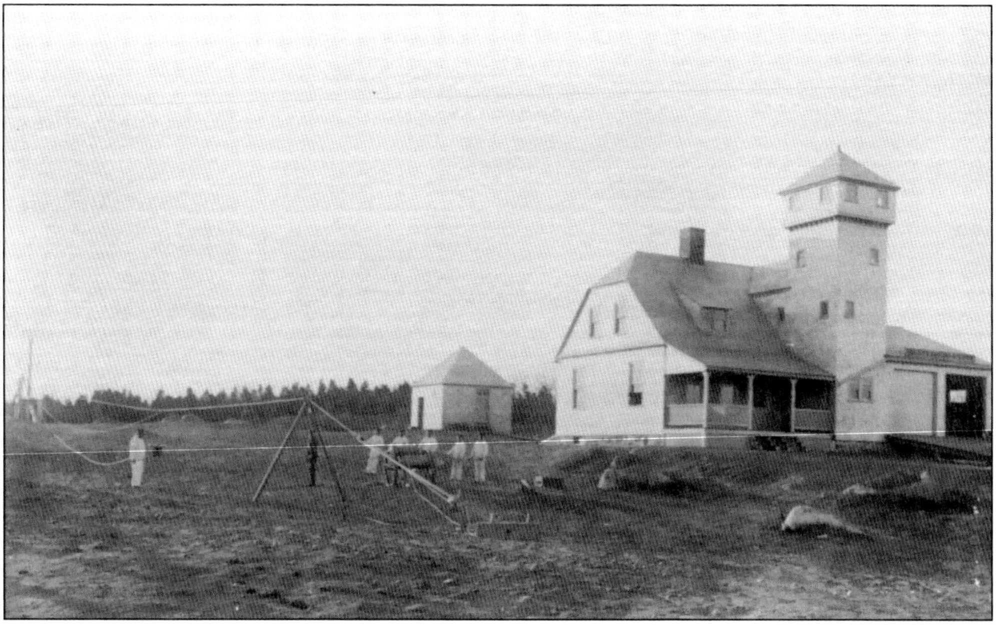

Lifesaving Crew Drilling, c. 1905. The crew often practiced working with the boatswain chair, which was an important tool in the arsenal of the service. During storms that were too rough for the crew to bring their boat alongside a floundering vessel, they could shoot a rope from their life-line cannon that would be tied to a high point on the ship to form a zip line. Victims could then be pulled to safety using the small rope chair.

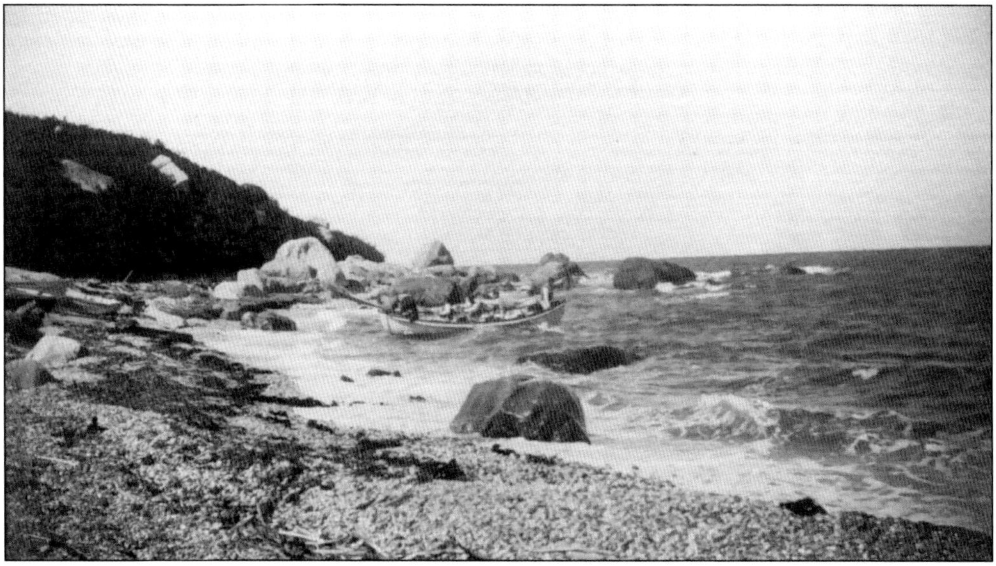

Lifesaving Crew Landing Drill, c. 1905. The Rocky Point Lifesaving Station's regular drills included the launching and landing of the lifesaving boats along the rocky shores of East Marion. Here, the crew is practicing their boat-handling skills on a relatively calm day on Long Island Sound.

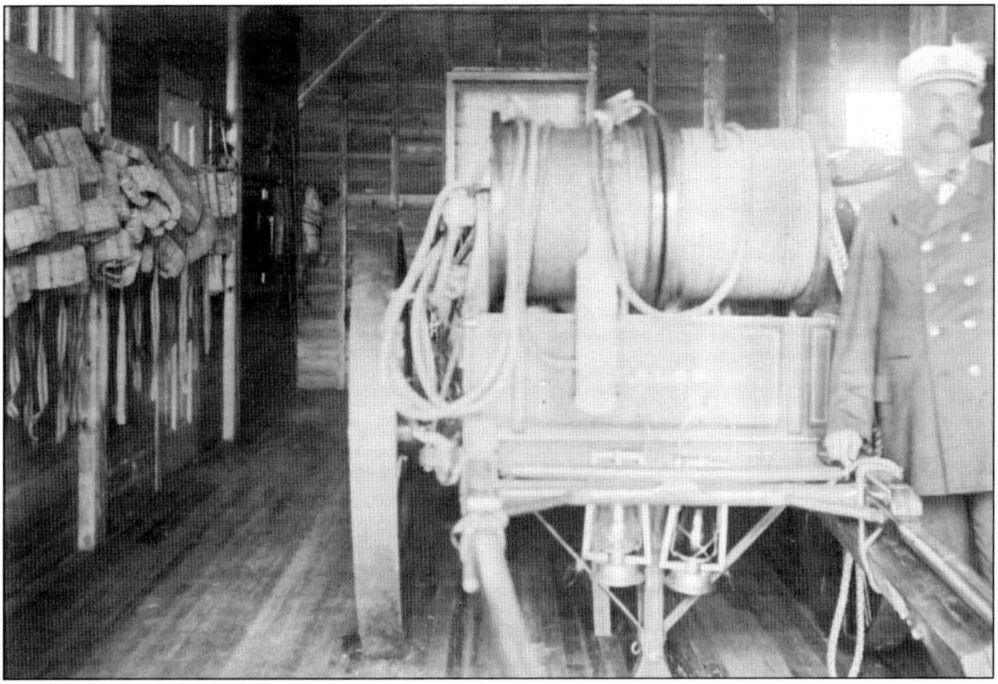

Lifesaving Station Equipment Shed, c. 1910. Pictured here is the interior of the attached equipment shed of the lifesaving station. The man posed next to the rope cart is either Capt. Harvey Brown or Wilbur Hedges. The cart was constructed so that it could be pulled along the beach by the lifesaving crew. Lined up along the wall are lifesaving vests made from cork.

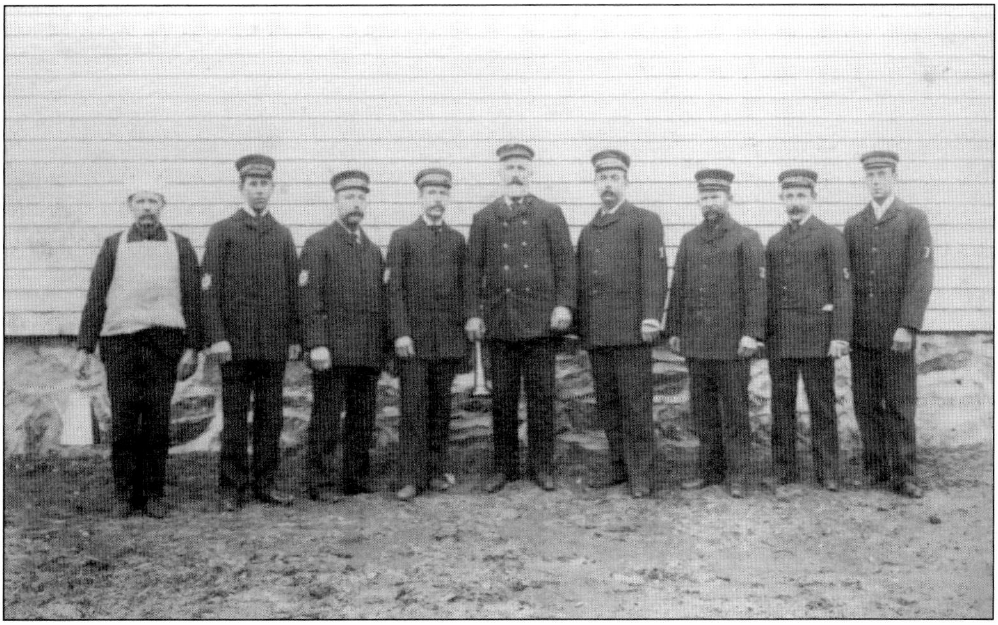

The Rocky Point Lifesaving Station Crew, c. 1905. Generally speaking, there were only seven men on the crew at a time. Although the men in this photograph are not identified, they are probably Harvey S. Brown, George V. Clark, Porter C. Rackett, William E. Paterson, Selden B. Case, George E. Udell, and Isaac B. Hallock.

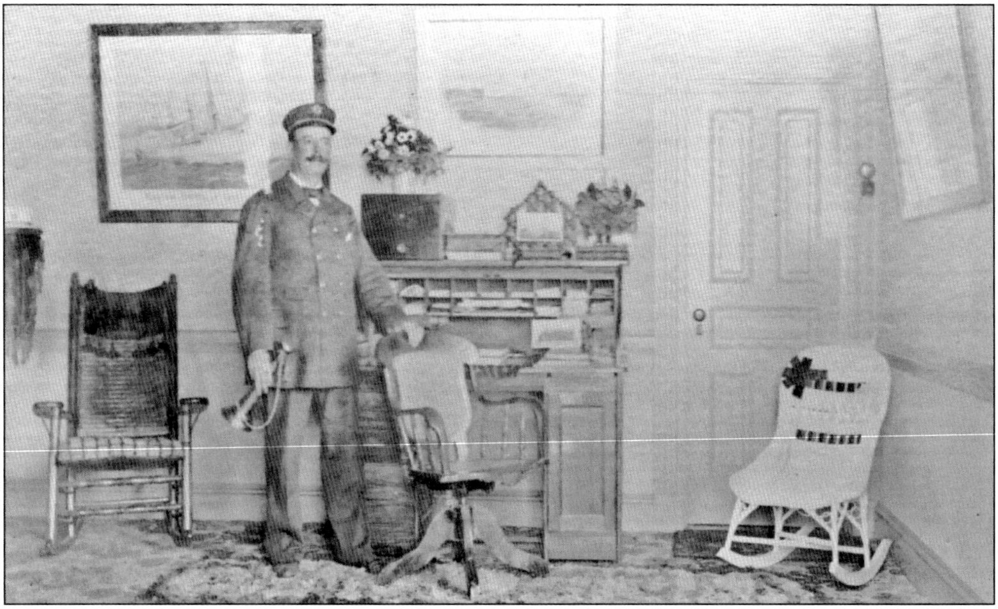

CAPT. HARVEY BROWN, C. 1910. Brown (1855–1927) poses in his office at the Rocky Point Lifesaving Station. Brown, a former fisherman, served at Rocky Point from its opening until 1919. He was replaced by Capt. Earl Suydam.

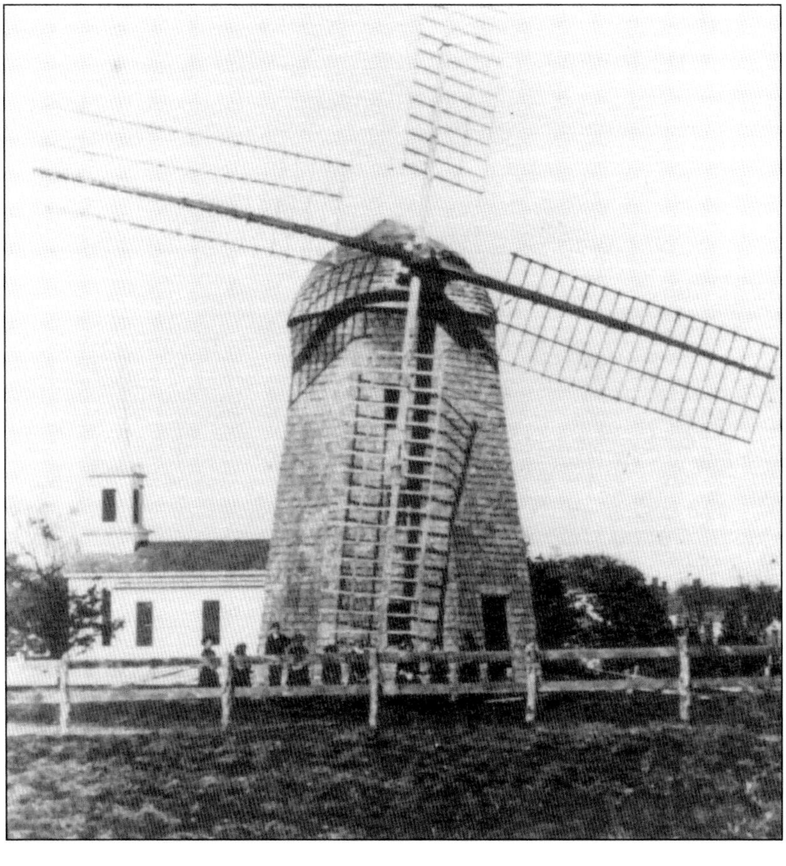

EAST MARION WINDMILL, C. 1870. Reputed to be the oldest mill in the area, the East Marion mill was moved to the hill at the intersection of Cemetery Road and Main Road from somewhere west of the village by longtime owner Daniel Vail. By 1873, the mill was run by Henry Horton, who also ran the Dam Pond Tidal Mill. It was still in use in 1878, but it burned down on May 10, 1885.

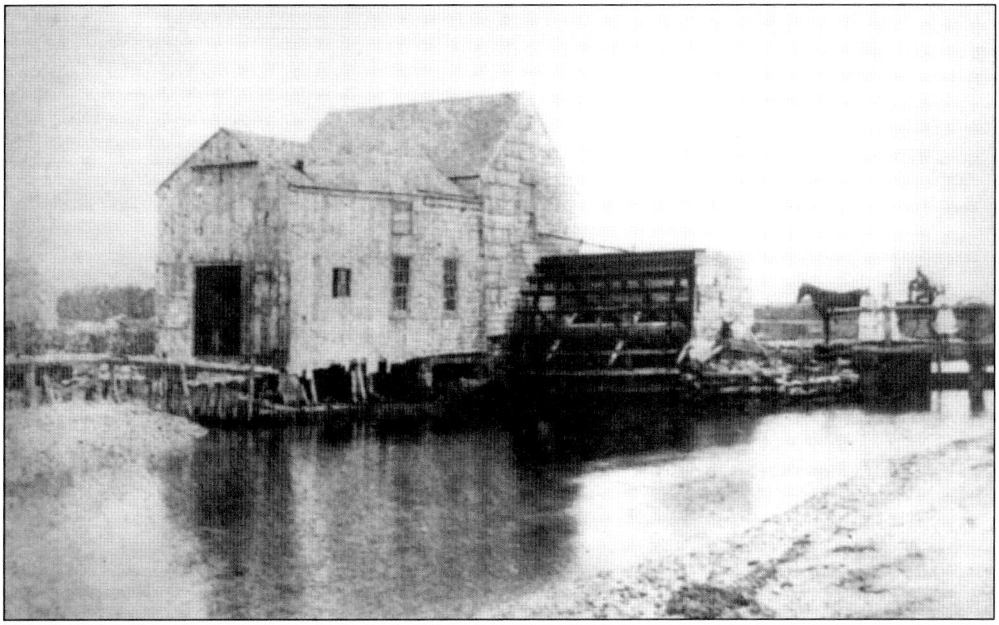

Dam Pond Tidal Mill, c. 1870. Originally built by Elizabeth Bailey, the tidal mill was located on the causeway where Dam Pond connects to Peconic Bay. In the 1850s, Henry Horton of East Marion decided that he did not like fishing, so he bought and ran the mill. Horton sold it to Usher Benjamin, who ran it for a time then let it decay. The mill was torn down in the late 1920s to build the seawall, but the foundation was still visible in 1946.

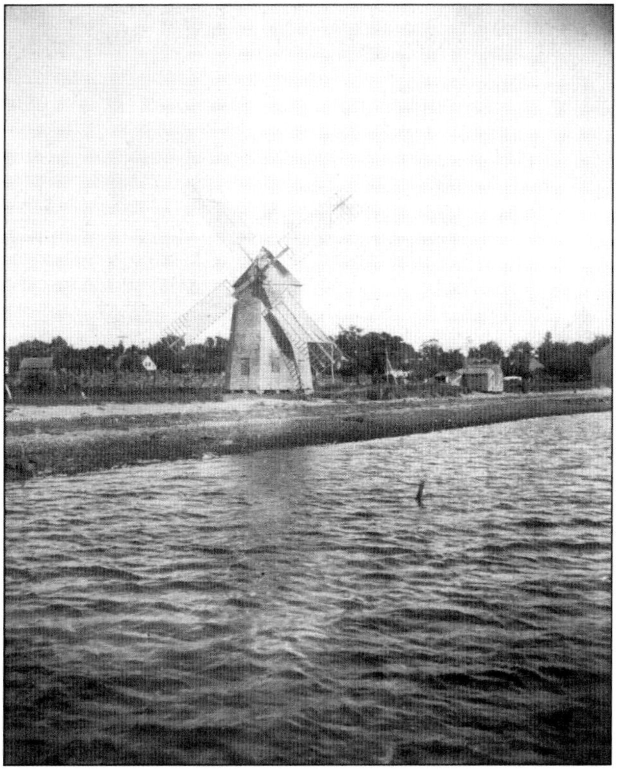

Orient Windmill, c. 1870. Built along the beach facing Orient Harbor, the windmill shown here is the third mill built to serve the Orient area. Known as the Orient Mill, the beloved landmark specialized in grinding grain from local farms. Constructed in 1810 to replace an earlier mill on the same spot, records are unclear about whether Nathaniel Dominey or John Terry was the builder.

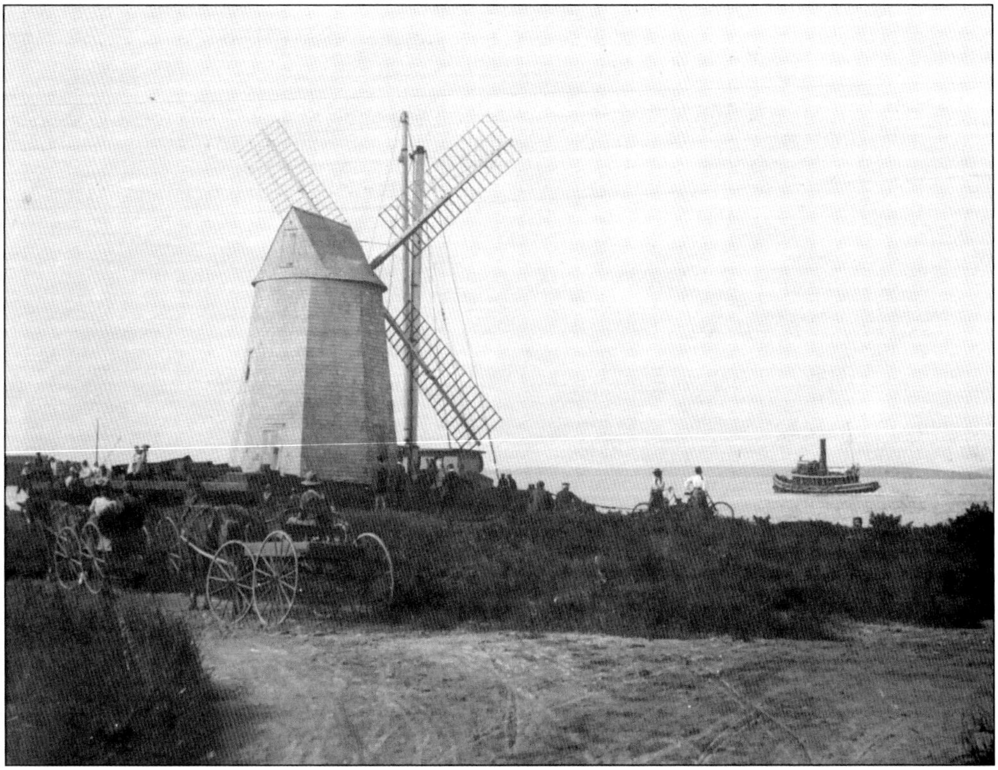

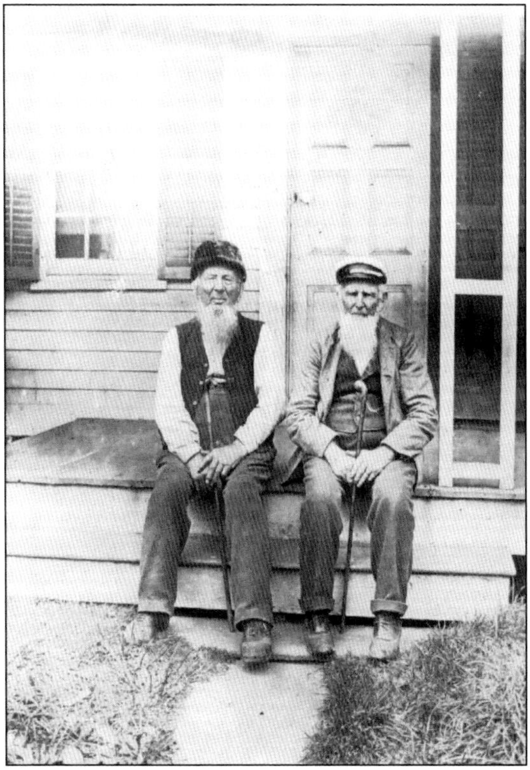

ORIENT WINDMILL, C. 1870. This is the view from the north looking south across Orient Harbor. One dangerous pastime of yesteryear was to ride the arms of the windmill one complete revolution. Only two people were known to have ridden the arms of the Orient windmill for the full circuit. One was Jim Ryan, and the other was Dick Brooks.

PAST MILLERS OF THE ORIENT WINDMILL, C. 1863. Relaxing on the front steps of a house are Samuel W. Young (left) and Baldwin Petty (right). Both Young and Petty had served the community as the miller of the Orient windmill.

John H. Terry, c. 1890. Terry sits in the doorway of the Orient windmill. Terry, who had run the mill for 40 years, was the last miller to work the mill. (Courtesy of Jean Letty.)

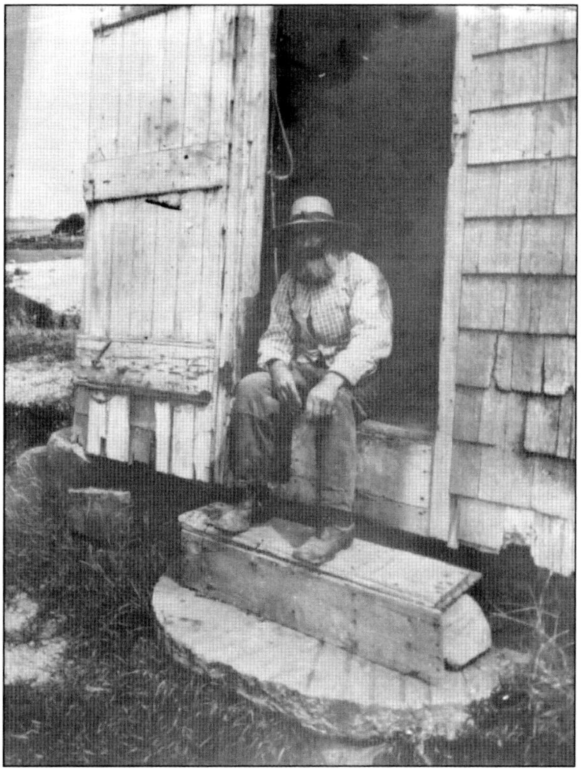

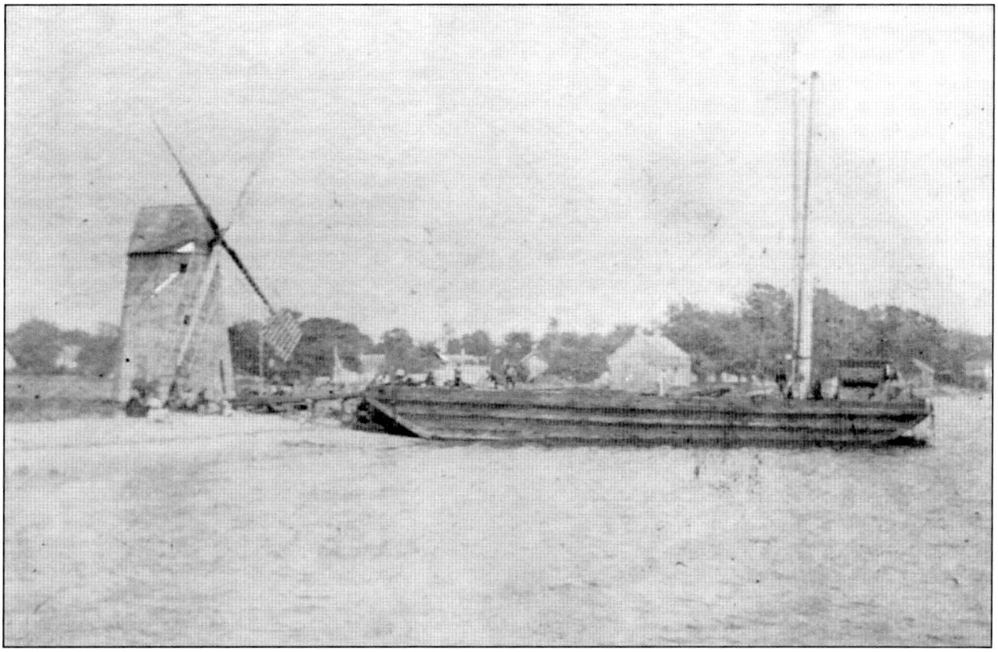

Orient Windmill, 1898. After the mill was rendered obsolete by the manufacturing of flour in factory mills, small local windmills were ignored or became tourist attractions. Not to let a good deal slide past, John H. Terry realized the mill would never be used again and sold it to an amusement park.

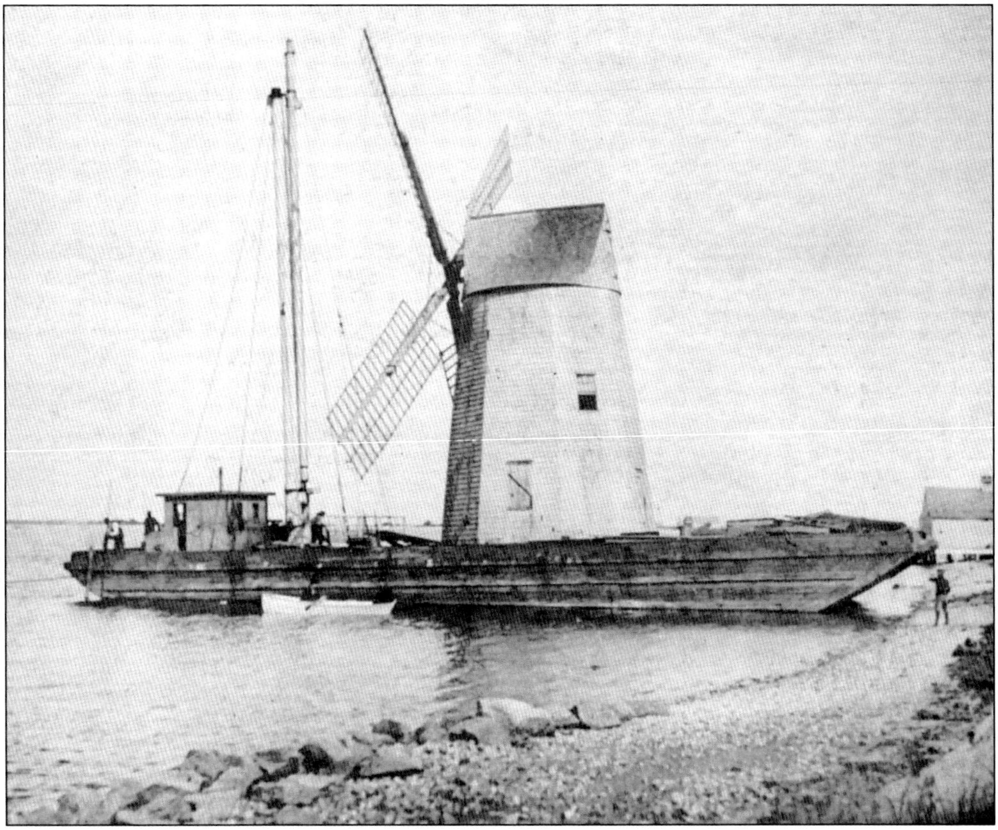

Moving the Orient Windmill, 1898. Unaware of the windmill's fate, the populace of Orient was astounded when a barge pulled up to the beach in front of the windmill and began to winch the beloved landmark onto its deck. As word spread, residents hastened down to shore. Many publicly decried the sale. It is said that for a long time, people in Orient were so mad about the situation that they ceased speaking to John Terry.

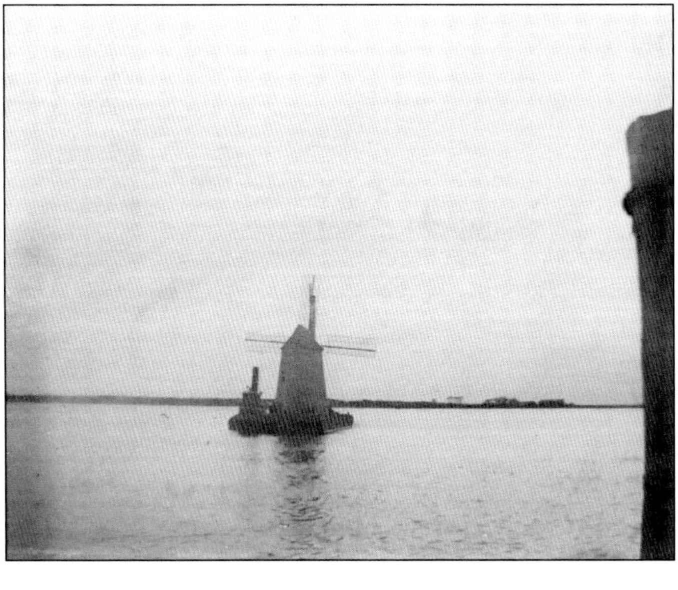

Moving the Orient Windmill, 1898. The mill was floated by barge to its new home at the Glen Island Amusement Park. The park, owned by John Starin, was a series of islands located just off New Rochelle. It featured buildings from around the world. The Orient windmill was passed off as a Dutch windmill. In 1910, the mill burned to the ground. Today, the park still stands and is run by Westchester County.

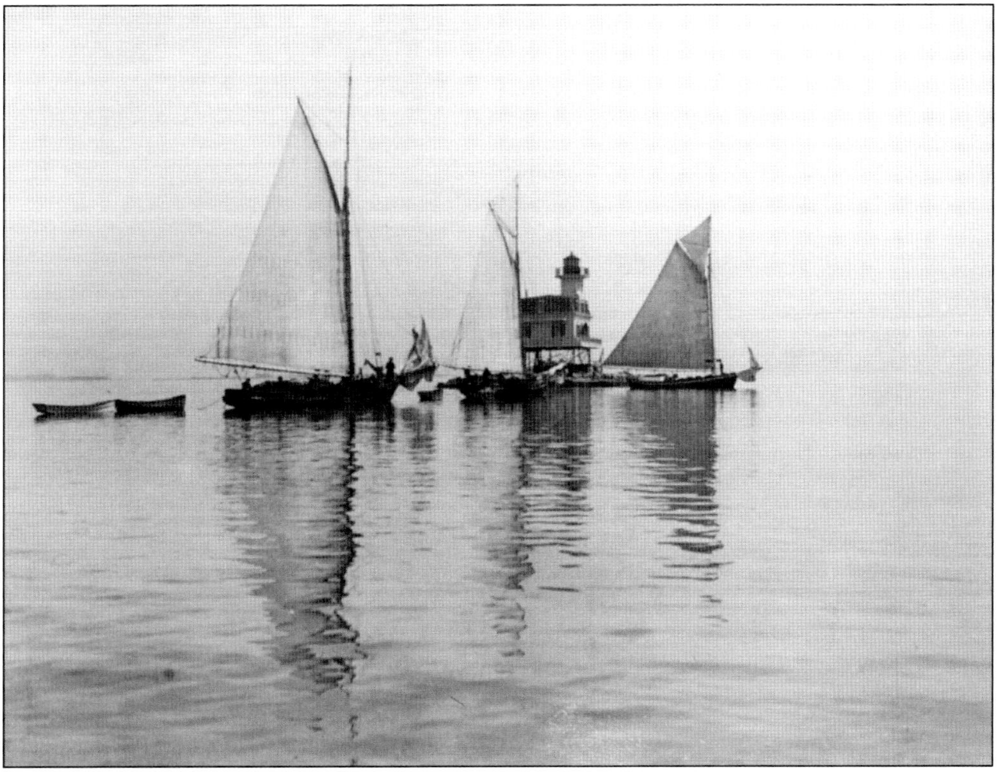

Long Beach Bar Lighthouse, c. 1880. Long Beach Bar is known locally as Bug Light. The open-framework base the light originally stood on reminded residents of the legs of an insect. Marking the end of a long, low sandbar, the light was installed and marks the entrance to Orient Harbor. Sailing before the light are, from left to right, the *New York*, the *Elmira*, and the *Black Eagle*.

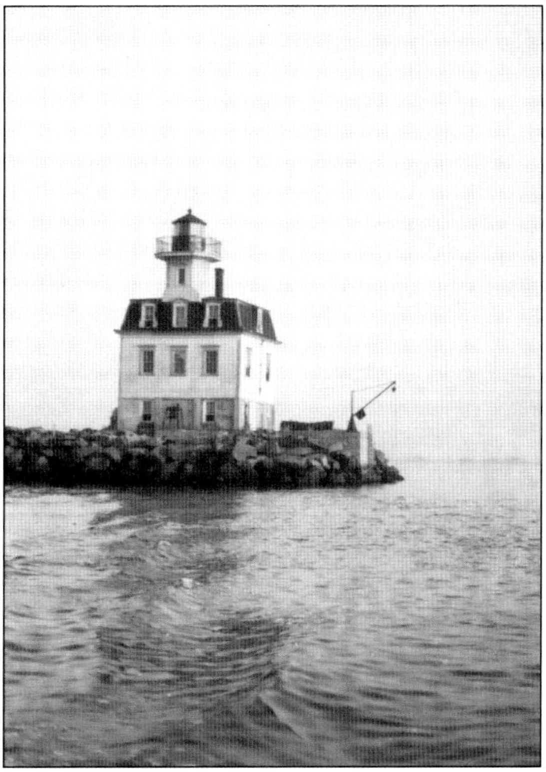

Long Beach Bar Lighthouse, c. 1930. In 1926, after a severe storm, the lighthouse board decided to enclose the open framework that supported the lighthouse. A stone wall was built that added strength and stability to the structure. By the 1950s, the light was automated, and the structure was left empty. On the July 4, 1963, the lighthouse was completely burned down in a suspected case of arson. Residents of East Marion and Orient were heartbroken.

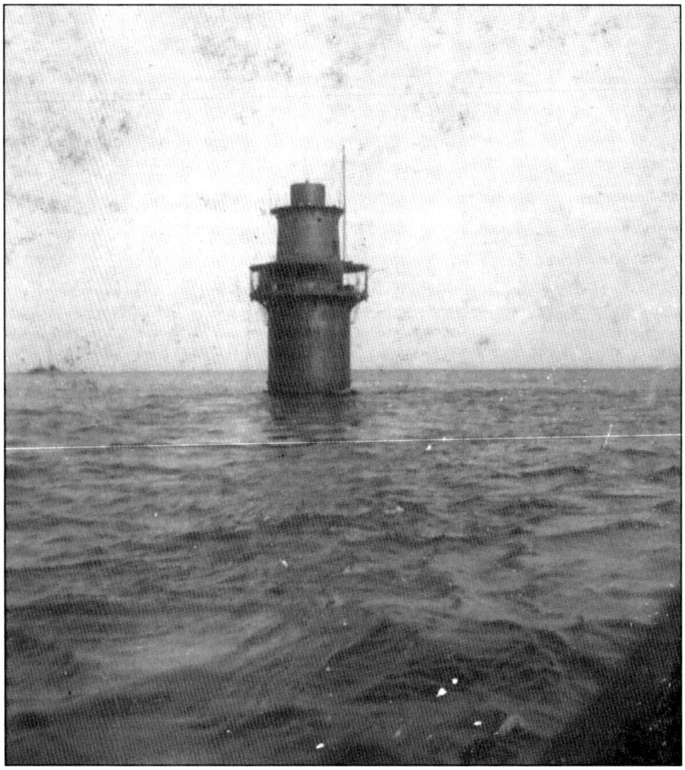

Orient Point Light, 1897. This image shows the Orient Point Light, still under construction in 1897. The light, which is affectionately known as the "Coffeepot" because of its resemblance to a stovetop coffeepot, is lacking the light and roof. The lighthouse marks the Orient Point Reef and stands just opposite the Plum Island Lighthouse. The Coffeepot stands on the side of one of the most dangerous channels in the area—Plum Gut.

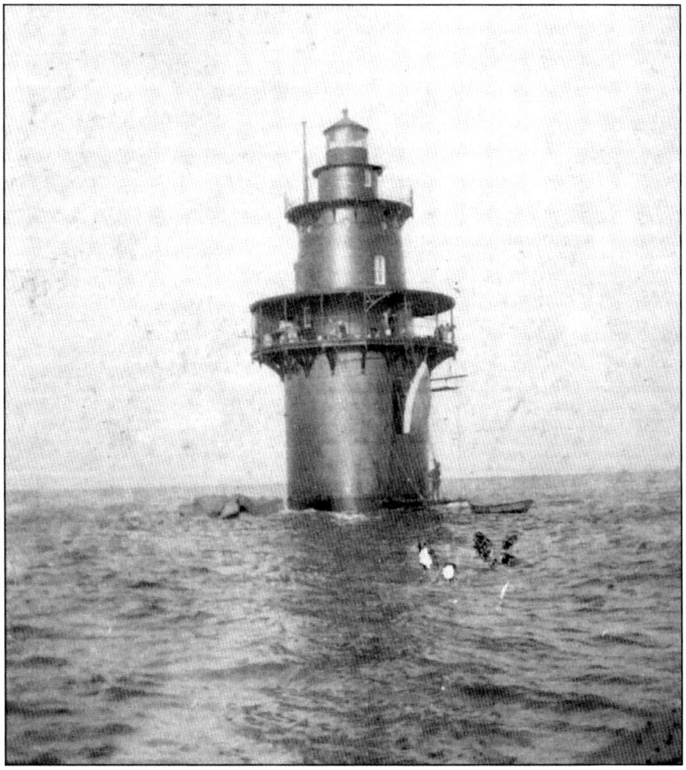

The Coffeepot after its Completion, c. 1900. This style of lighthouse is referred to as a sparkplug, after its resemblance to the automobile part. Regarded as one of the most dangerous lights in the area, the lighthouse board assigned a keeper and several assistants to the light, but they banned the families of the keepers from living at the light. The families lived nearby in Orient, East Marion, and Greenport.

Bibliography

ancestry.com

Brooklyn Standard Union, Brooklyn, NY: 1915–1919.

Chadwick, Henry. *New Association Score Book*. New York City, NY: Peck and Snyder, 1869.

Donald Boerum, interviews by Amy Folk, History of Orient, 2003–2013, notes in author's files, Orient, NY.

Elinor Williams, interviews by Amy Folk, History of Orient, 2003–2013, notes in author's files, Orient, NY.

Goodrich, Magdaline. *Southold Town Records* 1683–1856. Southold, NY: Academy Printing Services, 1983.

Gordon Rackett, interviews by Amy Folk, History of East Marion, 2009–2013, notes in author's files, Orient, NY.

Griffin, Augustus. *Augustus Griffin's Journal*. Orient, NY: Oysterponds Historical Society, 1983.

Hoadly, Charles J., ed. *Records of the Colony and Plantation of New-Haven, From 1638 to 1649*. Hartford, CT: Case, Tiffany, and Company, 1857.

Long Island Traveler, Southold, NY: 1871–1970.

Mattituck Watchman, Mattituck, NY: 1890–1970

Oysterponds Historical Society. *Historical Review*. Orient, NY: Oysterponds Historical Society, 1959.

———. *Historic Orient Village*. Orient, NY: Oysterponds Historical Society, 1976.

Robert Reeves Jr, e-mail messages to Amy Folk, October 2013–July 2014, notes in author's files, Orient, NY.

Suffolk County News, Sayville, NY: 1888–2015.

Wood, Clarence Ashton. Research Files. Unpublished documents.